STUDIES IN HIGHER EDUCATION

Edited by
Philip G. Altbach
Monan Professor of Higher Education
Lynch School of Education, Boston College

A ROUTLEDGE SERIES

Studies in Higher Education

Philip G. Altbach, *General Editor*

The Women's Movement and the Politics of Change at a Women's College
Jill Ker Conway at Smith, 1975–1985
David A. Greene

Acting 'Otherwise'
The Institutionalization of Women's/Gender Studies in Taiwan's Universities
Peiying Chen

Teaching and Learning in Diverse Classrooms
Faculty Reflections on Their Experiences and Pedagogical Practices of Teaching Diverse Populations
Carmelita Rosie Castañeda

The Transformation of the Student Career
University Study in Germany, the Netherlands, and Sweden
Michael A. Nugent

Teacher Education for Critical Consumption of Mass Media and Popular Culture
Stephanie A. Flores-Koulish

When For-Profit Meets Nonprofit
Educating Through the Market
Jared L. Bleak

Democratizing Higher Education Policy
Constraints of Reform in Post-Apartheid South Africa
Molatlhegi Trevor Chika Sehoole

Coming of Age
Women's Colleges in the Philippines during the Post-Marcos Era
Francesca B. Purcell

Does Quality Pay?
Benefits of Attending a High-Cost, Prestigious College
Liang Zhang

Adaptation of Western Economics by Russian Universities
Intercultural Travel of an Academic Field
Tatiana Suspitsyna

Dominant Beliefs and Alternative Voices
Discourse, Belief, and Gender in American Study Abroad
Joan Elias Gore

Inhabiting the Borders
Foreign Language Faculty in American Colleges and Universities
Robin Matross Helms

The Changing Landscape of the Academic Profession
The Culture of Faculty at For-Profit Colleges and Universities
Vicente M. Lechuga

The WTO and the University
Globalization, GATS, and American Higher Education
Roberta Malee Bassett

The WTO and the University
Globalization, GATS, and American Higher Education

Roberta Malee Bassett

Routledge
New York & London

Published in 2006 by
Routledge
Taylor & Francis Group
270 Madison Avenue
New York, NY 10016

Published in Great Britain by
Routledge
Taylor & Francis Group
2 Park Square
Milton Park, Abingdon
Oxon OX14 4RN

Transferred to Digital Printing 2009

International Standard Book Number-10: 0-415-97833-5 (Hardcover)
International Standard Book Number-13: 978-0-415-97833-0 (Hardcover)
Library of Congress Card Number 2005032922

Library of Congress Cataloging-in-Publication Data

Bassett, Roberta Malee.
The WTO and the university : globalization, GATS, and American higher education / Roberta Malee Bassett.
p. cm. -- (Studies in higher education)
Includes bibliographical references and index.
ISBN 0-415-97833-5
1. Education, Higher--Economic aspects--United States. 2. Higher education and state--United States. 3. General Agreement on Trade in Services (1994) 4. Globalization. I. Title. II. Series.

LC67.62.B37 2006
338.4'737873--dc22 2005032922

ISBN10: 0-415-97833-5 (hbk)
ISBN10: 0-415-80581-3 (pbk)

ISBN13: 978-0-415-97833-0 (hbk)
ISBN13: 978-0-415-80581-0 (pbk)

Contents

List of Abbreviations

AACC	American Association of Community Colleges
AASCU	American Association of State Colleges and Universities
AAU	Association of American Universities
AAUP	American Association of University Professors
ACCU	Association of Catholic Colleges and Universities
ACE	American Council on Education
AJCU	Association of Jesuit Colleges and Universities
APEC	Asia-Pacific Economic Cooperation Forum
ASEAN	Association of Southeast Asian Nations
CGS	Council of Graduate Schools
CHEA	Council for Higher Education Accreditation
CIC	Council for Independent Colleges
COFHE	Consortium on Financing Higher Education
CQAIE	Center for Quality Assurance in International Education
DOC	Department of Commerce
EI	Education International
FTAA	Free Trade Area of the Americas
GATS	General Agreement on Trade in Services
GATT	General Agreement on Tariffs and Trade

GDP	Gross Domestic Product
IHEP	Institute for Higher Education Policy
ITA	International Trade Administration
ITO	International Trade Organization
MFN	Most Favored Nation
NAFSA	NAFSA: Association of International Educators
NAFTA	North American Free Trade Agreement
NAICU	National Association of Independent Colleges and Universities
NASULGC	National Association of State Universities and Land Grant Colleges
NCITE	National Committee on International Trade in Education
NCSL	National Conference of State Legislatures
NEA	National Education Association
NICU	National Independent College Council
OECD	Organization for Economic Cooperation and Development
OEEC	Organization for European Economic Cooperation
OSI	Office of Service Industries (Department of Commerce)
STR	Special Trade Representative
UCEA	University Continuing Education Association
UN	United Nations
UNESCO	United Nations Educational, Scientific, and Cultural Organization
USTR	Office of the United States Trade Representative
WTO	World Trade Organization

Chapter One

Introduction

Why should you—higher education researcher, policy maker, student, administrator, observer—care about trade policy? Are you aware that you are part of the fifth largest service 'industry' in the United States? Indeed, the sheer monetary value of the enormous higher education system in the United States has inspired many officials and investors to examine ways to expand and profit from the successes of the U.S. system in today's global economy. How? Through trade: Trade policies have the potential to bring globalization to higher education in a way for which few, if any, campuses are prepared.

This book presents a much needed and timely examination of a key topic that lies at this intersection of globalization and higher education—international trade. Globalization is having a dramatic impact on higher education in the United States and around the world, affecting student populations, curricular decisions, funding sources, and, in reality, all levels of operation. International trade in higher education services is one mechanism through which globalization is beginning to infiltrate the relationship between American higher education and the federal government, an important shift that may have long-term ramifications for the higher education industry at all levels.

This book examines where American higher education falls within the General Agreement on Trade in Services (GATS), a World Trade Organization (WTO) initiative that seeks to diminish and ultimately eliminate all barriers to trade in service industries, including higher education. The Office of the United States Trade Representative (USTR) has elected to include higher education in its comprehensive offer to the GATS for trade liberalization in a broad array of service industries. If enacted, this agreement has the potential to dramatically change American higher education as it becomes subject to the requirements of international law. The purpose of this study, however, was not to evaluate the merit of the USTR's position on higher education or the views of those potentially impacted by it. Instead, it was to present an unbiased analysis of the on-going process that informs and influences the policy developments around trade in higher education services in the U.S.

In addition, this study extracted concerns about the commodification of higher education from the research data and utilized commodification theory to further inform the analysis of the issues raised by the participants. Whether higher education is a commodity or commercial product to be exchanged for money on the open international market, a culturally significant enterprise developed for the public good, or something in between is the consideration that informs the ongoing debate over the GATS and trade in education services. By encouraging trade in education,—the expansion of financial opportunities in education across borders—the GATS appears to accept that higher education is a commodity of sorts.

The diverse elements of the American higher education industry, on the other hand, largely oppose this interpretation of their efforts as being that of selling a service product (education as commodity) to consumers in the education marketplace. The term 'industry' is purposefully used throughout this book to underscore the market tensions affecting higher education and refers here to the broad collective of institutions—public and private, for-profit and non-profit, large and small—that make up the whole of higher education in the United States. It must be noted, however, that using the term industry in reference to the diverse and decentralized system of American higher education is somewhat controversial and not without critics. Commodification theory underscores and helps explain a portion of the tensions that exist on both sides of this debate over trade in higher education services.

WHY THIS ISSUE IS IMPORTANT

The United States has a world-renowned and historically decentralized system of higher education that is defined largely by institutional autonomy and academic independence. Any external, international policies affecting system-wide operating standards in the United States higher education industry would result in a major paradigm shift in this system. Passage of major trade agreements involving American higher education will truly alter the very core of how institutions define themselves and how they relate to government actors. And, the negotiations that will determine whether higher education joins insurance or banking or construction as internationally traded services are occurring right now.

The momentum for free trade in higher education services is clearly forging ahead, particularly as the U.S. government appears committed to its inclusion in U.S. trade agreements and as many American higher education organizations seek expansion opportunities abroad. The only way to affect how this movement toward free trade occurs is to be an informed and engaged part of the dialogue. If the leadership of the traditional, non-profit sector of American higher education chooses—either through ignorance or informed neglect—to remain largely outside of the debate on whether higher education should be traded freely, it risks being caught unprepared when the implementation of trade liberalization arrives on their campuses.

WHY THIS STUDY IS IMPORTANT

This study provides a direct examination of these emerging issues of trade in higher education services in the context of American higher education. Currently, few working within U.S. higher education are even paying attention to this issue. Those that are either can commit only a meager amount of time and resources to the issue or are fully immersed in their own interests and do not engage the full range of concerns about trade. Being an outside researcher, and not an active and biased party, allowed for broad access to and candid discussions with actors on both sides of this issue. This study provides a big picture perspective into the intentions, goals, and concerns of both sides of this debate, informing in, ideally, a neutral way, the broad debate about trade in higher education services.

The goal of this book is to present a balanced picture of the implications of including higher education as a regulated trade issue in the GATS. Again, this study will not, nor is intended to, take a position on or provide policy recommendations regarding the merits of the GATS or, more broadly, international trade in higher education services. Instead, it provides an important and novel perspective on the process through which policy decisions regarding trade are being developed today in the United States. If the actors involved, particularly those wanting to exclude higher education from trade agreements, hope to influence the debate and resulting policy outcomes, they must engage the process immediately and in an informed way. For all of these reasons, this study is critical in filling a gap in the research on globalization, trade, and American higher education.

HIGHER EDUCATION AS A TRADABLE SERVICE

In December 2000, the USTR publicly released its initial negotiating proposal to the WTO to remove barriers to trade in international higher education services. These barriers create "a series of 'obstacles' to colleges operating in other countries. These (obstacles) include special taxes, outright bans on higher education services from foreign institutions, restrictions on online instructional material from abroad, long delays in government approval of foreign programs, and difficult requirements for foreign academics entering and leaving countries" (Foster, 2002). This 2000 proposal by the USTR provided the earliest indication that the United States was seriously considering including higher education in its extended negotiations with the WTO about the GATS.

The USTR formally adopted this initial proposal on higher education as a small but significant area within its March 31, 2003, comprehensive offer to the GATS for broad liberalization of trade in services across industries. The GATS proposes liberalization consideration across 12 service sectors, including "business, communication, construction and engineering, distribution, *education* (emphasis added), environment, financial health, tourism and travel, recreation (cultural and sporting), transportation, and other" (Sedgwick, 2002). Education alone is merely one out of the 12, and higher education is an even smaller sub-sector within education. The USTR's offer also only lists higher education very briefly within the breadth of service industries being offered for trade liberalization, and includes traditional post-secondary education as well as adult education, technical training, and educational testing services. The decision to include higher education at all, however, indicates the USTR's perspective that higher education is an important service industry with significant potential for growth across national borders and deserving of international attention and agreements (USTR, 2003). While reserving the option of a future reversal, the USTR is currently proposing broad reductions in international trade barriers on higher education services.

Following similar statements made over the past decade by the European Union, Australia, Japan, and New Zealand, this proposal by the USTR is yet another indication of the marked change in how national and international governing bodies perceive higher education. No longer is international higher education made up merely of national systems that educate citizens for local employment and national service. Instead, higher education is being redefined at many levels as an international service industry to be regulated through the marketplace and through international trade agreements. It is modern international market forces meet historic domestic educational interests that tensions arise over international trade in higher education.

> Higher education, internationally, is experiencing changes on an unprecedented scale, driven by demand for access, staff mobility and

> cooperation, increased opportunities for the exchange and sale of services in teaching and research, and online technology. While the WTO has acknowledged the significance of an emerging global environment for higher education, . . . it is not evident that governments are collectively addressing the key issues. (Skilbeck, 2001, p. 14)

Higher education is undoubtedly being transformed by globalization, here defined as "the flow of technology, economy, knowledge, people, values, ideas . . . across borders" (Knight, 1997). In some countries, such as many of those in the European Union, the borderless, globalized nature of educational opportunities makes higher education inherently international. In others, such as the United States, individual institutions seem largely removed from any direct impact of globalization and, instead, respond to pressures from their own constituents in determining how extensive their international efforts and relevance will be. At both extremes, however, international issues are undoubtedly present. One particular area in which government and education intersect notably in the international arena is that of trade in educational services.

For developing and developed countries across the globe, trade in higher education has the potential to alter dramatically how and why their students seek and receive higher education. The global market worth of trade in education services is currently estimated at more than $2 trillion, including public and private spending on all forms of education (Patrinos, 2002). The United States earns over $13 billion from trade in higher education services in the form of foreign student enrollments alone (IIE, 2004), making higher education the United States' fifth largest service export (ACE, 2003; NCITE, 2003; Ascher, 2003). Due to its size and scope, it is no surprise that market competition and the drive to capitalize on the economic potential of higher education exports would become significant for such a lucrative international service industry. As the world's largest exporter of higher education services, the U.S. is in a powerful position to influence and benefit from international agreements removing barriers to expanding trade in higher education services.

"The liberalization of trade in educational services is high on the agenda of trade negotiators but is only just appearing on the radar screen of higher education managers and policy makers" (Knight, 2002). Examining this gap in interests and goals between U.S. trade representative officials and the American higher education establishment regarding trade in higher education services is the focus of this research. Such an examination also provides insights into the issues and concerns regarding the impact of free trade on American higher education.

A Worst-Case Scenario of the Impact of the GATS on Higher Education

To help the reader understand why there are such concerns over free trade in higher education services, it may be useful to present a worst-case scenario, to showcase some of the numerous ways in which trade liberalization could infiltrate American higher education. If one assumes that free trade has been applied unfettered across American higher education, then a basic fact in this scenario is that all WTO-member nation providers of higher education services, regardless of country of origin, are now subject to the legally binding terms of the GATS.

There are several levels at which absolute free trade, without any barriers protecting the industry, could force significant change onto American higher education. First, in examining the challenges to public higher education, it is possible to envision a case where another country would perceive having publicly funded higher education would constitute a monopoly, since the public financing helps hold down tuition prices at levels below what a private institution can offer. If challenged through an international dispute settlement process, it is possible that public higher education would be forced to privatize, in order to maintain a truly free market in which institutions compete for students.

Public institutions might also be challenged about their admission policies, through which they currently reserve a certain percentage of places for residents of their home state and other protective groups. Such a practice would illegally impact a foreign student's ability to be admitted and might be deemed illegal. (It is outside the scope of this research, but in this worst case scenario, one can envision, too, a challenge to admission policies requiring that all admitted students pass a high school graduation exam as unfair to foreign students without access to the exam or the language skills to pass the exam, which would extend the impact of free trade in higher education services down into the K-12 realm.)

For private institutions, the influx of formerly public providers as well as foreign suppliers could make competing for students even more challenging. These institutions might also face protests over admission and financial aid policies, if they once maintained different admission and aid standards for domestic and foreign student admission. For example, if an institution maintained need-blind admission for domestic students but took foreign students' financial status into consideration when evaluating their application, in a challenge this would be considered an unfair and illegal practice. In addition, if an institution provides full financial–need aid to its domestic students but does not offer the same aid structure to foreign students, this could be challenged as an illegal policy. Institution might lose their ability to admit students in any subjective way that might be deemed unfair to foreign students.

It is possible to imagine, too, a situation in which the traditional sector of higher education, in choosing to compete with the for-profit sector instead of fighting against the tide of trade liberalization, would focus on its financial interests. More market-susceptible institutions would have to consider eliminating departments that are not self-supporting, increasing activities that generate revenues, and outsourcing or eliminating altogether campus resources that might be provided by others at less cost. (This actually is already happening in higher education today, independent of the global imperatives discussed in this study.) These institutions would seek competitive advantages and eliminate all activities that affected the bottom-line.

The wealthier institutions would become the centers for studying all of those cash poor subjects (classics, perhaps, or comparative literature), resulting in elitism among academic fields. The liberal arts would become an educational luxury, where only those meeting the admission standards at the most elite institutions would have the privilege of studying these fields, and where only the privileged students would have the resources to commit to such studies.

To close out this worst case scenario, though there are numerous, perhaps limitless, additional examples of what might happen under uninhibited free trade conditions, it is possible to imagine entire fields of study becoming transformed due to international enrollments. Science and engineering are already facing intense enrollment pressures, as American students do not seek advanced degrees in the numbers needed to fill the classrooms and laboratories at institutions across the country. In many cases, domestic students with less impressive credentials are currently being admitted to programs over qualified international students to ensure some domestic presence in the program. Under an absolute free trade model, such protectionist admission policies would be illegal, and all applicants would have to be considered in the same way.

Under these conditions, one could predict, then, a rapid increase in East and South Asian students, for example, in graduate programs in computer science and engineering, programs that are vital for U.S. national security and economic development. It is not unimaginable that free trade could actually lead to diminished capacities to compete in business (in high tech, for example) and could pose a legitimate threat to national security—not because foreign students are studying here, which is already a current issue—but because there would be few, if any, domestic students qualified and eligible to for employment in classified areas and fields. Exporting this and other economically vital areas of expertise would, in fact, further disadvantage the U.S. economy, which is already suffering from extensive outsourcing of jobs to developing countries.

These examples within this worst-case scenario are extreme, of course, but they do offer insights into the nature of unfettered free trade in higher education services and why there is lingering skepticism over the value of free trade for American higher education. Perhaps protectionism is a necessary 'evil' for maintaining the quality higher education system that currently exists in the United States. This research will not, necessarily, provide mechanisms to refute or support the likelihood of any of these worst-case examples becoming a legitimate problem, but it does explain and elaborate on the environment in which they could.

Understanding the Global Forces Affecting Higher Education

Ideally, this book will provide a productive tool for understanding the complexities of the relationship between American government and the incredibly diverse higher education industry with regard to trade in education and, perhaps, offer a broader perspective on how globalization and internationalization will continue to change the American higher education system.

"If knowledge is fundamental to globalization, globalization should also have a profound impact on the transmission of knowledge" (Carnoy, 2002). "In the knowledge industries, of which education is a central part, globalization is already a key figure" (Altbach, Fall 2002). Globalization is affecting higher education, and the extent to which higher education is responding to the pressures of globalization is deserving of further examination and research. The significance of research on globalization and internationalization in higher education is in realizing the need to understand the breadth of the impact globalization is having and will continue to have on higher education systems and all of its constituencies. As noted at the beginning of this paper, globalization is not simply an economic issue. It is a broad force, affecting cultural, political, social, environmental, economic, and a myriad of other areas of interaction, and higher education falls in the crosshairs of all of these areas. Globalization is changing how we organize the world, and higher education will play a key role in helping mediate the effects of globalization, while simultaneously being transformed by globalization.

Internationalization provides a framework that can be researched in order to understand how individual institutions are responding to globalization. With organizations like the American Council on Education (ACE), Institute for International Education (IIE), and NAFSA promoting the collection of data on internationalization strategies and providing assistance to institutions looking to develop or improve upon their internationalization processes, it is apparent that institutions are becoming more open to being internationally relevant and globally aware. Much more research is needed in a broad spectrum of areas related to globalization and internationalization and higher education, including examining institutional leadership and how it affects decision-making around internationalization; faculty research and institutional and departmental support for area studies; the expansion of foreign campuses overseas; the expansion of campus programs to include greater exposure to international issues and studies; and much more. This research on trade and American higher education will provide a focused look at a specific and relatively unexamined area of the higher education industry as it evolves in this era of globalization.

For higher education to remain relevant as a tool for training all members of a functioning society and economy, from future leaders to laborers, it cannot ignore the transformation being imposed by globalization. Instead, higher education may need to embrace the fact that globalization is a force that cannot be ignored and look into strategies to make globalization work to the advantage of higher education. Ideally, research on internationalization strategies and outcomes will provide the information and data that allows institutions and leaders in higher education to embrace the potential of globalization, while pushing back against any negative ramifications.

PLAN OF THE BOOK

The following chapters present an overview of higher education in an international context, ultimately focusing on international trade policies and their potential impact on American higher education. Chapter Two details the research questions that guided this study and the methodology used to conduct and analyze the research. Chapter Three is a review of the literature on higher education and globalization, internationalization, and international trade and provides background information that establishes a context for the chapters that follow. Chapter Four highlights the emergence of higher education policies among the major multinational organizations, including the United Nations, the World Bank, and the Organization for Economic Development, that formed after World War II, describing and analyzing the circumstances in which higher education considerations grew in significance to elicit international dialogues and agreements. By providing this background information, Chapter Four sets the stage for the current climate in which higher education is being discussed and debated as an area of interest to the World Trade Organization and its General Agreement on Trade in Services, which is explained within the context of higher education in Chapter Five.

Chapter Six describes the USTR and its role in determining what elements of American commerce and industry are included in U.S. offers to trade agreements. This chapter also explains and analyzes the position that the USTR has taken regarding higher education services within its negotiating proposals and initial offer to the GATS. These chapters all establish the context for the presentation of the data collected through the research, which occurs in Chapters Seven, Eight, and Nine.

Chapter Seven introduces the participants in the research, the organizations that have either produced published or internal documentation regarding their position or had representatives willing to be interviewed about their organization's stance on trade in higher education and the GATS. From these interviews came the findings of Chapter Eight, which details the nuances and tensions of the environment in which the higher education 'industry' representatives and those of the USTR and Department of Commerce have been engaging in discussions about the ongoing GATS negotiations. And, Chapter Nine presents the specific issues and concerns regarding the inclusion higher education services in the U.S. offer to the GATS.

Examined collectively, the information provided in Chapter Nine points toward a theoretical explanation for the phenomenon of higher education's moving from being perceived as a public good to being regulated as a service industry. Chapter Ten utilizes theory on the commodification of higher education to inform the findings and present a broader perspective on the environment in which higher education operates in the United States today. Finally, Chapter Eleven concludes this book by summarizing the research and findings from the previous chapters and presenting ideas about potential future issues with regard to trade in higher education as well as ideas about future research that might be generated out of this research. In its entirety, this book seeks to expose the mechanisms by which international trade issues have begun to infiltrate American higher education, the challenges free trade poses for higher education at all levels, and the preparedness of the American higher education industry to respond to those challenges.

Chapter Two
The Research Questions

THE RESEARCH QUESTIONS

The main questions that grounded this study are:

- How has the federal government established its stance on trade in higher education services and why? How has the American higher education industry (as represented by higher education membership associations) responded to the U.S. initiative to liberalize international trade in higher education services and why? And, finally, what is each agency doing to pursue and promote its own interests regarding international trade in higher education?

Related questions that this research seeks to answer include:

- Who represents the interests of the American higher education industry in dealing with and influencing policy makers in the federal government and what are they thinking about these higher education trade policy initiatives?
- How do these representatives of higher education (ACE, AAUP, CHEA, NCITE, etc.) and of government policymakers (USTR) seek out the information from higher education leaders and researchers needed to best represent the interests of their constituents while establishing broad federal foreign policy?
- How aware are higher education campus leaders in the United States of these impending policy changes and the likely effects on their institutions?
- When these interests are in conflict, what mechanisms do these actors utilize, if any, to affect real change in the positions taken by the federal

government concerning international trade in higher education, and how effective are these mechanisms?

This study is also an examination of how this initiative on trade liberalization of higher education is redefining the role that the federal government is willing to take in regulating the American higher education industry and what this might mean for the historically independent, decentralized nature of American institutions of higher education. It explores how various constituencies—including representational organizations, individual campus actors, government policy makers—see their own interests regarding trade in education and how they are responding, if at all. This analysis offers new insights into why and how higher education chooses to involve itself in external concerns that may significantly affect its industry and operations. It aims to expose the complexities of the environment in which policies regarding trade in higher education services are being debated today, the specific concerns of those actors who are informed and engaged in the process, and the broad ramifications for American higher education of being treated as tradable service or commodity.

The perspectives represented in this study came from government officials, leaders of higher education associations, and consultants who have experience working on this issue. The campus perspective was eliminated from this study, in the end, when there was no response from the numerous campus officials contacted and after the representative organizations confirmed the lack of interest coming from their campus-level constituents. That this issue remains so completely removed from the campus but has the potential to impact campus-level operations dramatically indicates both the potential for significant surprises for the campuses, should these trade proposals be enacted into law, and perhaps, that their representative organizations have not presented the issue in a way that has grabbed their attention.

Gathering the specific data from the individuals and organizations that do examine international issues affecting American higher education, though a small subset of the higher education industry, provided a thoroughly comprehensive perspective on this issue as it is being addressed right now, as well as providing a foundation for future research. The main disadvantage of using such an inductive approach to applying theory to the research is that existing theory did not provide an up-front structure for my data collection or analysis. Useful theoretical explanations of the how and why questions behind initiatives to liberalize international trade in higher education services came out of the data collected through document analysis, historical research, and interviews, however.

Document Analysis and Historical Research

This study involved qualitative research, culminating in a case study of how American higher education is responding to the increased interest in liberalization of trade in higher education services by the federal government at this point in time. Data collection for the background historical sections and the section on the present international conditions of American higher education involved archival research through government documents, the websites of government and non-government organizations, and published materials, such as books and journals. For these initial chapters, the gathered data on the history of higher education as an international policy concern provided the background information necessary for understanding the context in which American higher education is currently operating, as it considers the implications of trade policies regarding higher education as a service industry. Further, using the documents published by experts and provided by the higher education associations regarding trade, the GATS, and the numerous responses to this new policy development provided significant and valuable data that complemented the data gathered through interviews.

Data Collection through Interviews

Thorough research into this trade issue and the positions of the federal government and higher education representatives on the issue required interviews of individuals at such places as the Office of the U.S. Trade Representative, the Department of Commerce, the American Council on Education, the Council for Higher Education Accreditation, and the National Committee for International Trade in Education. Using a semi-structured interview format in the interviews, the research resulted in a consistency among the data collected from the myriad sources interviewed. These interviews generated data on who is making decisions for these organizations around this trade issue, how the actors involved are gathering their own data in forming their opinions and positions on the issue, how they ensure that they are representing the position of their constituents, how they seek opportunities to influence national and international policy formation and through what means, and the similarities and differences of perceived implications of the current U.S. push for reduced/removed barriers to trade in higher education across borders. The interviews, therefore, included individuals at higher education organizations and membership associations, as well as representatives from the Office of the United States Trade Representative, the Department of Commerce, and the National Association of State Legislatures.

Higher Education Organizations and Associations.

Representatives of both "pro"-trade and "anti"-trade educational organizations participated in this study. Though, ideally, at least two individuals at each of these organizations would have been willing and able to contribute to the research, but, unfortunately, the reality of the trade issue is such that there were only two organizations in which there was a second person who had any capacity to speak to these issues of trade in higher education. In one case, the second individual was actually someone who had left the organization but was willing to speak about his prior work on trade in higher education. (Indeed, as noted above, at many of the representational organizations contacted, there was not even a single officer who knew enough about the issue and its implications to participate in my research.)

The participant organizations included two representatives from the American Council on Education (ACE), the Council for Higher Education Accreditation (CHEA), and the National Association of State Universities and Land-Grant Colleges (NASULGC), and one representative from each of the following associations: the National Committee for International Trade in Education (NCITE), the Council of Independent Colleges (CIC), the Association of Catholic Colleges and Universities (ACCU), the Association of Jesuit Colleges and Universities (AJCU), the Council of Graduate Schools (CGS), the National Educators Association (NEA), and the American Association of University Professors (AAUP). The Association of American Universities (AAU), the American Association of Community Colleges (AACC), the American Association of State Colleges and Universities (AASCU), the Center on Financing Higher Education (COFHE), and NAFSA: Association of International Educators (NAFSA) declined interviews on the grounds that there were no representatives of their organization well-versed enough to speak about these issues on behalf of their organization. These organizations are most significant in an examination of this trade issue in that they have each made public statements concerning their positions on higher education and GATS (ACE, CHEA, and NASULGC are against, AAU and AACC are publicly remaining neutral for the time being, and NCITE is for) and continue to be engaged in the debate about the USTR proposal.

There was a snowballing effect across the interviews, where those interviewed offered recommendations of others at different organizations who would be useful in this research. Altogether, fourteen interviews with representatives of ten education associations together with information gathered from another ten regarding their inability to participate in my research form the core of the data collected through first person interactions. Each of the interviews lasted between 45 minutes and an hour and a half, depending upon the interviewee's familiarity with the issue and the individuals' willingness to speak openly. (See Appendix A for the list of questions used to frame the interviews with these higher education representatives.)

Office of the United States Trade Representative.

In my next area of interviews for data collection (USTR), two officials from the Office of the United States Trade Representative participated—one in person and one by e-mail, providing insights into their policy development procedures and how those procedures are informed and/or affected by external actors and interests. Bernard Ascher, former director of service-industry affairs for the U.S. trade office, participated by e-mail. Dr. Ascher has repeatedly refuted criticism against the USTR's handling of its trade liberalization proposal by stating that federal officials warned these higher education organizations that higher education would be included well before the proposal was submitted to the WTO (Foster, 2002). In addition, Dr. Ascher's replacement as USTR Director of Service-Industry Affairs, Chris Melly, also agreed to be interviewed on two occasions. The first interview was truly valuable in understanding how policies get development and how much non-governmental input is allowed and/or welcomed into the process. The second interview helped put the information gathered in early rounds of data collection into a current context and helped clarify some findings from the initial data collection. (See Appendix B for the list of questions used to frame these USTR interviews.)

Other Interviews.

Finally, two additional interviews also emerged as significant contributions to the research. Both developed out of information gathered at earlier interviews. In the first, Jennifer Reason Moll, director of international services, at the U.S. Department of Commerce (DOC) agreed to discuss the DOC's perspective on trade and higher education. Ms. Moll also once worked for NCITE and served as a significant liaison between the USTR and Commerce Department and NCITE and other higher education associations. (See Appendix C for the list of questions used to frame this interview at the DOC.)

The other interview was with Jeremy Meadows, who directs committee development for the National Conference of State Legislatures (NCSL). Mr. Meadows came to my attention through an e-mail newsgroup concerning the Trade Representative's Office's plea to state governors for support of the new proposal to GATS. The governors had turned the issue over the legislators, and the legislators sought the assistance of NCSL in helping them both understand the proposal and craft a response. Mr. Meadows was seeking information on trade and provided interesting input into this examination of the issue of trade in educational services. (See Appendix D for the list of questions used to frame this NCSL interview.)

CONCLUSIONS

This study provides a comprehensive examination of the trade issue for American higher education today, its implications for the higher education industry in the United States, and the preparedness of the American higher education industry to respond to significant change in the status quo. Looking closely at public policies, in this case a very specific policy on international trade, provided a chance to investigate the flow of information and level of cooperation between the higher education industry, its representative non-governmental associations, and the federal offices that engage in creating policies that may affect operations industry-wide.

One important note about the particular role the author had as an interviewer: in some instances, the participants seemed to be seeking information about higher education or the specifics of this trade question in addition to providing information about their perspectives. In order not to affect the outcome of the interviews, it was important to temper external opinions within the conversations, in an attempt to minimize the extent to which outside opinions affected the interviewee's contributions. Maintaining as neutral a position as possible on the issues in all of the interviews was imperative, both to minimize the effect the researcher's opinions might have on the information being presented by the participant and to underscore a balanced presentation of the issue in the study.

Through the collected data and creating distinctive research findings, this book serves to synthesize and shed some light on individual organizational or institutional concerns that might be particular to one group; or, ideally, it illustrates an issue that should and will be of broader concern in the near future. The data and subsequent analysis serve as a basis understanding American higher education as it is impacted by and responds to globalization—in this case the globalization represented by international trade.

Chapter Three

A Review of the Literature: Globalization, Internationalization, and Higher Education

This chapter seeks to establish a core understanding of some of the key literature underscoring the intersecting research on globalization, internationalization, trade, and higher education. These are incredibly broad research areas with complicated histories, but when examined in conjunction with each other these areas provide a fascinating look at the modernization, innovation, and, even, commodification of higher education today.

Globalization in general is a hot topic these days, as a state of war exists in the Middle East, and as international terrorism and continued international unrest force a continued re-examination of the power dynamics between rich and poor, developed and developing nations across the globe. In addition, protest movements have emerged to attack the power and policies of international groups like the World Bank, International Monetary Fund, and World Trade Organization at their international meetings. Indeed, as the United States engages in a war on terrorism at home and abroad, using military, economic, and political power to influence and affect how nations around the world act, globalization has taken on greater significance in American foreign and domestic policy.

GLOBALIZATION, INTERNATIONALIZATION, AND HIGHER EDUCATION

> . . . (T)here is no doubt that globalization is an important issue for higher education. Around it is clustered many key matters: internationalization strategies; transnational education; international quality assurance; entrepreneurial approaches; . . . to name but a few." (McBurnie, 2001, p. 12)

Globalization is a concept that is often misunderstood, usually by being considered solely an economic issue, and is misappropriated to explain the multinational links that have become common and intertwined with domestic issues in many countries around the world (Wendt, 2000). While machines and technology have shrunk time and space and have created environments that transcend social norms, the impact of cross-national and cross-cultural relationships cannot be underestimated when try to understand the driving forces behind an array of political, economic, and social considerations today (Urry, 1998; Green, 1997). Globalization concerns the expansion of ideas, principles, and economic influence across national borders and requires effective leadership to ensure that its effects are positive. Technology, ecology, economics, corporations, civil society, politics, and culture all are significant dimensions of globalization today (Beck, 2000). Jane Knight's definition of globalization will serve as this research's primary definition: "Globalisation is the flow of technology, economy, knowledge, people, values, ideas . . . across borders. Globalisation affects each country in a different way due to a nations' individual history, traditions, culture and priorities" (Knight, 1997, p. 6).

The globalization of cultures—the blurring of national boundaries by such forces as entertainment and the media, multi-national corporations, and scholarly exchange—also demands effective educational leadership, to direct education systems that are preparing students and citizens for this new, international world. If higher education is in the "business" of creating and transferring knowledge, then the intersection of higher education and globalization seems inevitable according to Carnoy and Rhoten (2002). With the borderless quality of globalization reflected in the expansiveness of knowledge, education serves as a significant realm in which globalization can gain a foothold without too much structural change at an institutional level. It is where the borderless aura of education meets the day-to-day operations of higher education institutions that the major issues of trade in education as a service industry become apparent.

Higher education is an industry that cannot avoid the influence of globalization, particularly in light of the borderless quality and expansiveness of knowledge generation and dissemination. Indeed, with the inherent drive of scholars to seek out and share new information, higher education is especially well situated to serve as a center for this kind of globalization of education—internationalization (Scott, 1998).

"Internationalization" and "globalization" are used so frequently, broadly, and, often, interchangeably in academic and popular writing that no singular definition remains for either term (Scott, 2000). In some regards, particularly with general media usage, the terms are interchangeable; they both connote the cross-national exchange of ideas, economies, cultures, and the like. For the purposes of academic clarity, however, there are differences between internationalization and globalization which can distinguish between an individual institutional process and an external systemic force, resulting in a more specific application of each term in a research context. The following definitions by Jane Knight (1997) present highly useful distinctions between internationalization and globalization.

> - Globalisation is the flow of technology, economy, knowledge, people values, ideas . . . across borders. Globalisation affects each country in a different way due to a nation's individual history, traditions, culture, and priorities.
> - Internationalization . . . is one of the ways a country responds to the impact of globalisation yet, at the same time, respects the individuality of a nation.
>
> Thus, internationalisation and globalisation are seen as different but dynamically linked concepts. Globalisation can be thought of as the catalyst while internationalisation is the response, albeit a response in a proactive way. (Knight, 1997, p. 6)

The internationalization of higher education is a natural extension of and response to the many forms of globalization currently affecting cultures, governments, industries, and institutions. Higher education has been acutely affected by cultural and economic globalization, as nations and institutions reexamine their educational missions, as well as the educational product they dispense, to determine their effectiveness in this new international environment. For the purpose of this research, a further refined definition developed by Jane Knight and Hans de Wit is most fitting: "Internationalization of higher education is the process of integrating an international/intercultural dimension into the teaching, research, and service functions of the institution" (Knight and de Wit, 1997).

In this context, then, globalization is a broad force, while internationalization is a specific process undertaken by individual countries or, in this case, organizations. Globalization is a catalyst; internationalization is a response (Knight, 1999). Peter Scott (1998) presents a more extensive examination of the differences between internationalization and globalization and describes internationalization as an institutionally centered ethos toward cross-cultural and cross-national educational exchange; while globalization is a combination of external economic, technological, environmental, political, social, and cultural forces that pressure not only individual institutions but the systems in which they operate.

Finally, Jan Currie (1998) distinguishes between globalization and internationalization by focusing on the marketplace—globalization is the alignment of higher education practices to an international economic marketplace, while internationalization remains the processes by which institutions maintain international elements in their operations, programs, and curriculum (Currie & Newson, 1998). The causal relationship between globalization and internationalization are certainly having notable affects on campuses and systems of higher education today. And, again, for consistency, this research uses Knight's definitions to understand how the terms globalization and internationalization are being applied.

Globalization and Higher Education

Higher education is undoubtedly a global industry, particularly considering its international actors, expansion, and influence. It is a worldwide knowledge industry, with institutions of higher education existing on every populated continent, in all developed countries, and in the vast majority of developing countries. Its purposes and histories may vary by nation and culture, but its existence is part of a whole that extends back hundreds of years (Kerr, 1990; Knight, 1999). Higher education, the education of people beyond secondary school, exists across the entire globe and is at the core of economic expansion and globalization where the university now exists outside of its domestic sphere and at the center of an international knowledge system based on technology and advanced communication capabilities, while remaining concerned about its cultural significance (Altbach, 1998), three of the most significant elements that define globalization.

The changes to higher education brought on by the economic elements of globalization, particularly the expanding market orientation of many segments of higher education, include aspects that had been largely restricted to for-profit industries: market concerns, transnational centers and accounting, quality concerns, customer satisfaction, and other corporate models of operations (Currie, 1998). Globalization has added a neoliberal, capitalistic element to higher education as an industry, as higher education has become more responsive to international market forces as well as government and multinational organization policies and initiatives (Currie, 1998; McBurnie, 2001; Wendt, 2000).

According to Sheila Slaughter, globalization has four significant implications for higher education: 1) constricting of public funds for discretionary activities, as post-secondary education is increasingly viewed as a private good to be paid for by the student; 2) increasing importance being placed on "technosciences" and tying higher education to international and national markets; 3) tightening relationships with multinational corporations (MNCs) and state agencies; and 4) increasing attention being paid by MNCs and industrialized countries to issues of global intellectual property rights and strategies (Slaughter, 1998). The increasing privatization of higher education, as national governments proportionately decrease their financial support for institutions has contributed to and influenced the tightening bonds between institutions and corporations. As Altbach (1998d) notes, "University-industry relations have become crucial for higher education in many countries" (p. 15). Indeed, the shifting relationship between higher education and governments has been reinforced and influenced by these burgeoning relationships between institutions and the market.

The Tension Between Higher Education and the Nation-State

Thomas Friedman (1999) holds that globalization is built on three balances: 1) between nation states; 2) between nation-states and global markets; and 3) between nation-states and individuals. Among each of these three balances, the nation-state is the constant, ideally providing some guidance and leadership in the expansion of organizations and industries across borders and "providing an organizing framework for international affairs" (Friedman, 1999, pp. 6–7). "At the heart of the relationship between globalization and education in the current historical conjuncture is the relationship between the globalized political economy and the nation-state" (Carnoy and Rhoten, 2002, p. 3). In order to understand higher education's response to or place within globalization, it is imperative to acknowledge one additional balance: that between the nation-state and higher education (Kerr, 1990; Scott, 1998).

"Universities are, by nature of their commitment to advancing universal knowledge, essentially international institutions, but they have been living increasingly in a world of nation states that have designs upon them" (Kerr, 1990, p. 5). The relationship between higher education and the nation-state has changed dramatically over the past century, most notably due to the inception and conclusion of the Cold War (Kweik, 2001). According to Altbach (1998d) "Universities are simultaneously international institutions, with common historical roots and also embedded in national cultures and circumstances" (pp. 3–4). Perhaps, then, institutions seek to maintain an illusion of inherent international purpose to ward off encroachment by nation-states (Scott, 1998; Kweik, 2001) as pressures to prove their relevance become increasingly challenging for higher education institutions.

Globalization, however, is producing significant changes in how much governments can determine their own national educational policies. According to Carnoy and Rhoten (2002), "(g)lobalization forces nation-states to focus more on acting as economic growth promoters for their national economies than as protectors of the national identity or a nationalistic project" (p. 2). Being embedded in the national culture and circumstances is, perhaps, insufficient to protect national higher education from globalization, if, indeed, such protection is warranted. Regardless, the tension between the nation-state and higher education, particularly around the issue of economics, underpins the impact of globalization on higher education, particularly as higher education becomes an increasingly global industry (Readings, 1996).

Economic, Political, and Cultural Elements of Globalization in Higher Education

The rapid escalation of government financing of higher education began at the outbreak of the Cold War, in an attempt to develop technological superiority. At the end of the Cold War, globalization became the organizational paradigm for the new world (Friedman, 1999), and higher education is certainly not immune from its influence. With the rise of technology and the demise of the Iron Curtain, the United States has become further insulated as the lone super power, and the effects of this separateness, both self-imposed and inevitable given the politics and economic issues involved, undeniably extended to higher education. It is this sense of American higher education—as historically connected to the world, as the current leading system in the world and, yet, as a system highly alienated from the world—that makes the United States' system particularly compelling in an examination of the effects of globalization on higher education.

As the international economy moves toward a borderless, multinational model of financial and production flows, individual nations are being forced to examine their labor pool and the training necessary to have a competitive labor force. This dispersed global division of labor challenges both industrialized and developing countries to adjust and develop their education offerings in order to supply a prepared labor force (van Tilburg, 2002; de Wit, 2002). Higher education plays a crucial role in preparing workers for the job market, and the majority of local workers will come out of the local system of higher education. One legitimate concern about open trade in higher education, then, might be that the imported institutions or curricula may not be directly applicable to the local economy and the needs of the regional employer base. It is possible to imagine a scenario where the education offered is not applicable to the local economy, resulting in either an underemployed work force or an increase in outflows of well-educated people to countries that do have the need for their skills. In either case, the country would not be well-served by the increased educational opportunities afforded by external education providers, regardless of the appearance of a market for their service or their ability to provide an educational opportunity to the ever-increasing cohorts looking to enroll in higher education.

Indeed, though "(f)or most of their long history, universities were the preserve of the elite" (David, 1997), this is no longer the case in the developed world and increasingly even in developing nations. Over the past century and a half, the doors of higher education have opened wider to accommodate greater diversity among students, largely due to the economic benefits of attaining tertiary education. The economic significance of higher education exists on many levels. Peter Scott (1998) discusses the idea of higher education being translated into a competitive economic advantage for a country, as "knowledge" and highly skilled labor become primary resources in advanced economies (Scott, 1998). Beck holds that labor is being replaced by knowledge and capital and that a nation's ability to contribute to the world economy relies upon its ability to train a knowledgeable work force (Beck, 2000). The value of the labor of a nation's population is largely related to the skills that labor has and the ability to leverage those skills in the globalized economy, even more than at home.

The expansion of higher education came in response to economic pressures and the recognition of universities as centers for both research and knowledge generation as well as the training of human capital. In the "knowledge economy . . . the university (is) not just . . . a creator of knowledge, a trainer of young minds and transmitter of culture, but also (is) . . . a major agent of economic growth: the knowledge factory, as it were, at the center of the knowledge economy" (David, 1997). There continues to be an increased occupational demand for better-educated workers who can function in the new service- and technology-oriented economic environment. In addition, there has been a growth of new professional positions, again as new industries develop, that are less about production and more about service and that require a better-educated workforce. Together, the economy has provided incentives, demands, and direction to higher education—both to encourage existing institutions to respond and to develop new institutions to meet new demands.

Higher education in the U.S. has developed from a growth industry to a mature industry, meaning it not only has developed to its potential, as evidenced by massification, but has now become so established as to require oversight and supervision (Levine, 2001). It is facing a level of scrutiny and criticism from external actors and agents that is unprecedented in American higher education. Higher education for training a better-educated work force is seen as a requirement to be competitive in the world economy, but higher education, as an industry, is being threatened by diminishing support from public spending. In this way, the market forces of globalization have most definitely had an impact on higher education—workers need education to contribute to and find a place in the new economy, but they will have to fund it themselves. Even in the face of globalization pressures, the political will to fund higher education is not keeping up with the economic need for education.

The political elements of higher education often center around two key areas: funding and national security. With industrialization and, later, the tension between democracy and communism, higher education became a tool for government research and development, and in the post-war era, investment in education was a prominent tool for nation-building (Green, 1997). In much of the world, however, much of the expansion of higher education has had to occur in spite of the lack of economic growth and political stability. Universities across the developing world are facing the challenge of managing the rapid growth in demand for higher education at a time of severe cutbacks in government financial support for higher education (Salmi, 1992). In Africa and Latin America, enrollment in higher education increased by 500–800% between 1950 and the 1980s, though most nations did not have the infrastructure to support these levels of growth, resulting in systems that are overtaxed and under-funded (Neave, 1994).

Today, local and federal governments world-wide have cut back their spending on higher education, forcing institutions to become more financially savvy with their resources and to pass along more of the costs of instruction on to students. And, in reality, many of these nations do not have either the political will or economic stability to sustain the expansion of higher education that occurred during the past thirty to forty years. Many developing nations do not have economies developed enough to provide employment of college educated workers, creating an unbalanced internal efficiency between workers and the labor market and resulting in high unemployment levels for over-educated workers (Salmi, 1992). The political cutbacks in fact may result in a corrective force that levels the number of educated to the job market, but this correction may, in the long run, have a negative effect on growth.

Powerful cultural industries, like universities and colleges, also influence and are influenced by globalization (Urry, 1998). Indeed, as Sadlak (1998) notes, universities and other institutions of higher education have become "central in modern society and their role has shifted from being a *reflection* of social, cultural, and economic relationships to being a *determinant* of such relationships" (Sadlak, 1998, p. 106). Higher education is a significant conveyer of national identities and, for good or bad, national elites and social status (Scott, 1998; Readings, 1996; Green, 1997). As higher education becomes increasingly beholden to private industry and transnational concerns, due in large part to the economic and political issues noted above, the importance of institutional ties to the nation-state, and the cultural norms institutions once were expected to perpetrate, diminish (Readings, 1996).

Ideally, college graduates become economic, social, cultural, and political leaders in their countries. Unfortunately, and particularly among students from developing countries, the opportunities afforded in a global economy often result in graduates seeking the best opportunities available to them, and those opportunities are often not in their home countries. Globalization may in fact have dramatically negative cultural effects for nations whose best students seek work in other countries, while simultaneously contributing to the under-employment of a large number of college graduates at home. The resulting instability cannot be seen as positive for many nations.

Implications of Globalization on Campus

"Globalization (now serves) as the new pattern for administration, ordering, and arrangement of higher education" (McBurnie, 2001, p. 12). Indeed, globalization is having broad ramifications on the operations of higher education systems and institutions around the world, though those ramifications do differ significantly by country and influence in the global marketplace. Most notably, globalization has led to the development of entirely new areas of private international institutional development and a rapid increase in student and scholarly mobility, which often results in semi-permanent or permanent relocation of many nations' best students and faculty outside of their home countries (Altbach, 1999). The result for developed countries is more international students in the classroom, while for developing countries it is fewer top students in the classroom and in leadership roles on home campuses.

As fiscal issues become increasingly significant in the existence and operation of higher education, particularly in cases where individual nation-states cannot afford to compete to keep their own students at home institutions, colleges and universities will not be able to remain inured from market forces as they execute their operations in areas like designing their curricula or constructing their student bodies. Instead, issues like marketability of skills and access to jobs will play increasingly important roles in how institutions operate and what students and society will expect from higher education (Altbach, 1998).

Globalization is also impacting how campuses develop their curricula to compete in the global marketplace for students and faculty; what language is used for instruction and operations, as English expands to become the language of knowledge distribution; and whether Western education models will continue to be seen as the standard-bearers for higher education around the world. The breadth of implications of globalization on higher education, even at the campus-level and in the classroom, illustrates the importance of understanding the complicated relationships that will continue to evolve between higher education and external agents as higher education responds to both marketization and international economic cooperation within the scope of globalization.

As economic issues become increasingly significant in the existence and operation of higher education, particularly in cases where individual nation-states cannot afford to compete to keep their own students at home institutions, colleges and universities will not be able to remain inured from market forces as they execute their operations in areas like designing their curricula or constructing their student bodies. Instead, issues like marketability of skills and access to jobs will play increasingly important roles in how institutions operate and what students and society will expect from higher education (Altbach, 1998c). Because of the impact globalization has had across higher education, from practitioners to consumers, it has also served as an impetus for further examination and implementation of campus and system-wide internationalization policies and programs.

International Higher Education?

Higher education is more than simply a nation's system of post-secondary training opportunities. Instead, colleges and universities are often part of extensive education systems and represent the best a nation has to offer to the international community—scholars, knowledge, investment in people and the betterment of their country. Though current developments in higher education and its relationship with the world market for advanced education indicate a shift in higher education from an international enterprise to an international industry, at its core higher education has been and will continue to be oriented toward the international or borderless nature of knowledge generation and dissemination.

From the earliest scholarship of Greek and Muslim academies to the earliest universities at Bologna and Paris, scholars and students traveled to and from academic centers and home nations, establishing higher education as an international enterprise. Higher education continues to have an international profile and visibility, but two schools of thought exist regarding the extent to which higher education is an inherently international arena. The first holds that higher education is, by its nature, international, regardless of national government; the second promotes the belief that higher education is not inherently international but only chooses to be so when it serves the domestic self-interest.

Clark Kerr (1990) and Philip Altbach (1998) outline the origins of higher education as that of migrant, international scholars gathered together to seek information and truth. This model of the mobility of scholarship remained the norm until approximately 500 years ago, when higher education began to expand as a domestic concern (Kerr, 1990; Croxford, 2001; Altbach, 1998). Regardless, as Richard DeAngelis (1998) notes, "Higher education institutions, especially universities, are remarkably international, diverse, flexible, adaptive, and enduring phenomena" (p. 123), and "(a)t one level, university life has always been inherently global, universal, and cosmopolitan, at least as compared to other social institutions, allowing constant interchanges of personnel and ideas across boundaries of time, space, and types of knowledge" (p. 130). In this way, higher education is, fundamentally, a borderless enterprise.

Peter Scott (1998), on the other hand, does not believe that higher education has had an inherent international bent or orientation. On the contrary, Scott believes that historically higher education has been inwardly focused on developing institutional autonomy and promoting developments in the disciplines, but not necessarily on spreading or sharing knowledge internationally. If higher education has been international, according to Scott, then it is a byproduct of individual investments and institutional self-preservation (Scott 1998). It is a fact that the earliest American scholars sought their education abroad, particularly prior to the development of advance degree programs in the United States (Lucas, 1994; Kerr, 1990; Rudolph, 1990). But, the fact that individuals experienced international scholarship does not necessarily mean that higher education was international.

Much of early higher education, particularly in the United States for example, was developed to ensure economic and social development domestically. Welcoming foreign scholars, sharing information abroad, and otherwise being institutionally focused on global relations or issues were simply not priorities during the earliest days of higher education, nor are they today. From this perspective, it was largely in the face of government regulation and corporate interference that higher education institutions and higher education as an industry look internationally in their operations. And, it is this tension between the international nature of knowledge and the self-protective needs of nations that is being exacerbated by globalization and its impact on higher education.

Internationalization and Higher Education

The internationalization of higher education is a natural extension of and response to the many forms of globalization currently affecting cultures, governments, industries, and institutions. Higher education has been acutely affected by cultural and economic globalization, as nations and institutions reexamine their educational missions, as well as the educational product they dispense, to determine their effectiveness in this new international environment. For the purpose of this research, a further refined definition developed by Jane Knight and Hans de Wit is most fitting: "Internationalization of higher education is the process of integrating an international/intercultural dimension into the teaching, research, and service functions of the institution" (Knight and de Wit, 1997).

Historic Elements of Internationalization in American Higher Education

The American system of higher education was modeled after both the British college and German university systems. The British model served as the ideal in the development of the earliest colleges in the American colonies—small, religious, focused on teaching—while the German, Humboldtian, model brought graduate education and research to the forefront of American higher education (Haskins, 1965; Readings, 1996; Rudolph, 1990).

The most significant expansion of higher education in the United States occurred around the turn of the 20th century, with the establishment of the Morrill Land Grant Acts of 1862 and 1890, which set aside parcels of land throughout the country for states to use to establish public institutions of higher education (Lucas, 1994). These institutions, with their mandate to provide instruction and, most importantly, research relevant to the needs and issues of their home states, were modeled after the German research institutions, which encouraged faculty to be as involved in creating and furthering knowledge as they were in teaching it (Readings, 1996).

At the earliest points of American higher education, foreign influences were most evident in organization structures and research models. Faculty were almost expected to study and research abroad, bringing the superior training of Europe back to their home campuses. On American campuses, however, foreign students and foreign studies (outside of the classics—Greek and Latin) were unusual. This changed dramatically throughout the twentieth century.

At the turn of the twentieth century, industrialization was becoming a major mode for economic growth and expansion throughout Europe and the United States. In addition, the post–World War II economic and political stabilization came largely from the United States, as it evolved from a colonial country on the periphery of Europe to the great power sitting in the center of the world stage (Goodwin & Nacht, 1991). As is the case with the globalization forces at work today, political and economic forces dramatically influenced higher education around the world throughout the twentieth century, with productivity and practicality the driving concerns pushing modernization within and outside of higher education.

Areas of Internationalization

Internationalization on a college campus comes in both obvious and ambiguous forms. Obvious international elements on any campus include the presence of international students and campus supported study abroad programs. Less visible international institutional elements like the hiring of foreign faculty, increasing international areas of study, encouraging foreign language skill development, and providing financial aid to international students are equally significant in encouraging internationalization on campus. According to Jane Knight (1999), there are four general approaches to internationalization: activity, which includes programs and curricular developments; competency, which involves emphasizing skills, knowledge, and attitudes; ethos, which emphasizes creating an open culture or climate to support international initiatives; and process, which calls for the integration of international elements across institutional operations (Knight, 1999). Regardless of the form, internationalization of higher education is a response, ideally a structured and focused response, to the multiple influences of globalization, through which individual campuses and systems focus energy and resources on supporting a wide array of methods for making their institutions and operations more internationally oriented.

Economic, Political, Cultural, and Academic Rationales for Internationalization.

The need to respond to globalization is, indeed, at the core of the current expansion of internationalization efforts today. During the cold war, foreign policy norms called for some attention to foreign scholarship, to assist allies and know enemies (American Council on Education, 1995; Knight, 1999). Today, however, the rationale behind internationalization is more varied and lacks a single motivating factor, such as national security during the cold war. Instead, globalization is the catalyst—economic integration and interdependence, technological innovations, cultural exchange. The breadth of globalization extends thoroughly into higher education and affects the value of educational outcomes for students, faculty, and institutions. The industry of higher education, therefore, is looking for ways to respond, particularly at the urging of its constituents, from politicians, to faculty, to students, parents, and employers.

Jane Knight (1999) and Hans de Wit (2001) both present four rationales (motivations) for internationalization: political, economic, academic, and social/cultural. First, political motivations for internationalization remain the most historically consistent. As a foreign policy tool throughout the cold war, a method of preparing future foreign service workers, a way to strengthen relationships with allies through educational exchanges, and a means for spreading democratic ideals through international scholarship, international efforts in higher education served real political goals. The economic rationales correspond closely with the more explicit pressures of globalization: market competitiveness for corporations and employees; meeting increasing levels of demand for tertiary education brought about by massification efforts, which are expanding the sheer numbers of students seeking education beyond the secondary level; and the burgeoning market for international students, who often pay higher rates for attendance and, therefore, bring greater per student revenues to campuses. Serving the market by training students for future employers and creating opportunities for students to study are primary economic globalization issues.

The academic rationale is more idealistic but no less real for higher education. Knowledge is borderless and should not be contained by national boundaries. Internationalization brings out opportunities for sharing research and teaching methods, as well as information, which ideally results in improvements in quality and breadth of operations and opportunities. Increasing mobility of students, staff, and faculty might result in broadening the academic horizons of those who benefit from the exchange of ideas and cultures, while institutions benefit by having greater international visibility and credibility.

Finally, the cultural and social rationales for internationalization stress the personal benefits and utility of developing international consciousness in individuals. Learning about the cultural norms and values of different peoples can make individuals and, by extension, societies more empathetic and understanding of differences. Being able to teach or work with others from different countries with different cultures and social mores can make people more appreciative of their own cultures and more savvy in recognizing and dealing with issues brought on by cultural and social differences. Together, Knight (1999) and de Wit (2001) show how every facet of human relationships and academic operations are impacted by internationalization and how the political, economic, social, and academic motivations for internationalization intertwine to form a cohesive understanding of why internationalization is useful and important and why institutions and systems should consider internationalization as a fundamental area within their operations.

International Organizations, Globalization, and Trade in Higher Education Services

> It is the mission of global organizations like UNESCO to promote the global vision of Higher Education in which people are enabled to function in their personal, professional, and community lives, and are able to be perpetrators and repositories of knowledge, ideas, and local and national cultural traditions. (Sadlak, 1998, p. 107)

Organizations like the World Trade Organization (WTO), and the Organization for Economic Cooperation and Development (OECD) are asking nations to liberalize their state regulations concerning higher education, particularly with regard to opening domestic higher education to foreign institutions (Altbach, 2002). Others, like UNESCO, are promoting a more culturally sensitive approach to cross-bordered education. As noted above, the evolving relationship between higher education and the nation-state is largely influenced by the emerging power of transnational entities, including non-governmental organizations, like those listed above, and corporations (Readings, 1996).

Multinational, somewhat supranational, organizations like the WTO and UNESCO provide important contrasting perspectives on the foreign provision of higher education through trade by presenting contrasting approaches—one based on consensus and mutually developed accords (UNESCO) and the other based on removing barriers to trade and letting the market decide what will work (WTO)—to the internationalization of higher education (Larsen and Vincent-Lancrin, 2002; Barblan, 2002). As nations are forced to cut back their public funding for higher education, institutions will be forced to seek allies and support from outside actors (Scott, 2000), and with that support undoubtedly will come pressures to accept alternatives to domestic public providers, including foreign suppliers of education. What remains to be determined is the form that such transnational higher education provision will take.

Trade in higher education services is a controversial issue related to how these voids created by cuts in public funding might be solved by foreign providers and is growing in significance in much of the world. The General Agreement on Trade in Services (GATS) is one mechanism among many through which higher education is being manipulated within an international sphere, and its effectiveness is still to be determined. Jane Knight (2002) provides the best and most articulate examination of the specific elements of the GATS as they related to higher education services in her piece,

> The GATS is controversial, and the literature on the GATS has been divided between those who support the initiative to include higher education within a broad serves trade liberalization agenda and those who are opposed to it.
>
> Critics focus on the threat to the government role, 'public good' and quality aspects of higher education. Supporters highlight the beliefs that more trade can bring, in terms of innovation through new delivery systems and providers, greater student access and economic values. (Knight, 2002, p. 3)

Looking at the literature from the American perspective, the support for free trade in international higher education focuses on the foreign opportunities for American education providers. The removal of trade barriers would open markets in higher education into which American providers, including for-profits such as Laureate Education, Inc. and the Apollo Group, could export their operations and educational products (Sedwick, 2002; Foster, 2002; Altbach, 2003). The debate around this issue is largely grounded in this sense that the policymakers are showing preferential treatment to the for-profits over the objections of the larger non-profit sector and that free trade threatens the nature of public higher education (Larsen, et al, 2002; Foster, 2002; Sauvé, 2002; OECD, 2004).

These issues of regarding the true purpose of higher education, the tension between the public and private sectors, and the rise of the for-profit sector's significance and influence appear through the literature on trade in higher education services (Larsen and Vincent-Lancrin, 2002; ACE, March 2003) and throughout the data presented in this book. These are issues that will remain well into the future of liberalized trade in education services. It is important to note, however, that trade policies do not, necessarily, determine whether trade exists. On the contrary, trade policies often develop out of a need to respond to existing trade issues (Sauvé, 2002; OECD, 2004) and while significant in moving the debate about the benefits and detriments of trade to higher education, the policies are not independently significant within the debate. The significance of the policies, including the GATS, is that they codify market behaviors into modes for regulating operations, and it is this movement toward regulation that has stirred the greatest controversy in the higher education arena internationally.

Critics of the GATS and free trade cite the potential for privatization of public services and the transformation of 'public good' industries into competitive market products (OECD, 2002, Altbach, 2002; Flower, 2003). Rachel Pasternack (2004) presents a compelling look at this process as a reality in Israeli higher education, though for Pasternack this convergence of privatization and globalization is a positive outcome for Israel, expanding educational opportunities. Ultimately, it is this compelling tension between the positive expansion possibilities that free trade in education services might bring and the removal of publicly valuable but not-profitable elements from higher education in order to maximize revenues that makes an examination of the burgeoning agenda around trade in higher education services most important today.

The United States has not seen dramatic responses from the public or from campuses to the burgeoning issue of trade in higher education services, but that may not be the case for long. As more representative associations publicly acknowledge their concerns and publish pieces concerning trade policies and implications (Ward, 2002; Foster, 2002; Lenn, 2002), the debate among the actors and campus officials can be expected to gain momentum, particularly if speculation about ramifications transform into actual operational issues. All of this remains in the future, however.

CONCLUSIONS

The autonomy of institutions and systems of higher education may continue to be challenged by external forces, as they have been by national government influence on operations and by the inputs and expectations of outside actors. Globalization and trade merely extend the possibility that challenge will come from abroad, as well. In the U.S., groups like the American Council on Education (ACE), Council for Higher Education Accreditation (CHEA), the National Education Association (NEA), and the Council of Graduate Schools (CGS) will continue to serve as representational agents for higher education around areas such as globalization and to provide leadership and ideas for how to enhance and develop institutional and system-wide responses to globalization (de Wit, 2001).

In highly decentralized, independent higher education systems, like that of the United States, these agencies will be even more important in representing the interests of the higher education industry, as broad and diverse as it is, in negotiations on policy initiatives and proposals that will directly and indirectly affect how higher education operates domestically and internationally. With regard to trade, the opinions and actions of these industry representatives are the only ones currently being articulated on behalf of higher education, making their input into the negotiations and dialogue on the burgeoning policy of including higher education in trade agreements on service industries the sole perspective from the higher education side.

Throughout the following chapters, the literature on trade in education services is presented in conjunction with the collected data and findings, which detail the potential benefits and threats of trade in higher education services. The chapters that follow also detail the history of higher education in an international policy context, the response of the traditional sector of American higher education to the potential reality of higher education's being included in the American offer to the GATS, and the current trend within the USTR toward supporting policies that remove the trade barriers that currently regulate international higher education investment and endeavors.

Chapter Four

Higher Education as an International Policy Concern

Higher education has been an inherently international enterprise from the time of its origins (Altbach, 1998). Students, scholars, and the pursuit of knowledge have ignored national boundaries from the earliest universities in Bologna and Paris. Colleges and universities, on the other hand, have largely been national institutions, financially supported by governments and seen as important conveyors of individual national interests and culture. It was only after the industrial revolution of the late 19th Century and the two World Wars of the early 20th Century that the significance of scholarship as both a national and international economic engine brought the 'industry' of higher education into the realm of international treaties and agreements.

This chapter will present an historical examination of higher education as an international policy concern, looking specifically at the most visible and influential organizations that formed following the end of World War II. Since the post-war mid-20th Century, the value and influence of higher education on national and international development has only increased, and this shift has been reflected in the inclusion of education—higher education, in particular—in the social, cultural, and, ultimately, economic spheres of international organizations and agreements.

THE INTERNATIONAL ORGANIZATIONS AND AGREEMENTS AND HIGHER EDUCATION

From the United Nations (UN) to the World Trade Organization (WTO), an important cadre of international organizations and assemblies have set their sights on education as a policy concern. Though these organizations all serve overlapping nations and address many overlapping issues, their purposes are not the same. The United Nations and its branches serve in a supra-governmental role, in which representatives of member states come together to form governing bodies whose authority independent nations, by and large, willingly recognize and respect. Organizations such as the OECD and WTO also seek the input of multilateral accords to affect international relations and policies, but their authority is not so much a matter of governmental authority as working in the best interests of members.

While independent self-interest is, of course, present in the UN, the commitment to the UN often supersedes national self-interest for the benefit of the international community as a whole. The OECD and the WTO, being economically oriented, do not encompass the same broad commitment to international peace so much as they seek to create solid international relations through committed economic, market, and trade relations. The World Bank, which has the highly complicated role of distributing funds from the North to the South and monitoring development within certain applied programs, bridges the operations of the market and the public sector. As UNESCO's aims continue to focus on individual access and opportunity for the betterment of international relations, the WTO's purposes are more directly related to economic exchange and the establishing, in this case, of higher education as an internationally traded service industry. (The OECD has come down clearly in support of the WTO and GATS.) This tension, between access and opportunity and the power of the market is the core issue, in the arena of globalization and education, and, ideally, this research helps to shed more light on how these issues are playing out in intergovernmental, national policy, and national educational organizations.

The following organizations are the most visible and most significant international bodies that have been and remain involved in incorporating education in their operations. The decision to include these organizations and not others was based solely on the size and significance of these organizations and their sphere of influence. Though there certainly are other important international and regional organizations addressing with higher education policy issues, the European Union (EU) and the Association of Southeast Asian Nations (ASEAN), for example, their policies are restricted to issues within their regions. This research, which is concerned with the World Trade Organization's policies toward higher education services, seeks to provide context to the WTO's stance by examining the following multi-regional and influential organizations below.

The United Nations Educational, Scientific, and Cultural Organization (UNESCO)

Following its establishment in 1945, the United Nations (UN) began what continues to be a long evolution of developing initiatives and organizations that meet the needs and realities of cross-national interactions and relationships, developing an arm that was to focus on broad social and cultural issues, the United Nations Educational, Scientific, and Cultural Organization (UNESCO). UNESCO was formed after the end of World War II and chartered in November of 1945 to promote peace and security in part through supporting education initiatives worldwide (Daniel, 2002) and was the first major international body to introduce education as a broadly defined area of international concern. UNESCO evolved out of a 1942 meeting of the Conference of Allied Ministers of Education (CAME) of the European wartime allies against Nazi Germany. This meeting was called during World War II to prepare for the reconstruction of education sectors across Europe. Out of these discussions emerged the idea that an organization, ultimately UNESCO, would be able to address directly issues of transnational education.

Representatives of 37 countries signed the UNESCO constitution in November 1945, and it was ratified in November 1946, by the original 20 signatory nations: Australia, Brazil, Canada, China, Czechoslovakia, Denmark, Dominican Republic, Egypt, France, Greece, India, Lebanon, Mexico, New Zealand, Norway, Saudi Arabia, South Africa, Turkey, the United Kingdom, and the United States—developed and developing countries, from the North and the South. With a constitution that specifically addresses education and advocates for the significance of education in promoting positive international relations, UNESCO became the first, and continues as the most, prominent multinational organization to include education in its organizational charter. Initially, however the initiatives of UNESCO focused on primary and basic education.

Other noteworthy predecessors of UNESCO were: the International Committee of Intellectual Co-operation (CICI), Geneva 1922–1946; its executing agency, the International Institute of Intellectual Co-operation (IICI), Paris, 1925–1946; and the International Bureau of Education (IBE), Geneva, 1925–1968, which has, since 1969, been part of the UNESCO Secretariat under its own statutes (UNESCO, 2004). These earlier organizations had acknowledged that there were issues specifically around international education, including the sharing of knowledge and emerging scholarship among nations, that deserved international attention and oversight. UNESCO continues that educational aim—including having a specific focus area on higher education—while also serving as a particularly significant arm of the UN, focusing on non-political areas of international exchange, such as the protection of significant cultural landmarks, the promotion of copyright protection and intellectual property rights, and the preservation of library treasures and collections, as well as promoting basic education for all. Advanced scholarship and higher education also remain important programmatic and policy areas for UNESCO.

From 1960s onward, the major issue of transnational higher education concerned the recognition of earned degrees across international lines, and UNESCO continued to examine this particular issue area repeatedly through the 1970s and 1980s while broadening its scope of attention to a myriad of higher education issues (Uvalic´-Trumbic´, 2002). UNESCO continues to serve as a forum for examining issues around international higher education. UNESCO presents itself as an important leader in recognizing the importance of higher education in the development of individual nations, as well as in the emerging realm of globalized higher education and promoting transnational education as a mechanism for economic development and improved international relations.

> UNESCO is the only UN body with a mandate to support national capacity-building in higher education.
>
> The Organization plays a leading role in the worldwide reflection on higher education reform. It also provides a platform for dialogue on how best to adapt education systems to the emergence of knowledge societies and the new social, cultural and economic challenges of an increasingly globalized world.
>
> UNESCO builds international and regional networks to assist with a range of issues in higher education: academic mobility, international exchanges of excellence, research on education systems and knowledge production, curriculum innovation, leadership roles for women educators, teacher development, and the defense of quality in higher education qualifications. (UNESCO, 2004)

That the United Nations deems higher education worthy of specific attention points to the significance of higher education as both a national investment and an international industry. UNESCO incorporates issues such as democracy, women's rights, economic development, and scholarship into their higher education endeavors, expanding the sphere of influence of higher education from merely that of the few who actually enter into higher education worldwide. Trade in higher education, particularly cases in which foreign providers enter into domestic markets, could have a significant impact on national capacities to expand higher education and offer it to larger segments of their populations; and issue that is of both interest and concern to UNESCO as well as many other international and higher education organizations. Globalization and international trade are both issues of significance for UNESCO in its higher education area.

UNESCO has established globalization as a specific and significant focus on its work in higher education.

> Globalization: Once viewed as mainly economic in nature, this phenomenon has profound social and cultural aspects. Borders between countries have become more open to intellectual exchange, and the search for uniformity and for common solutions continues to increase in many domains. In the field of higher education, the international aspects reach into numerous university activities. Many universities are part of international agreements, and mobility is facilitated by the rapid increase in international exchanges. In the field of research, there is an increased interest in the concerns of global governance e.g. democracy and human rights, collective social responsibility, the rising impact and interconnectedness of phenomena such as conflict-resolution, multiculturalism, environmental matters and the advent of technology. (UNESCO, 2004)

Indeed, UNESCO's attention to higher education and the globalization of many elements of scholarship and acknowledgement of the inclusion of higher education in many international agreements, provides an important forum for debating the importance of providing regulatory guidelines as higher education expands internationally.

UNESCO has established the Conventions on the Recognition of Qualifications, which, according to the UNESCO website, "represent the only existing regulatory frameworks for transborder mutual recognition of qualifications. These Conventions have been ratified by over 100 Member States in Africa, Asia and the Pacific, the Arab States, Europe and Latin America" (UNESCO, 2004). The UNESCO Conventions seek to promote cross-border recognition of degrees and qualifications between the countries that have ratified them. Ideally, such international cooperation in higher education would reduce actual and perceived obstacles to the mobility of teachers and students, with such mobility being increasingly popular and significant as higher education becomes more thoroughly globalized.

The UNESCO Conventions seek to promote "non-profit internationalization" (Knight, 2002), pitting UNESCO, in many instances, against organizations like the OECD and the WTO, which are focusing much of their efforts regarding higher education on trade and investment in the for-profit arena. UNESCO stands out among all of these major international organizations in its skepticism about the benefits of the GATS. UNESCO launched the Global Forum on International Quality Assurance, Accreditation and the Recognition of Qualifications in 2003, as part of its mission "to respond to emerging ethical challenges and dilemmas as a result of globalization" (UNESCO, 2005) and in part to address the potential implications of trade liberalization of higher education through the GATS. UNESCO notes on its website the tension between trade and education and the need to mediate how trade policies in education are developed:

> In the heated debates worldwide there is a growing polarization between the education and the trade communities. Some of the stakeholders of higher education, the teachers' unions and the students being the most vocal, followed by institutions, consider that education is not a tradable commodity, and that higher education should remain a public good and a public responsibility. GATS is perceived as a threat to national sovereignty and culture and as a serious attack on the core values of the university and the quality of teaching. Trade promoters, on the other hand, try to point to its benefits—competition, motivation for traditional institutions to innovate, establishment of professional networks, providing enhanced opportunities for access to higher education etc. Preserving the quality of higher education and protecting/empowering the learner become key issues in response to this phenomenon.
>
> UNESCO is well positioned to overcome this conflict and provide some common ground, primarily by providing a platform for dialogue. UNESCO has its normative instruments as a legal framework for action. Reinforcing, revising and updating the existing conventions on the recognition of studies could provide an international qualifications framework—relevant in the context of the GATS debates. Reinforcing links between recognition of qualifications, quality assurance and accreditation networks could constitute a more acceptable approach to overcoming obstacles in cross-border mobility as well as promoting non-profit internationalization and 'fair trade,' in the interest of the learners. (UNESCO, 2005)

UNESCO has also created the UNESCO Forum on Higher Education, Research and Knowledge out of two major international conferences: The World Conference on Higher Education in Paris, 1998, and the World Conference on Science in Budapest, 1999. From these conferences came the goal of establishing regular gatherings around the world during which researchers and policymakers can discuss the most pressing challenges and issues facing higher education both regionally and internationally. The GATS has become an issue of focus for the Forum, and in 2005, the Forum will host seminars on the GATS in Asia and in Latin America and the Caribbean, to gather feedback and research data on the issue as it directly relates to those regions. Between these two ongoing initiatives—The Global Forum on International Quality Assurance, Accreditation and the Recognition of Qualifications and the Forum on Higher Education, Research and Knowledge—UNESCO has established itself as a significant actor in the international dialogue about globalization, trade, and higher education.

The Organization for Economic Cooperation and Development (OECD)

The foundations of the Organization for Economic Cooperation and Development (OECD) also emerged from World War II, in this case from initiatives developed out of the European Aid Program—the Marshall Plan. The Marshall Plan, named after U.S. Secretary of State George C. Marshall, was initiated in June 1947 and outlined the United States' commitment, through multilateral cooperation, to help Europe rebuild following the devastation of the two World Wars. Shortly after the announcement by Secretary Marshall of the U.S. intentions for assisting in the economic recovery of Europe, the Organization for European Economic Cooperation (OEEC) emerged as the multinational organization that would work with the U.S. and Canada to administer aid most effectively in rebuilding the economies of Europe. The OEEC became the OECD in 1961, with the ratification of the OECD charter in September of that year.

Unlike with UNESCO—at the time of its founding and today—the OECD is not a culturally oriented organization but is an economic and market oriented organization, a distinction which is significant in understanding how these organizations both target their research and projects and interpret their collected data. The Convention that established the OECD stipulates three main concerns the organization is to consider as it promotes policies:

- to achieve the highest sustainable economic growth and employment and a rising standard of living in member countries, while maintaining financial stability, and thus contribute to the development of the world economy;
- to contribute to sound economic expansion in member as well as non-member countries in the process of economic development; and

- to contribute to the expansion of world trade on a multilateral, non-discriminatory basis in accordance with international obligations (OECD, 2004, p. 4)

It is no surprise, then, that as the OECD has examined education issues in its context, it has presented arguments in favor of trade liberalization and open markets for education as a service industry.

According to the OECD, education has been a core issue for the OECD from its inception. During 1960s, the early years of the Cold War and the "race to space," the OECD focus on education centered on developing scientific personnel. Later, as the unemployment levels and economic woes of many OECD nations became severe in the 1970s, the OECD moved its educational focus away from scientific innovation toward more general employment issues. And, in September 2002, the Secretary-General of the OECD, Donald J. Johnston, announced the creation of an independent Directorate for Education to raise the profile of OECD's work. He noted that "education is a priority for OECD Member countries and the OECD is playing an increasingly important role in this field. Society's most important investment is in the education of its people. We suffer in the absence of good education: we prosper in its presence" (OECD, 2004, p. 5).

The OECD Directorate for Education established six "strategic objectives" to help orient the focus of their education initiatives within member countries. The six objectives are:

- Connecting lifelong learning policy with other socio-economic policies
- Evaluating and improving outcomes of education
- Promoting quality teaching
- *Rethinking tertiary education in a global economy* (emphasis added)
- Building social cohesion through education
- Building new futures for education (OECD, 2004, P. 6)

The global economy (a.k.a. globalization) is, again, a core issue for an international organization that understands that education worldwide is not immune to the impact of international economic influences and must evolve to ensure that higher education, in particular, continues to serve its constituents well. According to the OECD and other similarly important international organizations, globalization is a force so strong that it requires a re-examination of existing tertiary (higher) education to ensure that it remains relevant.

The OECD focuses its attention regarding tertiary education to the market forces currently impacting higher education in its member countries.

"Governments are major players in the (tertiary education) sector, but they are not the only stakeholders: there is competition on the supply side and greater sophistication in demand" (OECD, 2004, p. 16). With this focus on understanding the market for higher education internationally, the OECD has established five "activities" in which they are conducting research and focusing their work on tertiary higher education: evaluating tertiary education policy, monitoring internationalization and trade in tertiary education, improving governance and management of higher education institutions, improving indicators on tertiary education, and building future scenarios of universities (OECD, 2004, p. 16). The OECD produces research that fills a void by generating data on macro and micro level shifts in both domestic and cross-border markets for higher education as supply (institutions and governments) and demand (students, employers) pressures continue to impact the international tertiary education market. By examining national and international policies, as well as the roles and impacts of "suppliers" and "consumers," the OECD provides important data and analysis of the "numbers" behind the often emotional and anecdotal responses to the evolving globalized nature of higher education today.

The OECD currently remains the most prominent international organization conducting research specifically on trade in higher education services and provides the broadest database of information and statistics on the international market for higher education. It also is the most visible proponent of the GATS outside of the WTO and has published numerous books and articles in support of open markets for service industries, including the market for higher education.

> Many of the arguments put forward today against liberalisation of trade and investment in services are based on misinformation and a lack of understanding of the GATS. At the same time, the significant economy-wide benefits deriving from liberalisation of trade and investment in services do not receive enough attention, and this reinforces less than positive views of the liberalisation of trade and investment in general and participation in the multilateral trading system through membership of the WTO in particular. (OECD, 2002, p. 4)

The OECD presumes that any opposition to the GATS must be due to "misinformation," a position that sets it firmly in line with the goals of the WTO and completely disconnected from the numerous legitimate and credible agencies who remain either firmly opposed to the GATS or, at least, wary of complete acceptance of the term and condition of the GATS.

This conspicuously one-sided perspective held by the OECD diminishes its capacity to provide a nuanced argument regarding the concerns of those opposed to the GATS and renders its own contributions important but notably biased in any attempt to develop a broad understanding of benefits and negative attributes of including education services in the GATS.

The World Bank

Formed originally in 1944 in Bretton Woods, New Hampshire, USA, as the International Bank for Reconstruction and Development (IBRD), the World Bank arose, like many of these other significant international agencies, out of the recognized need to be prepared to rebuild the world after the destructive chaos of World War II. The World Bank was developed and remains an organization that, very simply, provides low-cost loans to nations working to improve their economic capabilities. The original twenty-eight governments that signed the IBRD's Articles of Agreement (Belgium, Bolivia, Canada, China, Czechoslovakia, Ethiopia, France, Greece, Honduras, Iceland, India, Iraq, Luxembourg, Netherlands, Norway, Philippines, South Africa, Egypt, United Kingdom, United States, and Yugoslavia) largely overlap the signatories of the charter documents for many of the organizations discussed here. There are currently 184 member countries, both developed and developing, who provide both the funding and oversight for the distribution of the funding, "Along with the rest of the development community, the World Bank centers its efforts on the (sic) reaching the Millennium Development Goals, agreed to by UN members in 2000 and aimed at sustainable poverty reduction" (The World Bank, 2004). According to the World Bank's website, the Bank is the largest external financial source supporting education around the world.

Higher education, as part of the overall picture of education funded through World Bank loans, has been elevated to a real policy concern for the World Bank over the past few decades. According to the World Bank's website, tertiary education (teacher education) was an element of the Bank's very first educational loan in 1963, to Tunisia. From teacher education and the development of buildings and ground-level operations, the World Bank's funding for higher education has focused more on "systemic reforms and capacity building" (World Bank, 2004). All together, the World Bank loaned over$84 billion to over 107 countries for 336 education projects with tertiary education components, and over the past decade, lending for tertiary education projects has averaged $343 million per year (World Bank, 2004).

After three decades of policies that prioritized primary and secondary education over tertiary, the World Bank has shifted its position dramatically and is now focusing its education efforts on post-secondary education:

> The Bank is commonly perceived as supporting only basic education; systematically advocating the reallocation of public expenditures from tertiary to basic education; promoting cost recovery and private sector expansion; and discouraging low-income countries from considering any investment in advanced human capital. Given these perception, the rapid changes taking place in the global environment, and the persistence of the traditional problems of tertiary education in developing and transition countries, re-examining the World bank's policies and experiences in tertiary education has become a matter of urgency. (Salmi, 2003, p. 52)

Explaining its commitment to higher education, particularly in contrast to the long-standing priority given to primary and basic education, the World Bank (2004) states:

> Higher education is a key piece to the holistic puzzle of a country's entire education system, providing the advanced skills required by teachers, doctors, scientists, civic leaders, technicians and entrepreneurs. Adequate education capacity is key to a competitive workforce, and that includes higher-order skills. Even to promote literacy, good health, and other aspects of human development in disadvantages segments of the population, countries require good quality tertiary education—teacher training institutes, nursing schools, medical colleges, universities, and local avenues for lifelong learning—so that sufficient numbers of appropriately trained professionals are generated to support these development goals that are proven to reduce poverty. Investments are being made at all levels of education to support the comprehensive and equitable expansion of human capital needed to better the lives of all people. (World Bank, 2004, online)

The World Bank also supports research on higher education and produces publications, conferences, and other mechanisms for disseminating their research findings. Starting in the mid-1990s, the World Bank undertook new policy reviews on its decades-old position that marginalized tertiary education, resulting first in the publication of *Higher Education: The Lessons of Experience* in 1994, which began the World Bank's redeployment of efforts into the tertiary education sector. This undertaking was soon followed by the convening of the Task Force on Higher Education and Society, which was an international body of higher education leaders and researchers from across the developed and developing world, assigned to focus their attention specifically on the state of higher education in developing countries. *Higher education in developing countries: Peril and promise* (2000) is the outcome of two years of collaboration by the task force.

This report is noteworthy in the context of this research as it examines a breadth of concerns and challenges facing higher education worldwide and offers suggestions for re-investing in higher education, particularly in the developing world. It also touches briefly on the impact of globalization, specifically, on higher education in noting: "The globalization of higher education can have damaging as well as beneficial consequences. It can lead to unregulated and poor-quality higher education, with the worldwide marketing of fraudulent degrees or other so-called higher education credentials a clear example" (Task Force, 2000, p. 43). This perspective on globalization—here referring to the economic pressures to expand for-profit higher education in worldwide markets and the ramifications of such expansion—provides a skepticism about the benefits of unchecked growth in higher education, even where a real need for expansion of opportunities for higher education exist. With trade policies and agreements that facilitate the expansion of the higher education service industry worldwide, such skepticism is, itself, a useful check on the value of globalized higher education today.

The most recent major World Bank publication regarding international higher education is the most pointed and developed rationale for World Bank support for tertiary education initiatives to date. *Constructing Knowledge Societies: New Challenges for Tertiary Education* (2002) specifically addresses globalization and the need for a well-educated work force in order to participate in the new global economy. The report "describes how tertiary education contributed to building up a country's capacity for participation in an increasingly knowledge-based world economy, and investigates policy options for tertiary education that have the potential to enhance economic growth and reduce poverty" (Salmi, 2003, p. 52). The report also offers a specific critique of the current state of trade agreements regarding tertiary education.

> The threat of increased competition by virtual and other nontraditional providers is leading some governments to take protectionist stands against foreign suppliers. In this context, the World Bank will work at both international and national levels to help define rules of conduct and appropriate safeguards to protect students from low-quality offerings

and fraudulent providers, but without erecting rigid entry barriers. (Salmi, 2002, p. 126)

The Bank appears to acknowledge both the benefits of free trade and the need to maintain some level of domestic oversight regarding the quality of education being offered by outside, non-traditional providers. This compromise stance places the Bank is a powerful position, in that it appears to recognize the valid points on both sides of the debate and seems willing to serve as a bridge between the pro- and con- sides of the GATS issue. The seemingly countervailing ideals of free trade in educational services and national oversight in order to meet domestic cultural and economic needs will undoubtedly remain in conflict as free trade and other broad trade agreements begin to include areas educational services.

The World Bank, though a lending body with high levels of accountability to the most powerful and wealthiest nations, examines issues that affect the least powerful nations, and the expansion of globalization in educational services through trade is one area that will likely continue to receive attention by the Bank in the future. The Bank has the potential to dramatically affect the course of trade liberalization in tertiary education, as it wields influence in the First and Third Worlds. The role it will choose to take in the debate, however, remains ambiguous.

The International Trade Organization (ITO) and the General Agreement on Tariffs and Trade (GATT)

The period between the first and second World Wars was notable for the protectionism that governed trade, and, in 1943, in response to concerns about the economic ramifications of protectionism, the U.S. and UK began bilateral discussions to develop an international trading system that was free of protectionism (Cohn, 2000, p. 205). The following years saw increased activity regarding international commercial and economic cooperation. In 1945, at the same time that the UN was rising out of post-war diplomacy, the U.S. offered a proposal on trade and employment that was to be the basis of an International Trade Organization (ITO), and a group of 23 of the most developed nations met in 1946 to discuss the more narrow trade issue of tariffs (Rikowski, 2003).

While the U.S. proposal did not ultimately result in the development of the ITO, it did establish some of the founding principles for what ultimately became the General Agreement on Tariffs and Trade (the GATT), which became effective in 1948. The GATT emerged as an organized attempt to reduce tariffs on tradable goods between member countries, resulting, ultimately, in a dramatic reduction in tariffs and an equally valuable increase in international trade and economic growth (Papovich, 2004). After World War II, during a period of idealized international cooperation, the GATT was envisioned as a precursor to a more broadly defined ITO, which would serve as one of many arms of the United Nations and would cover trade as well as "employment, international investment, economic development, services, competition, restrictive practices, and commercial policy and commodity agreements" (Rikowski, 2003, p. 2).

The GATT was not an organization, per se, but was, instead, a legal framework for eliminating discriminatory trade practices among participating nations while also allowing individual countries to alter their commitments to the GATT if their commitments ultimately proved too great a burden to the home economy. Countries that agreed to conform their policies to this framework were considered signatories of the GATT. Among the key components of the GATT was the principle of Most Favored Nation (MFN) status. It was under GATT that member nations developed and agreed to adhere to the principle of Most Favored Nation (MFN) status, which dictated that each signatory member nation of the GATT be offered the lowest tariff rate applied by any one member nation to any other member nation (NEA, 2004, p. 7) and supported the equal treatment of all nations in burgeoning trade agreements. Being a signatory nation of the GATT provided market access at the best terms to the other members' markets and was a compelling impetus for complying with the terms and conditions of membership.

With this one main principle guiding the development of the GATT, the member nations continued to meet during eight negotiating trade rounds from 1948–1995. These rounds included rounds in 1949 (Annecy, France), 1951 (Torquay, England), 1956 (Geneva), and 1960–62 (Geneva—the Dillon Round), all of which focused exclusively on tariff reduction among member nations. The 1962–67 GATT Round in Geneva (the Kennedy Round) included negotiations around both further tariff reductions as well as the development of additional rules to govern the GATT negotiations, most notably the introduction of anti-dumping measures to protect weaker markets from being manipulated by foreign providers offering low cost, and often low quality, products at prices below those in their home countries.

It was not until the 1973–79 Tokyo Round that broader trade issues, outside of tariff concerns, became part of the GATT negotiations and included such non-tariff barriers to trade as government procurement, customs laws, subsidies, and antidumping measures, among other concerns (WTO, 2004, Pacific Commerce, 2004). Finally, it was the Uruguay Round of 1986–1994, and the further broadening of trade issues being addressed by signatory nations that ultimately led to the evolution of GATT into the World Trade Organization (WTO).

From the GATT to the World Trade Organization (WTO)

As noted above, it was during the eighth and, ultimately, final round (the Uruguay Round) of negotiations under the GATT that the World Trade Organization (WTO) emerged as a new model for international cooperation regarding trade—this time focusing on both goods and services. The GATT had begun to include issues other than tariff concerns, and a logical extension of these growing international economic concerns was a more broadly defined international agreement to provide structure and guidance to international financial relations. This agreement, seen as a more cohesive body—no longer merely a framework for negotiations but a fully recognized 'international institution" (USTR, 2003)—is the WTO.

From its inception, the overarching purpose of the GATT was the reduction of tariffs on the trade of goods between nations. After the 1995 Uruguay Round of GATT, the agreement evolved into a more comprehensive organization—the WTO—which would both maintain the commitment to reduced barriers to trade and seek to promote improved trade relationships both in goods and, significantly, in services. The WTO emerged as a "multi-country treaty that promoted liberalization of international trade" (NEA, 2004, p. 7). According to its own website, the WTO is "the only global international organization dealing with the rules of trade between nations. At its heart are the WTO agreements, negotiated and signed by the bulk of the world's trading nations and ratified in their parliaments. The goal is to help producers of goods and services, exporters, and importers conduct their business" (WTO, 2004).

The WTO is made up of 148 countries that account for 97% of the world's trade in goods and services (WTO, 2005). The WTO holds that its main purpose is to promote free trade through "administering trade agreements; acting as a forum for trade negotiations; settling trade disputes; reviewing national trade policies; assisting developing countries in trade policy issues, through technical assistance and training programmes; and cooperating with other international organizations" (WTO, 2004). The WTO maintains its rules through two main agreements—the GATT and the General Agreement on Trade in Services (GATS). The GATT, though no longer the stand-alone agreement, was heavily revised during the Uruguay Round and remained as an agreement within the WTO, maintaining its rules and regulations over trade in goods. At the urging of many of its wealthiest member states, including the United States, the WTO has looked beyond the GATT's focus on goods to include initiatives on trade in services industries, as well, through another agreement, the GATS.

> In February 1997 agreement was reached on telecommunications services, with 69 governments agreeing to wide-ranging liberalization measures that went beyond those agreed (sic) in the Uruguay Round.
>
> In the same year 40 governments successfully concluded negotiations for tariff-free trade in information technology products, and 70 members concluded a financial services deal covering more than 95% of trade in banking, insurance, securities and financial information. (WTO, 2005, online)

After these large service negotiations proved successful, the WTO decided to expand its efforts into agriculture and a broader array of service industries, including education. Starting in 2000 and developed further at the November 2001 WTO Ministerial Conference in Doha, Qatar, this expanded commitment to increase efforts for trade liberalization across service industries has kept the GATS at the forefront of the debate about trade in services, particularly services that are considered within the domain of the "public good." Because of its blanket goal of promoting free trade, the WTO is seen as a kind of villain, out to break down those areas of policy that are designed to protect public interests outside of the marketplace.

The WTO efforts to promote free trade in have encountered heated debate and all-out conflict with regard to trade liberalization through the GATT, as opponents have charged the WTO with pushing policies that diminish the protections offered by such domestic regulations as labor laws and the environmental regulations. There is no question that the WTO's positions on free trade in goods and services will continue to attract supports and opponents, as the effects of the WTO's policies stretch into areas long seen as domestically protected, such as higher education.

CONCLUSIONS

There is currently little debate about whether higher education is now operating in an international sphere. Indeed, as noted in the opening of this chapter, certain elements of higher education have always been international in some form. It was only in the latter half of the 20th Century, however, that newly formed international organizations began to examine environment in which higher education operates internationally. The organizations described above are the most significant and well-represented international organizations to focus a portion of their operations specifically on higher education. In the early years, the efforts were about assisting in the domestic development of higher education systems. Today, these organizations are all engaged to some degree in examining the effects of globalization on higher education in terms of the capacity of domestic systems to develop the work force (human capital) the local economy needs and the market pressures promoting international trade in higher education services.

The most prominent effort to promote and regulate international trade in higher education services is happening through the on-going negotiations of the WTO's General Agreement on Trade in Services. The following chapter will expand upon the defining elements, areas of controversy, and specific requirements of the GATS, to situate the this entire research project within the policy realm and present the issues against which many representatives of traditional American higher education are working.

Chapter Five

The General Agreement on Trade in Services (GATS)

This chapter will first present the background and then examine the terms of the General Agreement on Trade in Services (GATS), the first major international initiative to focus on trade in service industries, including higher education services. By including higher education services as an industry to be considered for trade liberalization, the GATS is now at the center of an international debate being waged among scholars, policy analysts, higher education officials, and government agencies about the role of higher education in society and the relationship between higher education and government.

The GATS is still in the process of being developed through international negotiations among WTO member nations. Though not yet operational as international law, the GATS nonetheless serves as a lightning rod for the large storm brewing around trade in higher education services. In order to investigate the tensions and issues surrounding the GATS and higher education, it is necessary to understand the context and nuances of the GATS' terms and conditions.

FROM THE GATT TO THE WTO AND THE GATS

Since the inception of the GATT in 1948, tariffs and other trade restrictions on the flow of goods internationally have been reduced dramatically, and during the Uruguay Round of the GATT, the focus turned toward services. The "Final Act" of the Uruguay Round of the GATT officially closed out the GATT and its last round and established both the World Trade Organization and its foundation agreements, all listed as Annexes, on goods (Annex 1A), services (Annex 1B), intellectual property (Annex 1C), dispute settlement processes (Annex 2), trade policy review mechanism (Annex 3), and plurilateral trade agreements (Annex 4) (WTO, 2004). Together, these Annexes dramatically expanded the arena of influence of the WTO into new areas of trade.

"The GATS ranks without a doubt amongst the chief accomplishments of multilateral trade diplomacy at the end of the 20th Century" (OECD, 2002, p. 3). Even without final ratification of national commitments within the GATS, the mere presence of the GATS in promoting and providing a forum for free trade in services has transformed international trade from an environment of goods crossing borders to one that examines all sources of international revenue, including service industries and products. The importance of focusing on trade in services seems particularly obvious given that services account for close to 70% of all production and employment in OECD countries, which include the world's largest economies (OECD, 2002). What may not be as obvious but is equally significant is that services are becoming increasingly more important to the economies of developing countries, where the share of services in terms of national GDP increased by an average of nine percentage points in mid- and low-income countries between 1980 and 1998 (World Bank, 1999). It was, perhaps, inevitable then that governments and international agencies would begin to focus more pointedly at services, given the size and returns of service industries to national and international economies.

Negotiated by the governments of WTO member nations, the GATS established the multilateral rules governing international trade in services and provides a structure in which individuals and companies are able to operate (WTO, 2004). The agreement has become one mechanism through which governments are looking to influence the liberalization of the international marketplace for trade in services. The GATS is "a legally enforceable agreement governing international trade in services" (National Education Association, 2004, p. 15) and seeks "to establish a multilateral framework of principles and rules, aimed at progressively opening up trade in services worldwide" (Sedgwick, 2002).

According to the Office of the United States Trade Representative, the GATS is designed

- to reduce or eliminate government measures that prevent services from being provided across national borders or that discriminate against foreign-owned service producers in their market;
- to provide a legal framework for addressing barriers to trade and investment in services;
- to provide a vehicle for further negotiations to open services markets around the world and progressively liberalize conditions for trade. (Papovich, 2002)

One of the conditions for participation in the GATS requires all member nations to abide by the two core components of the GATS: the general obligations, and the schedule of commitments. A third component of the GATS is the Annexes, which outline limitations individual nations are applying to their schedule of commitments. The Annexes, though structurally important, are more like complementary elements to the schedules and are not as independently significant in understanding the application of the GATS as the general obligations and the national schedules.

The general obligations, the framework agreement containing the general rules and disciplines of the GATS, and the national schedules, which list individual countries specific commitments on access to their domestic markets by foreign suppliers (WTO, 2001), provide the structure in which nations are able to understand the GATS and their ability to create proposals and commitments to the GATS that are in their best interests.

The GATS general obligations and their sub-principles are described in detail below, but it is important to understand the concept and realities of the national schedules of commitments to put these principles and obligations in the proper context. In their national schedules, member nations present their plans for including specific industries and the levels at which they are willing to provide domestic market access to foreign service suppliers to those industries. Each schedule is developed independently by national governments, often and ideally with input from local industry representatives, and the WTO does not maintain guidelines or restrictions on the appearance of any nation's schedule.

The GATS, unlike other bilateral or multilateral trade agreements, is an "opt-in" agreement; meaning, nations must specify in their schedule which industries will be included, when, and to what extent. If an industry is not included, then that industry is not subject to any of the principles or regulations of the GATS. The national schedules are the mechanisms that each nation has to indicate what and how industries are open for expansion within the scope of the GATS. It is with an understanding of the flexibility provided by the national schedule idea that the general obligations and principles of the GATS are best examined.

GATS: PRINCIPLES

Within the general obligations are four major principles—most-favored nation (MFN) status, transparency, market access, and national treatment. Two, MFN and transparency are principles that are also broad obligations to which all members must adhere. The other two—market access and national treatment—are applicable only to those service areas that a member nation lists in its national schedule for liberalization. Each principle, however, is important in understanding the climate for trade created and enforced by the GATS.

Most Favored Nation (Article II)

First, "the MFN obligation means that a country will treat the service suppliers of another member no less favourably than it does the service suppliers of any other member" (OECD, 2002, p. 59). MFN status was a core principle of the GATT and, subsequently, the WTO, though WTO members were given the opportunity to list MFN exemptions in the Uruguay Round of the GATT for application to the GATS. Such exemptions are structured to end after about a decade and are subject to an interim 5-year review, to confirm their validity (OECD, 2002). MFN status exists to ensure that there is not an environment of discrimination in an industry, regardless of national origin, so long as the providers are from a member nation. MFN status does not assure, however, that the market will be specifically open to any provider; it merely assures that there will not be structural barriers to the trade opportunity. A company from an MFN nation could try to compete in the marketplace, but success in the marketplace could not, of course, be guaranteed any more than it is for any other company competing in the market.

Transparency (Article III)

The obligation for transparency involves ensuring that all any and all "barriers" to trade, including such concerns as legal statutes, international agreements, taxes, etc., must be clear and easily comprehensible to anyone looking to engage in that trade concern. Transparency is as it sounds—an ideal of completely clear and unambiguous policies regarding barriers to trade in a nation's economy.

> Given the high degree of regulation of many service activities, effective access to markets can depend crucially on services suppliers gaining accurate knowledge of the laws and regulations in force in a perspective market. The need for predictability is considerable in services trade, and is reflected in the fact that disciplines on transparency, . . . are one of the Agreement's core general obligations. That is, it applies to all services subject to GATS coverage, regardless of whether members have scheduled (*i.e.*, undertaken legally bound) liberalization commitments. (OECD, 2002, p. 59)

Indeed, transparency provides a core of understanding among all member nations, that industrial leaders and other interested parties will have real access to all pertinent and relevant information regarding trade in any particular country. The principle of transparency best represents the borderless quality and ideals of the GATS.

Market Access (Article XVI)

Market Access commitments are developed by member nations within their liberalization schedules. Member nations determine which industries are being included in their proposals to the GATS and specify which levels of market access will be available to trading nations.

> Market access commitments do not affect the right to regulate service and they do not oblige Governments to permit the entry of unlimited service suppliers. They can include limitations on the number of suppliers, the total value of transactions, the number of service operations, the number of persons to be employed, the types of legal entity permitted and the share of foreign capital. The entry "none" in a schedule is an undertaking that limitations of these kinds will not be imposed. (WTO, 2001, p. 8)

The ideal of market access is consistent with the other guiding GATS principles in that its purpose is overtly to allow for equal opportunities for service providers regardless of national origin. Market access does not limit a national government's ability to regulate and industry nor does it provide greater or special rights to providers over the goals of domestic governments. Instead, it establishes the parameters of operations for all providers—foreign and domestic—within the market for an industry.

National Treatment (Article XVII)

The rules on national treatment hold that while a nation may develop any regulations and conditions to operations that it wishes, if an industry is scheduled to be included in a country's GATS proposal, foreign suppliers in that industry must be held to the same standards and national suppliers. As in all parts of the GATS, national treatment is an "opt-in" ideal, meaning the principle is not applied to an industry unless the national government's proposal to the GATS opts to include that industry in its liberalization proposal. Once included, that industry is required to treat foreign and national providers the same, If not included, however, the issue of national treatment does not apply to that industry. As with the other three main principles of the GATS, the goal of establishing national treatment protections in the GATS was to provide protection against discrimination against foreign suppliers to the benefit of domestic ones (WTO, 2001; OECD, 2004).

Progressive Liberalization (Part IV)

Perhaps the most controversial and least understood element of the GATS, progressive liberalization is less a stand-alone principle than an operating procedure for the GATS. While not a mandated regulation, per se, progressive liberalization is a fundamental tenant of the GATS. In the WTO's ideal expansion of the GATS, each member nation of the WTO and/or signatory of the GATS would strive over time to remove any officially sanctioned barriers to trade. This could happen in stages and over time, ideally within a decade after the conclusion of the most recent GATS round. The controversy or confusion around progressive liberalization concerns the elimination of protections that may have been provided within original national commitments to the GATS. Groups and individuals that have sought influence in the negotiations and ultimate development of their government's commitment to the GATS are anxious that the ideal of progressive liberalization will ultimately remove their hard-fought compromises from their nation's trade relations and will expose their industries to trade forces that might, theoretically, threaten their home industry.

Dispute Settlement (Article XXIII)

One final issue that is particularly noteworthy in the GATS is the need for a clear dispute settlement process. As the GATS regulates relations between nations—not individuals, companies, or, even industries, the dispute settlement process comes into play when an actor from one nation appeals to his/her government about a situation in another country that is affecting his/her ability to trade there, It is up to that government, then, to appeal to the WTO to challenge the legitimacy of that barrier. The other nation would then present its own case for why that barrier is legitimate. The WTO would determine after hearing from both governments, whether a promise for free trade had been breached, according to the "defending' country's commitments to the GATS and apply sanctions on in cases where that country was acting against its own stated policies for free trade. Governments, of course, remain sovereign and could respond to a negative finding in numerous ways, including appealing the finding, agreeing with the finding, withdrawing from that area of the GATS, or, even, withdrawing entirely from the GATS. The WTO/GATS dispute settlement process, regardless, provides a forum for hearing complaints and through which governments can continue to discuss issues regarding their position on GATS and their service sectors.

GATS: INCLUDED INDUSTRIES AND "MODES OF SUPPLY"

The GATS encompasses all services industries with two key exceptions: "services provided in the exercise of governmental authority and, in the air traffic sector, air traffic rights and all services directly related to the exercise of traffic rights" (WTO, 2001). The important question in the debate about the GATS and higher education involves the first exception—"services provided in the exercise of governmental authority." In GATS Article I.3(c), such governmentally supplied services are defined as "any service which is supplied neither on a commercial basis, nor in competition with one or more service suppliers" (WTO, 2001).

This exception, however, does not clarify entirely, and, in fact actually complicates, the picture of higher education services in the United States. Public higher education and private higher education often do not appear to be entirely distinct in the U.S., where public higher education receives ample funding from private sources and citizens and where private higher education is heavily subsidized by public funding. Public institutions do compete with private institutions for students, faculty, research grants, and more. Such institutions may even offer largely identical curricula and other educational services. For these reasons, the debate about the effect of the GATS on trade in higher education services remains complicated, and there do not appear to be concrete or specifically identifiable answers to questions about how and where the GATS could be applied to higher education. There are areas, or modes, of supply, however, that are clearly outlined in the GATS and that can be applied to trade in higher education services.

Mode1: Cross Border Supply

Mode 1 concerns the ability of a service provider to accommodate a consumer who is located in another nation. Cross border supply does not necessarily require the physical presence of the provider in another country; merely the ability of a consumer from one country to partake of the service in another country. A higher education example of Mode 1 supply would be e-learning and distance learning opportunities over the internet or through correspondence courses from universities.

Mode 2: Consumption Abroad

In mode 2 types of supply, the consumer actually crosses over their national border and purchases an educational service abroad. Undergraduate and graduate level study abroad is the most obvious example of mode 2 supply, but other examples would include short and long term language immersion courses or executive training courses. Any situation in which the consumer of the educational product traveled to another country to study falls under Mode 2, which currently describes the largest mode of international, trans-border consumption of educational services.

Mode 3: Commercial Presence

Commercial presence, Mode 3 supply, involves the supplier of the service physically moving into a foreign country to provide its service to foreign consumers. In a time when traditional campuses such as the Wharton School at the University of Pennsylvania or the Medical School at Cornell are opening branch campuses in Europe, Asia, and the Middle East, this mode of supplying educational services across borders in gaining in visibility and, in many cases, notoriety. Where education is seen as an important transmitter of national culture and norms, the presence of foreign institutions can seem threatening, and questions about how to regulate these foreign providers remains at the forefront of the debate on their utility and validity as education providers abroad. Mode 3 is the most controversial of the modes of supply and the mode that seems to feel the most threatening to educational critics of the GATS.

Mode 4: Presence of Natural Persons

Mode 4 involves the movement of individuals abroad in order to provide a service. Currently, having faculty, researchers, and staff members hired from overseas is neither uncommon nor, for the most part, controversial. As noted at the beginning of this chapter, higher education has always been defined by the mobility of scholars and scholarship, and in this age of easy travel and technological innovations such as online databases, e-mail, and internet journals, the borders between nations seem even more porous with regard to the movement of knowledge and those that produce and disseminate it. Individuals will undoubtedly continue to be recruited for and seek independently opportunities for employment overseas from their country of citizenship.

These different modes of supply are broad categorizations and, to some degree, simplifications of the many and varied elements of the educational industry, but they are very useful in understanding how the "industry" of higher education can be broken down into "tradable" parts.

GATS: EXCLUSIONS

Three specific exclusions were codified into the GATS: 1) the GATS does not apply to "services supplied in the exercise of government authority, defined in the GATS as any service which is supplied neither on a commercial basis, nor in competition with one or more service suppliers"; 2) the GATS does not include air transportation services; and 3) the GATS does not apply to government procurement of services (USTR, July 2002). The GATS also allows for governments establishing protections they deem necessary for the protection of their domestic policies and interests. According to the GATS, no government is expected to usurp their own autonomy in order to abide by WTO/GATS commitments.

By and large, then, these exclusions exist to protect government interest and autonomy in their operations. Of particular note and, to some extent, concern for the U.S. higher education industry is the first exclusion, which seems to "protect" public (government run) entities from trade liberalization. Since American higher education blurs the lines between public and private in terms of funding and competition, determining what levels of exclusions apply to higher education remains very challenging, if not impossible, without greater clarification on the part of the WTO.

GATS: TIMELINE

The GATS schedule of negotiations includes key dates by which certain elements of the GATS negotiations regarding both requests of other members for access to their markets and offers of market access to other member nations must be completed. The most recent round of GATS negotiations began in early 2000, and had a June 2002 deadline for requests to member nations, a March 2003 deadline for initial offers for market access, and was to be completed with the submission of all final offers by January 2005. After the collapse of GATS negotiations in Cancun, September 2003, it became clear that the January 2005 deadline would pass without final enactment of a completed GATS, and the deadline is now open-ended. Negotiations among WTO member nations, therefore, remain ongoing.

CONCLUSIONS

The GATS specifically notes the commitment of the WTO to work alongside the UN and other international organizations "concerned with services" (Article XXVI), such as the organizations detailed in the previous chapter. UNESCO, the OECD, and the World Bank are the most notable of such international actors engaging in the current examination of trade in services. Higher education encompasses a global market with an estimated annual value of $30 billion as of 1999 (American Council on Education, 2002), and, as such a significant service industry area, it seems inevitable that higher education was going to become an industry of interest to trade officials and entrepreneurs. By 2002, the United States alone generated approximately $12.85 billion from trade in the form of foreign student enrollments alone (IIE, 2003), making higher education the U.S.'s fifth largest service export (USTR, July 2002). With demand to education increasing worldwide, trade in the supply of education services seems destined for continued growth.

As member nations of the WTO look to the GATS to treat higher education as a commodity to be regulated (or deregulated) as another international trade concern, higher education may become less autonomous as an industry of independent institutions and more like a system to be influenced, regulated and controlled by outside markets and actors (Altbach, Fall 2002). Indeed, the newest proposals/offers submitted to the World Trade Organization by Australia, New Zealand, and the United States are just the latest in a series of international proposals to minimize the impact of trade regulations on higher education as a globally traded service area, allowing providers and consumers to have greater influence on the "product" of education being traded.

Not all higher education providers are excited about this access to free trade in higher education, however. The American proposal to remove barriers to trade in international higher education services has come as an unwelcome surprise and area of significant concern for many organizations representing the traditional base of U.S. higher education around issues of internationalization, government relations, and trade. The next chapter examines the details of the different USTR proposals and ultimate offer to the GATS, as they related to higher education, to ground the explanation and analysis of the current debate about the USTR's stance on the GATS and, more broadly, trade in higher education services.

Chapter Six

The USTR, the GATS, and U.S. Higher Education as a Tradable Commodity

As noted in the previous chapter, the GATS is an agreement within the World Trade Organization (WTO), is the first international agreement to focus on trade in services (as opposed to goods), and aims to "expand free trade in services, open markets, and facilitate economic growth" among member nations by "removing restrictions on market access and barriers to competition" (ACE, 2003). The WTO is made up of member nations, and within the WTO, a subset of members are signatories of the GATS. The responsibility for representing individual national interests in the WTO falls to government agencies, and the representative agency for the United States is the Office of the United States Trade Representative (USTR). This chapter introduces the USTR's origins within the executive branch of the federal government and then details the USTR's position and actions with regard to the GATS.

WHAT IS THE USTR?

The USTR is an agency within the Executive branch of the federal government, reporting directly to the President. From its origins in the Trade Expansion Act of 1962 and through numerous additional trade acts and executive orders since that time, there has been some form of trade office and trade advisor to the president, and the current structure of the Office of the Trade Representative of the United States places the head of the USTR in an ambassadorial role, serving on the President's Cabinet as the President's "advisor, negotiator, and spokesperson on trade issues" (USTR,

2004). Two particularly noteworthy expansions of the role of the trade representative came in 1979/80 and 1988.

President Jimmy Carter submitted the Reorganization Plan No. 3 of 1979 and the Executive Order 12188 in 1980 with the goal of improving "the capacity of the Government to strengthen the export performance of United States industry and to assure fair international trade practices, taking into account the interests of all elements of our economy" (Carter, 1979). The Reorganization officially renamed the trade representatives office from the Special Trade Representative (STR) to the USTR and "assigned overall responsibility to USTR for developing and coordinating the implementation of U.S. trade policy" (USTR, 2004a). Among many focused responsibilities officially assigned to the USTR in this Reorganization Plan made the USTR responsible for overseeing all issues regarding trade in services, notable for specifying the interest of trade in services as independent and significant from trade in goods, which had been the main focus of all trade negotiations (largely through the GATT) until this time.

The Omnibus Trade and Competitiveness Act of 1988 was passed by the U.S. Congress which "codified the status and responsibilities of USTR previously established through Reorganization Plan No. 3 and Executive Order 12188" (USTR, 2004a). Through this legislation, Congress reinforced the ties between the legislative and executive branches with regard to trade policy and made particular note of the USTR's role as advisor to both the President and Congress. According to the USTR (2004), the Act specifically noted such responsibilities as:

- To have primary responsibility for developing and coordinating the implementation of U.S. international trade policy;
- To serve as the principal advisor to the President on international trade policy and advise the President on the impact of other U.S. Government policies on international trade;
- To have lead responsibility for the conduct of, and be chief U.S. representative for, international trade negotiations, including commodity and direct investment negotiations;
- To coordinate trade policy with other agencies;
- To act as the principal international trade policy spokesperson of the President;
- To report and be responsible to the President and the Congress on the administration of the trade agreements program, and to advise on non-tariff barriers, international commodity agreements, and other matters relating to the trade agreements program; and
- To be Chairman of the Trade Policy Committee. (USTR, 2004a)

The Uruguay Round Agreements Act (1994) further solidified the USTR's position as the lead organization for U.S. international trade interests by legislating the USTR's responsibility for leading U.S. interests in all negotiations within the World Trade Organization. Between these Presidential and Congressional acts regarding the USTR, the role of the USTR has been well defined and codified as the primary agency for overseeing all international trade efforts for the United States.

The USTR notes that its primary responsibilities include "providing leadership and negotiating expertise" on behalf of the U.S. in:

- Bilateral, regional and multilateral trade and investment issues;
- Expansion of market access for American goods and services;
- International commodity agreements;
- Negotiations affecting U.S. import policies;
- Trade, commodity, and direct investment matters managed by international institutions such as the Organization for Economic Cooperation and Development (OECD) and the United Nations Conference on Trade and Development (UNCTAD);
- Trade-related intellectual property protection issues;
- World Trade Organization (WTO) issues (USTR, 2004b)

It is within the context of these specific responsibilities that the USTR has developed and is continuing to negotiate the U.S. position on trade in services through the GATS.

BRINGING HIGHER EDUCATION INTO THE SERVICES NEGOTIATIONS

According to Dr. Bernard Ascher, the former director of service-industry affairs at the USTR:

> Education has been included as a service sector from the beginning, that is, from the late 1970s and 1980s when the U.S. initiated its efforts to get other countries to focus on service industries as part of the negotiations. Service industries, which at that time accounted for about 70 percent of U.S. non-agricultural employment (and now accounts for 80 percent), urged that the U.S. Government provide services with treatment equal to that accorded to agricultural and industrial goods in trade agreements. In 1986, other countries agreed to discuss services during the so-called Uruguay Round negotiations. The Trade Act of 1988 contains a definition of services, which specifically

> includes education. During the Uruguay Round, agreement was reached on provisions for services. (B. Ascher, personal communication, November 10, 2003)

The agreement reached by the broad WTO membership during the Uruguay Round was the initiation of the GATS. From the start of the negotiations on trade in services outlined through the GATS, the United States has consistently maintained a position that included higher education alongside the myriad other service industries. As the negotiations regarding the U.S. offer to the GATS developed, the USTR sought input from different sources in the higher education community for feedback on its evolving position regarding how and to what extent higher education was to be included in its GATS offer. The negotiations and discussions are on-going.

KEY DATES FOR THE GATS NEGOTIATIONS

The structure of the GATS, outlined earlier, has been developed with a listing of key dates for all GATS signatories, providing a timeline and deadlines for making requests of other members for access to markets and for providing offers of market access to other member nations. The negotiation period of the most recent round of GATS began in early 2000 and was assigned a completion date of January 2005 (which passed without a final implementation of the GATS). During this period, the USTR has been actively developing requests for access to higher education markets abroad and a proposal for offering access to the U.S. higher education market.

The United States is a member of the WTO and a signatory of the GATS. As such, the United States, represented by the USTR, has followed the prescribed timeline and submitted documentation to the WTO to meet each deadline. The USTR submitted to fifteen negotiating proposals between the summer of 2000 and the summer of 2002, on a variety of areas and concerns, and these proposals ultimately served as the foundation for the official USTR request for market access filed in the summer of 2002. These negotiating proposals were timed to lead into the most significant dates of this round of negotiations: 30 June 2002, when initial requests of member nations to other member nations for market access were to be filed; 31 March 2003, when initial offers of market access to domestic markets for other member nations were to be filed; and 1 January 2005, by which time all offers are to be finalized and completed. The following is a description of the submissions presented by the USTR as they relate to higher education.

18 December 2000: The Higher Education Negotiating Proposal

As noted above, the USTR submitted fifteen negotiating proposals between the summer of 2000 and the summer of 2002, each proposal offering opinions and position the U.S. was looking to include in the broad dialogue that was developing around the GATS. One proposal in particular brought attention to the direct inclusion of higher education in the USTR's proposal for liberalization of services.

For the purposes of this research, the 18 December 2000 negotiating proposal, entitled "Communication from the United States: Higher (Tertiary) Education, Adult Education, and Training," is the most significant of all of the USTR's official documents leading up to the Initial Offer of Market Access, because it expresses specifically and clearly the rationale and operating philosophy that the USTR was using in including higher education in its liberalization plan for trade in services, as well as the goals for higher education service liberalization it was hoping to achieve through the GATS proposals. The December 2000 proposal presents the background of and predicts the position on education that the USTR would ultimately take in its March 2003 initial offer of market access.

In the December 2000 proposal, the USTR outlines its goal in addressing trade in education through this proposal as seeking to establish an environment that would be most conducive to removing barriers to trade in post-secondary education services while, simultaneously, protecting national interests in public education. The proposal opens with an acknowledgment "that education to a large extent is a government function, but that most countries permit private education to coexist with public education" (USTR, December 200, p. 1). The U.S. position, then, was to promote private higher education opportunities as a complement to the public services already available in countries around the world.

The USTR continues in the document to explain that the purpose of the specifically focused proposal on higher education was to help *suppliers* of higher education by pushing for the removal and reduction of barriers to cross-border trade. As the USTR acts on behalf of American business interests, the focus on suppliers of education seems in keeping with mission of the USTR, although the proposal does not define the term supplier within the document, and, considering the vast diversity of higher education providers in the American system, the lack of clarity on this point may illustrate a purposeful vagueness in the language or at the very least an oversight in acknowledging the complexity behind defining a supplier of higher education that would want and benefit from open markets in higher education services.

Indeed, from an educator or student perspective, this focus on the supplier of education seems too simplistic considering the complexity of American higher education, including the diversity and variable interests of the many higher education "suppliers," specific concerns of students, and the 'public good' element of the provision of education. Outside of making reference to the economic value of education for employment, the USTR's negotiating proposal on higher education focuses on the business of international higher education and its ability to "develop a more efficient workforce, leading countries to an improved competitive position in the world economy" (USTR, December 2000, p. 1).

The December 2000 proposal both compels the U.S.'s trading partners to be purposeful in their willingness to open their markets to trade in post-secondary education and lists what the USTR saw as fundamental obstacles to free trade in post-secondary educational services. The USTR offers to continue expanding its offer on liberalization in higher education (as well as training and education testing) so long as other trading nations were willing to match the offer being proposed by the U.S. Finally, the December 2000 proposal ends with the USTR asking other member nations to address existing barriers to educational services in their impending offers of market access in. The listed obstacles presented by the USTR were:

- Prohibition of higher education, adult education, and training services offered by foreign entities
- Lack of an opportunity for foreign suppliers of higher education, adult education, and training services to obtain authorization to establish facilities within the territory of the Member country
- Lack of an opportunity for foreign suppliers of higher education, adult education, and training services to qualify as degree granting institutions
- Inappropriate restrictions on electronic transmission of course materials
- Economic needs test on suppliers of these services
- Measures requiring the use of a local partner
- Denial of permission for private sector suppliers of higher education, adult education, and training to enter into and exit from joint ventures with local or non-local partners on a voluntary basis
- Where government approval is required, exceptionally long delays are encountered and, when approval is denied, no reasons are given for the denial and no information is given on what must be done to obtain approval in the future
- Tax treatment that discriminates against foreign suppliers

- Foreign partners in a joint venture are treated less favorably than the local partners
- Franchises are treated less favorably than other forms of business organization
- Domestic laws and regulations are unclear and administered in an unfair manner
- Subsidies for higher education, adult education, and training are not made known in a clear and transparent manner
- Minimum requirements for local hiring are disproportionately high, causing uneconomic operations
- Specialized, skilled personnel (including managers, computer specialists, expert speakers), needed for a temporary period of time, have difficulty obtaining authorization to enter and leave the country
- Repatriation of earnings is subject to excessively costly fees and/or taxes for currency conversion
- Excessive fees/taxes are imposed on licensing or royalty payments.

USTR, December 2002, p. 3–4

This list addresses concerns as basic as breaking through national bureaucracy to adjusting tax policies, to creating economic models to help expose the level of need for more open trade in education services. In addressing this list of issues to the entire WTO membership, the U.S. also opened itself to criticism should it retain any of the obstacles in its own treatment of foreign providers of education services. By elaborating on these concerns, the USTR established the reality of its commitment to including post-secondary education in its offers to the GATS for market access and trade liberalization. As will be discussed later, it was this December 2000 proposal that particularly caught the attention of the U.S. domestic higher education industry and spurred a rapid attempt to infuse greater and broader influence of the higher education industry in the development of the USTR position on trade in higher education.

As with the December 2000 negotiating proposal, the goal of each of the fifteen negotiating proposals was either to specify issues related to the 12 service sectors included in the GATS, to focus the issue of transparency within domestic policies, and to put specific issues on the table so as to assure some level of redress prior to the upcoming request and offer rounds of 2002 and 2003. They also provided a structure for the USTR to lobby other member nations to address concerns specific to the United States well in advance of the deadlines for presenting specific requests for market access (2002) and offers of market access (2003).

30 June 2002: Initial Request for Market Access

The USTR's "Proposals for Liberalizing Trade in Services," the executive summary of the USTR's "Initial Request for Market Access" was released on 1 July 2002, following the request's submission to the WTO the day before, meeting the deadline for making requests of other nations regarding specific areas of market access. This request's executive summary begins with an analysis of the importance of service industries on the U.S. economy, perhaps to justify the requests it's chosen to make it the proposal. According to the USTR,

> (s)ervices are what most Americans do for a living. Service industries are a major component of U.S. economic activity, accounting for 80 percent of U.S. employment and 63 percent of the U.S. Gross Domestic Product (GDP). The United States is also the world's largest exporter of services. U.S. services exports have more than doubled over the last 10 years, increasing from $137 billion in 1990 to $279 billion in 2000, according to U.S. Department of Commerce data.
>
> USTR, July 2002, p. 1

By establishing the scale of the service market in the USTR provides a rationale for seeking greater opportunities for trade in the service sector.

With regard to education, the USTR 's initial request for market access highlights the breadth and economic value of trade in education services for the United State in noting that the "U.S. balance of payments receipts from incoming students amount to some $10 billion annually (USTR, July 2002, p. 5). The proposal calls for: " . . . increased access for higher education . . . in traditional institutional settings, such as universities or schools, or outside of traditional settings, including workplaces, or elsewhere." It continues by clarifying what educational services are not included in the request: "The United States is not requesting commitments . . . with respect to public institutions, subsidies, or other assistance in the education sector." And, finally, it seeks to assure those with concerns about public autonomy with regard to trade in education that the goals of liberalization of education markets is to provide greater access to a highly demanded service. "The U.S. approach does not seek to displace public education systems, but rather proposes to help upgrade knowledge and skills through privately provided educational . . . programs, while respecting each country's role of prescribing and administering public education" (USTR, July 2002, p. 5–6).

Since this phase of the GATS proposals involves asking for access to the domestic markets of other countries (as opposed to offering access to the U.S. domestic market), the USTR used the proposal to promote the importance of increased access to educational services around the world (in order to develop skills needed to participate fully in modern economies) as well the success and attractiveness of American education services (in noting the number of international students who come to study in the U.S.). Again, as with the negotiating request on higher education, the USTR opened the U.S. to criticism regarding its own openness to foreign providers of services on its domestic soil, and the 31 March 2003 Initial Offer of Market Access sought to face any such critiques with offers of broad access to service providers from other WTO member nations.

31 March 2003: Initial Offer of Market Access

The March 2003 offer of market access submitted to the WTO by the USTR opens with a six-point introduction, with specific references to progressive liberalization goals; responding to market access requests by other nations; acknowledging the offer's focus on private, non-governmental operations and the fact that nothing in GATS supercedes any nations' right to promote policies that are best for its own national stability and security; offering the U.S.'s openness to bilateral and other trade agreements that could result in greater U.S. obligations; securing the U.S.'s right to withdraw from any and all elements of the offer should the need arrive prior to its final ratification; and noting that the U.S. was reserving the right to make corrections to the text of the offer to correct "errors, omissions, or inaccuracies" (USTR, March 2003, p. 1).

The structure of the initial offer of market access is that of a matrix in which a sector or sub-sector is named and which then describes any limitation on market access or on national treatment within each of the four Modes of Supply—1) cross-border supply, 2) consumption abroad, 3) commercial presence, and 4) presence of natural persons. Educational services is just one of twelve service sectors specifically named by the USTR to be included in its offer, and higher education services (defined here as post-secondary education, training services, and educational testing) are the only education services being considered for a final commitment for market access. The section of the offer regarding higher education services, however, contains numerous clauses and caveats (limitations) to any broad liberalization that the scale of access to be offered through any final commitment, which is still being developed.

The limitations to any future commitment regarding higher education include the right of "individual U.S. institutions to maintain autonomy in admissions policies, in setting tuition rates, and in the development of curricula or course content" (USTR, March 2003, p. 57). Other limitations involve the right of federal and state government to fund or provide subsidies only to

U.S. schools, the right to restrict scholarships to U.S. citizens or citizens of particular states, and the right to set different tuition rates for in-state and out-of-state students. Finally, the offer provides a long list of regulatory structures that would remain in place even with broad liberalization in higher education services: admission policies regarding equal opportunity, setting standards for the granting of degrees, state regulations on institutional facilities, accreditation, the application of tax or other public benefits to institutions, and the requirement that any foreign entity wanting to have its students be eligible for the federal student loan program would have to abide by the same requirements applied to U.S. institutions (USTR, March 2003, p. 58).

The 31 March 2003 offer does not explicitly include higher education as much as it implies that higher education, ultimately, will be included and all interested parties should be on notice for future reference. With the extensive introduction to concerns around higher education, the USTR appears to be readying higher education constituents for inclusion by the finalization of the Doha Round. What are explicitly included, however, are adult education and "other education services," including training and testing services. These sectors have been listed as largely having no restrictions/ limitations regarding market access for Modes 1–3, with one odd exception.

Adult education has one restriction regarding the commercial presence (Mode 3) of a foreign provider in that "the number of licenses for cosmetology schools in Kentucky is limited to 48 total licenses, with a total of 8 licenses allowed for operation of such schools per congressional district" (USTR, March 2003, p, 58). Why are Kentucky cosmetology schools being specifically protected? Lobbying on behalf of that sector is most likely why this protection was included, and this random-seeming protection seems to highlight the somewhat serendipitous nature of deciding what is and is not to be included in such broad and detailed negotiated document such as a GATS offer.

In both adult education and education service, the presence of natural persons (Mode 4) supply issue with regard to market access limitations is presented as "unbound," meaning the USTR is not taking a specific position in this offer but the government is reserving the right to add restrictions on access in this mode and, by explicitly stating that position in this offer, will not face any future sanctions for that. National treatment is being restricted in all found modes of supply with regard to limiting access to higher education financial support to U.S. citizens and/or residents of individual states, protecting scholarship programs and government funding priorities from being challenged through GATS.

IMPLICATIONS OF HIGHER EDUCATION IN THE USTR'S GATS NEGOTIATIONS

The implications of higher education's being included in the U.S. GATS offer, even if not at the level, yet, of a fully committed service area, seem to extend beyond the actual terms of the offers being made. In examining the request for and offer of market access documents, as well as the specific document concerning trade in higher education, it seems apparent that there is a tension between the complexity of the higher education "industry" in the U.S. and the need to simplify all industries down to a few methods of supply and access issues.

None of the documents produced by the USTR involving higher education and the GATS go into detail about the multiple layers of tension in American higher education—private versus public, for-profit versus non-profit, professional versus liberal arts, degree granting versus certification-based, religious versus secular, regional versus national, national versus international, and so on. Even grouping higher education with adult education and education services oversimplifies the vast differences in the scale, purpose, and audiences of these kinds of education operations. No doubt simplification of the issues makes for less challenging negotiations, particularly when international education systems are so vastly different from those in the U.S. Simplifying the issues down to commonalities might make sense in order to have all nations negotiating from the same basic point.

It is this seeming simplification, however, that requires further examination, in order to determine whether at the core, the USTR's works are legitimate in their representation of the interests of American higher education—if there is a collective 'industry' that is coherent enough to go by that singular title. If the ideal ramification of opening trade in higher education services is to provide opportunities to the suppliers of higher education, it seems reasonable to ask the suppliers and related interested parties about their stake in the matter and whether and how their interests are being represented by the USTR in their trade negotiations.

CONCLUSIONS

Considering the vast array of trade issues that fall within its oversight, the USTR cannot be expected to be experts on higher education. As will be discussed in the following chapters, the USTR developed a stance on free trade in higher education services with little internal expertise on higher education and input from higher educations sources that do not represent a broad spectrum of American higher education, forcing interested parties within higher education to become rapidly familiar with trade policies and the specific parameters of the GATS. As these higher education representatives began to engage the USTR, the USTR, in turn, developed its own understanding of the areas of higher education worth consideration with regard to trade.

The research presented in the following chapters derives from this circular relationship between the USTR and representatives of the traditional sector of American higher education. In order to determine the validity of both the USTR's stance and the resulting industry concerns about that stance, one needs to examine the actors, their stake in the issue, and the relationships that exist within this sphere of trade in higher education services. By exploring the dialogue and debate that informed the USTR's official submissions regarding higher education, this research sheds light on the complex relationships that remain between the USTR and higher education and among the higher education actors themselves. The following chapters first provide information about the representative agents of traditional higher education sector and their position, if any, on the GATS, explores the complex environment in which the trade discussions took place, and then details the specific concerns regarding trade liberalization of the engaged higher education representatives.

Chapter Seven

The Associations Representing American Higher Education

The response to the USTR's decision to include higher education in its initial offer to the GATS was highly varied. While the issue of trade policy and its possible effects on higher education were, and remain, too abstruse an issue for campus leaders to tackle, it is exactly the kind of broad policy concern that higher education representative associations would consider addressing, on behalf of their campus constituencies. These kinds of representative associations serve dual roles for their constituents—providing pre-emptive information on issues that may soon filter down to the campus level and responding to concerns brought to their attention by constituents on the campus level. The emerging issue of trade and its impact on American higher education remains largely removed from the campus level, so the efforts on the part of many of these associations are particularly important in representing the interests of their constituents and American higher education in any negotiations. This chapter provides an overview and "biography" of the participant associations in this research, including higher education associations and federal government agencies. In order to understand the relevance of each association on this research on trade in higher education services, it is important to know who they are, what their purpose and roles are, and who they represent as they investigate these issues and take positions on them.

These associations were selected for participation in this research through multiple means, most notably by pulling their names from the long list of signatory associations of a March 2003 letter to the USTR's Office that was authored by the director of the American Council on Education (ACE), David Ward. ACE, whose members include the presidents of over 1800 American college and university, is one of the most respected higher education representative organizations, particularly with regard to international policy issues. The credibility of ACE is widely recognized and provides validity to the decision to use an ACE initiative to inform this research. This letter authored by ACE purports to represents all of American higher education: "The education organizations listed (in this letter) "represent every public and private, two- and four-year college and university in the United States and their 15 million students" (Ward, ACE, March 7, 2003), providing an ideal starting point in establishing a contact list.

In addition, associations were identified and cross-referenced for validity by gathering names from articles and websites in which higher education associations were referenced; researching the primary representative associations for a particular segment of higher education; and through a snowballing effect, with recommendations made by other individuals or associations. Some of these are associations that simply could not be ignored in a canvassing of significant higher education associations, regardless of whether they had taken a position on the GATS. Discovering their capacity for and willingness to engage in this international policy issue was part of the broad research agenda.

Each association contacted was asked to name the groups to whom they looked when seeking internationally-oriented information, and the same few names came up again and again. Information gathered from these individuals and associations from the higher education sector form the basis of the findings and those higher education associations are presented first below. Also included in this research are two government agencies and one legislative representative association. Taken together, these groups cast a wide net that encompasses the vast majority of both American higher education institutions and the governmental agencies engaged in issues of international higher education. In cases where an association's inclusion would have been useful but was thwarted in some way, the explanatory information is provided here.

WHICH ASSOCIATIONS WERE CONTACTED AND WHY?

The following associations were asked by e-mail and phone calls to participate in this research, by granting an interview with a representative in-person, over the phone, or by e-mail. Associations that responded are noted in **bold**, and those that agreed to be interviewed in the research are noted with an asterisk (*).

Higher Education/Other Education Associations (30)

American Association of Community Colleges (AACC)

American Association of State Colleges and Universities (AASCU)

American Association of University Professors (AAUP)*

American Council on Education (ACE)* (2 contacts)

APPA: Association of Higher Education Facilities Officers

Association of American Law Schools

Association of American Universities (AAU)

Association of Catholic Colleges and Universities (ACCU)*

Association of Community College Trustees

Association of Governing Boards of Universities and Colleges

Association of International Education Administrators

Association of Jesuit Colleges and Universities (AJCU)*

Career Colleges Association

Center for Quality Assurance in International Education/National Committee on International Trade in Education (CQAIE/NCITE)*

Consortium on Financing Higher Education (COFHE)

Council for Christian Colleges and Universities

Council for Higher Education Accreditation (CHEA)*

Council for Independent Colleges (CIC)*

Council of Graduate Schools (CGS)*

Education International (EI)

Institute for Higher Education Policy (IHEP)

NAFSA: Association of International Educators (NAFSA)

National Association of College and University Business Officers

National Association of Independent Colleges and Universities (NAICU)

National Association of State Universities and Land Grant Colleges (NASULGC)* (2 contacts)

National Collegiate Athletic Association

National Education Association (NEA)*

National Independent College Council (NICU)

United States Distance Learning Association

University Continuing Education Association (UCEA)

Government Agencies and Non-Education Associations (5)

American Council for Trade in Services

National Conference of State Legislatures (NCSL)*

United States Department of Commerce (DOC)*

United States Department of Education

United States Trade Representatives Office (USTR)*

For-Profit Higher Education Institutions/Corporations (5)

Apollo Group

Education Management Corporation

Jones International University

Sylvan International University (now Laureate Education, Inc.)

University of Phoenix

Again, beginning with the signatories of ACE's March 2003 letter to the USTR provided a well-informed starting point from which to develop a list of potential participants. The listing of organizations actually contacted, however, is actually more comprehensive than the ACE signatories list, as it includes, in addition to the signatories, a few additional higher education agencies and institutions, as well as government representatives. Out of the 40 associations contacted, 24 responded with some level of information (60% response rate), and 13 agreed to participate in the research through interviews (33% overall, 54% of respondents). In addition, if one were to remove the non-higher education groups from the overall list, the response rate is slightly better. Of the 30 higher education representative associations contacted, 20 (67%) responded with some level of information, and 10 (34%) agreed to participate in interviews. In a few cases, with associations that were particularly engaged in this trade issue, there were interviews with multiple members of the association. In four cases, an initial interview was followed by a second, to "member check" the findings developed from the first round interviews. The high response rate to requests for participation and the ability to share early findings with the most engaged of the participants lends a high level of confidence to the findings of this study.

Unfortunately, the participant list is not as comprehensive was intended when structuring this study. For what are undoubtedly numerous and different reasons, many organizations did not respond to repeated requests for their participation. In instances where their participation may have proven particularly useful, information from their website and/or publications is used where possible to present their public perspective on the issues. And, in the case of the numerous requests to the for-profit institutions, the initial goal of getting their input had to be eliminated altogether, due to their complete lack of response. (Only one for-profit, Education Management Corporation, responded in any way, albeit indirectly, by mailing their annual report.) The organization that represents the for-profit sector, the Career Colleges Association, also did not respond to repeated requests for information.

The lack of response from the for-profit higher education sector was disappointing and may be explained by their being uninterested in participating in such research. Or, the organizations may have assumed a bias in the research approach to the issue and were wary of participating. Its also possible that they chose to remain closed off from the outside because of increased public and legal scrutiny over their operations and the credibility of their educational services. There may be other reasons that cannot be known from the outside. It was not entirely surprising perhaps that none of the for-profits were able to or interested in participating in this research, but there is no question that their participation would have resulted in an even more compelling examination of this trade policy issue.

Regardless, the input from the organizations that were willing to participate does present a comprehensive and informative perspective on the question of how the higher education industry influenced and has responded to the prospective inclusion of higher education in the GATS. These groups present a varied and useful array of perspectives on the issue of trade in higher education services, and taken together their input provides a kind of 'member checking' redundancy to the research, supplying confidence to the findings.

The following are brief 'biographies' of the actively participating education and government organizations/agencies, to better understand the sources of the data that informed this study. Collectively, these organizations represent the interests of all non-profit higher education in America in some form, with a few representing the interests of the for-profit sector, as well. By including the wide spectrum of these organizations, the resulting data and information has a real resonance as information representing the broad interests and issues of the American higher education industry.

American Association of University Professors (AAUP)

According to its website, the mission of the American Association of University Professors (AAUP) is "to advance academic freedom and shared governance, to define fundamental professional values and standards for higher education, and to ensure higher education's contribution to the common good" (AAUP, 2004). The AAUP is an academic union, founded in 1915, to provide leadership and guidance to the evolving structures and institutions of American higher education by developing standards and procedures that promote quality and ensure academic freedom for faculty across all institutions of higher education in the United States. The membership of the AAUP includes approximately 45,000 faculty members, who also form the core for more than 500 local AAUP chapters, as well as 39 state organizations affiliated with the association.

The AAUP has a 37-member staff at its headquarters in Washington, DC, though the staff engaging the core issues of this study is made up of the Director of Public Policy and Communication and one staff member working in government relations. The entire DC staff works with Congress and state legislators to promote legislation in support of the core interests of their membership. Among its myriad domestic policy operations, the AAUP also makes a particular point to have an international policy focus within its public policy area. One example of an international policy issue that became a focus of the AAUP involved legislation on monitoring U.S. international studies programs.

According to the AAUP's website, "the Senate Committee on Health, Education, Labor and Pensions is considering legislation that would establish an advisory body (the International Studies Advisory Board) to 'review, monitor, apprise, and evaluate the activities' of international studies programs, to assure that the programs are designed and implemented to 'meet the national need' and 'reflect diverse perspectives and the full range of views on world regions, foreign languages and international affairs'" (AAUP, 2004). The AAUP does support reauthorization and expansion of these international studies programs ["they are even more critical under present global circumstances" (AAUP, 2004)] but it does not support the language in the reauthorization which would establish an "International Advisory Board," largely on the grounds of its passing along responsibility for enforcing federal policies onto university personnel. The AAUP "oppose(s) legislation naming English as the official language of the United States and (o)ppose(s) legislation that would require educational personnel to enforce federal immigration laws or deny educational opportunities to any resident of the United States" (AAUP, 2004).

The AAUP took a forceful position on the issue of the GATS in 2003, through an article by Ruth Flower, the AAUP Director of Public Policy and Communication, in Change Magazine, entitled *Education as Commodity* (July-August 2003), which specifically calls for greater input into the GATS negotiations on the part of higher education. She notes:

> Based on these (accreditation, distance education, and publicly funded research) and other concerns, the AAUP believes that including higher education in GATS may pose a threat to the vitality of public and private nonprofit institutions while favoring the commercial success of private companies proposing to offer higher education in domestic and international markets. (Flower, AAUP, 2003, p. 69)

Though Dr. Flower was on sabbatical during the period of this study, she recommended meeting with Mark Smith, the AAUP Director of Government Relations. Dr. Smith was particularly not well–versed in the specific nature of the GATS but was aware and supportive of the position taken by Dr. Flower on behalf of the AAUP. He discussed the unknown implications of the GATS and free trade on funding for both research and hiring, as just two of the numerous potential results of free trade. Dr. Smith also acknowledged that AAUP was not investing much time into following the GATS more closely, outside of the efforts of Dr. Flower, but was monitoring the information coming out of ACE, the USTR, and other sources. Nonetheless, in the scheme of the broader higher education industry, the attention being paid to the GATS issue by the AAUP is more than at most other associations.

American Council on Education (ACE)

ACE proclaims in its mission statement that, "ACE, the major coordinating body for all the nation's higher education institutions, seeks to provide leadership and a unifying voice on key higher education issues and to influence public policy through advocacy, research, and program initiatives" (ACE, 2004). Made up of a membership of approximately 1,800 higher education institutions (as represented by their presidents), associations, and corporations, ACE notes that "three key strategic priorities drive ACE's activities: (1) Representation: Serve as principal advocate for all of higher education, influencing the federal agenda, state policy, and public opinion; (2) Leadership Development: Enhance the diversity and capacity of American higher education leaders; and (3) Service: Support colleges, universities, and other higher education and adult learner organizations in their efforts to serve students and society" (ACE, 2004).

ACE was founded after World War I to serve as a kind of "umbrella group" to help higher education representative associations work through differences on major issues to present a unified and common position to the outside. ACE's role has been to try "to get the major associations to reach agreement ..." (Burd, 2005, p. 2). ACE has also been the organization within American higher education to provide leadership and representation on issues of public policy, including international issues. Coupled with its establishing internationalization as a specific focus area for its operations, this focus on being a voice for American higher education places ACE in a compelling position to be engaged in this question about GATS. (The other three areas of focus are: access, success, equity, and diversity; institutional effectiveness; and lifelong learning.)

ACE seeks to promote internationalization by providing "programs to help colleges and universities prepare students to work and live in a globally interdependent world" (M. Green, personal communication, May 13, 2004). This internationalization focus along with ACE's stated priority of serving as a representative of its members in influencing "the federal agenda," led ACE to become both increasingly engaged in the issue of trade in education services and sought after by member institutions and other higher education industry associations to provide information and leadership on the question of GATS and how it relates to American higher education. It has also led to ACE's trying to be constantly proactive on any developments regarding globalization and American higher education. Indeed, within their strategic goal regarding *representation*, ACE focuses on leading American higher education in predicting and responding to significant policy concerns:

- Be the most visible and influential higher education organization in public policy deliberations.
- Identify emerging federal and state policy issues and assess their implications for higher education.
- Develop strategies to shape federal initiatives in student aid, scientific research, tax policy, and international education.
- Strengthen higher education's voice in public policy by developing a unified position on legislative and regulatory issues.
- Intervene in important judicial proceedings.
- Advance public understanding of higher education through the popular media and trade press. (ACE, 2004)

This comprehensive listing illustrates ACE's breadth of operations and position in higher education as a bridge between what local campus leaders and officials can tackle and what issues are of concern for higher education more broadly.

In his message on the *Challenges of a New Century*, David Ward, President of ACE, states, "The increased movement of faculty members and students across international boundaries, along with the export of more educational programs and services, has broadened the reach of colleges and universities even as it has generated a new set of complex issues for them" (Ward, ACE, 2004). ACE is engaging those complex issues, including trade policy concerns and negotiations, as it strives to remain current and engaged in the realm in which American higher education interests intersect with government policy development. Dr. Madeleine Green, ACE's Vice President and Director of its Center for Institutional and International Initiatives, has been one of the most active, knowledgeable, and engaged individuals addressing this GATS issue as it relates to higher education.

Association of Catholic Colleges and Universities (ACCU)

According to the ACCU website, the mission of the association is "to promote Catholic higher education by supporting the member institutions, especially with reference to their Catholic mission and character and to serve as The Voice of Catholic Higher Education in the United States" (ACCU, 2004). In the international realm of their operations, the ACCU regards its responsibility as being "to build coalitions as appropriate with international and national higher education associations." This official statement about creating international links is unusual and significant in understanding Catholic higher education as it focuses on its Catholic mission over its national position.

The ACCU has a membership of 214 American institutions and cites its objectives by stating, "through research, collecting and coordinating data, publications, and conferences, ACCU encourages and facilitates sharing of ideas and cooperative efforts among its member institution" (ACCU, 2004).

ACCU's relationship with the Catholic hierarchy in the United States is through the Unites States Conference of Catholic Bishops Joint Bishops and Presidents Committee, and the Congregation for Catholic Education of the Holy See. The ACCU also represents Catholic Higher Education and its member institutions more broadly, to the United States' Catholic community, as well as to the Federal government and the media. ACCU also "maintains international and ecumenical higher education contacts through membership in the Washington Higher Education Secretariat of the American Council of (sic) Education, the Association of Executives in Church-related Higher Education, the National Association of Independent Colleges and Universities, the International Federation of Catholic Universities, and the International Forum of Associations of Christian Higher Education" (ACCU, 2004). Of these associations, the American Council on Education is the most visible and often cited leader for American higher education regarding international issues, and the fact that ACCU looks to ACE for leadership in this area is not surprising. Many of the following organizations state similar relationships to ACE. (This leadership role of ACE also came out repeatedly in the data discussed in the following chapter.)

Association of Jesuit Colleges and Universities (AJCU)

The Association of Jesuit Colleges and Universities (AJCU) is a U.S.-based service association, serving its 28 Jesuit college and university members. On its website, AJCU notes: "the 28 schools are bonded together by a common heritage, vision and purpose, and engage in a number of collaborative projects" (AJCU, 2004). AJCU is included in this study for two reasons: 1). Boston College is a member of AJCU, and 2) the history of Jesuit higher education includes significant international efforts in establishing institutions around the world. In addition, AJCU's president, Dr. Charles Currie, SJ, also participates in international higher education conferences regarding Catholic higher education, and globalization has been a topic of debate within the Catholic higher education sector over the last few years. While AJCU has not established a statement or position on international issues within their mission or operations, including AJCU in this research seemed necessary to present a more comprehensive picture of American higher education as it relates to trade.

Center for Quality Assurance in International Education (CQAIE): National Committee on International Trade in Education (NCITE)

Two of the most active organizations in this trade debate are the National Committee on International Trade in Education (NCITE) and its mother organization, the Center for Quality Assurance in International Education (CQAIE), a 501(c)3 non-profit higher education organization. Their activities regarding this particular issue of trade in international higher education include lobbying and maintaining close relationships with the USTR and the U.S. DOC, holding conferences on issues of trade that include such significant participants as the OECD, WTO, UNESCO, ACE, and other international organizations, and publishing articles and their conference proceedings, to distribute their data and other research to as broad an audience as possible.

Background information on CQAIE taken directly from the organization's website states:

> The Center for Quality Assurance in International Education, a membership organization made up predominantly of U.S. accrediting bodies, was founded in 1991. It grew out of the Council on Postsecondary Accreditation [COPA] (the umbrella organization for U.S. accreditation) where the Center's Executive Director [Dr. Marjorie Peace Lenn] was Vice President... (CQAIE, 2003)

The CQAIE website also presents the mission of the organization as serving as:

> ...a collaborative activity of the higher education and quality and competency assurance communities both within the United States and between the United States and other country associations concerned with issues of quality and fairness in international academic and professional mobility, credentialing and recognition. The Center facilitates the comparative study of national quality and competency assurance mechanisms to improve efforts within countries and promote mobility among national systems. To these ends, the Center's activities fall into three categories:
>
> 1. Assisting countries in the development or enhancement of quality assurance systems for higher education
> 2. Promoting the globalization of the professions; and
> 3. Monitoring issues of quality in the transnational movement of higher education. (CQAIE, 2003)

In addition, NCITE, founded within CQAIE in 1999, focuses directly on this issue of trade in higher education services and notes that its mission is fourfold:

1. To provide a forum for discussion and education to its corporate, institutional and organizational members related to our common interests in light of the trade agreements;
2. To act as an advocate and information clearinghouse for driving forces in the globalization of education and training, including but not limited to the globalization of the professions;
3. To provide accurate, current and organized information related to U.S. education and training interests to the proper U.S. government agencies, and particularly the Office of the U.S. Trade Representative (USTR), as

well as keeping NCITE members informed of governmental and other related activity; and

4. To develop and maintain a national database of global providers of education and training services in order to provide ourselves, our government and interested parties accurate information related to the true scope of growing international activity in the delivery of these services. (NCITE, 2004)

Much about the CQAIE and NCITE remains unclear—even after reading their materials, poring over their website, digging into recent tax filings, and interviewing their director—particularly regarding their membership. Though their websites offer membership to subscribers, neither organization offers for public access a list of their members, the number of member organizations, nor any specific information about their members. When pressed for greater details regarding their membership and a list of members, their director, Marjorie Peace Lenn, Ph.D., stated that CQAIE/NCITE are not a membership organizations, though their "activities are supported by a wide range of educational institutions and organizations, including accrediting and certifying bodies, higher education associations (including testing organizations), and institutions of higher education interested in quality and mobility issues as higher education crosses borders" (M.P. Lenn, NCITE, personal communication, November 4, 2004).

There is no way to substantiate this statement, since the organization does not release its membership information to non-members, and it would not supply more detailed information when asked. It was also impossible to gather specific data on CQAIE/NCITE's sources of funding. An examination of the tax returns for the organization, which files under the name of the Council in Quality Assurance in International Education, shows that less than 10% of the listed revenues of the organization come from contributions ($24,754 of $283,963). The bulk of the listed revenue for the organization comes from international consulting ($153,716), the NCITE program ($60,250), and conferences/workshops ($27,560). In addition, $5,000 of income came from government fees and contracts. All together, these sources of income for CQAIE appear to refute the idea that NCITE/ CQAIE represents a wider array of educational institutions and actors. The organization—on paper, at least—appears to be more of an international higher education quality assurance consulting firm than a representative organization/association.

Dr. Lenn, according to her own input and the perceptions of others who have worked with her, is a highly sought after consultant, working with governments and institutions around the world, and the fees for that work are substantial, as noted above. She appears also to be the only high-level administrator at both organizations, serving as the director of both. According to her own published statements and in conversation, Dr. Lenn has served as the U.S. representative to the UNESCO Working Group on Transnational Education in the late 1990s and as the Vice President of the Council on Post-Secondary Accreditation around that time, as well. Her individual credibility, in terms of her experience in and commitment to issues of international education is undeniable.

What is also undeniable is the influence of the CQAIE and NCITE on the development of the USTR's position on trade in higher education, and the extent of their influence became clear through the data collection of this research. The credibility of these two organizations as representative membership associations, however, is dubious and could not be fully substantiated through any available data nor through direct questions to Dr. Lenn. Dr. Lenn's willingness to participate in the interview and supply supplemental data about the GATS issue, however, proved absolutely generous and pertinent to this research. CQAIE/NCITE is enormously significant in this examination of how higher education entered the negotiations of trade agreements, and their participation was invaluable. Without it, this research would have been incomplete.

Council for Higher Education Accreditation (CHEA)

Formed in 1996, "Presidents of American universities and colleges established CHEA to strengthen higher education through strengthened accreditation of higher education institutions. As its mission statement provides, 'The Council for Higher Education Accreditation will serve students and their families, colleges and universities, sponsoring bodies, governments, and employers by promoting academic quality through formal recognition of higher education accreditation bodies and will coordinate and work to advance self-regulation through accreditation'" (CHEA, 2004). Since its founding, the Council for Higher Education Accreditation has become the largest institutional higher education membership association in the United States, with approximately 3,000 member colleges and universities and more than 60 participating national, regional, and specialized accrediting organizations.

According to CHEA, its organizational purpose is to provide advocacy, service, and recognition for American higher education with federal and state governments and agencies. Further, CHEA also lists its seven operating principles as quality assurance, leadership, advocacy, service, core values, independence, and inclusion, which "provide the foundation for the CHEA mission statement, the organizational functions (of CHEA)... , and the CHEA Recognition Policy" (CHEA, 2004).

Since the accreditation of higher education institutions in the United States is a voluntary process, CHEA serves a vital role of providing a singular body to which all institutions can look for a consistent understanding of the requirements for accreditation. Since federal financial aid and admission to graduate schools and professional organizations often depend upon attending or having attended an accredited institution, CHEA provides a level of reliability to the credibility to a college's operations and legitimacy to the degrees granted at these institution. This role places CHEA squarely in the debate on trade in higher education with regard to providing a level of quality control through somewhat uniform accreditation standards for institutions, regardless of country of origin.

Along with ACE, CHEA is among the most watched and respected higher education membership organizations, particularly with respect to broad federal policy developments, including this trade policy proposal. And, like at ACE with Madeleine Green contributing significant leadership on this issue of trade, CHEA has a dynamic authority heading up its position on trade in Dr. Judith Eaton, CHEA's president. At an international conference on trade in education services, Dr. Eaton described CHEA's efforts to maintain a legitimate international profile:

> CHEA provides assistance to accrediting organisations and higher education through several types of international activity. These include functioning as a forum for international quality review issues through conferences and meetings, undertaking policy research and publications on a range of issues related to international quality review, representing the interests of U.S. accreditors with multinational organisations such as United Nations Educational, Scientific and Cultural Organisation (UNESCO) and the Organisation for Economic Cooperation and Development (OECD) and representing the interests of U.S. accreditors to the U.S. federal government especially as this relates to the negotiations of the World Trade Organisation (WTO) and the General Agreement on Trade in Services (GATS). CHEA uses its convening and advising functions to encourage various international initiatives by individual accrediting organizations. (Eaton, 2003)

Chapters Eight and Nine include information about and from CHEA, because of the position of influence and respect CHEA has with both higher education institutions and other higher education member associations. CHEA serves as a leader on important but, perhaps, abstruse issues like international trade in higher education services. CHEA, in partnering with ACE, has taken a strong and conspicuous position on the GATS, and their contribution to this research was significant.

Council of Graduate Schools (CGS)

The Council of Graduate Schools is an international organization of institutions of higher education that engage in graduate-level education, research scholarship, and the preparation of candidates for advanced degrees. For more than forty years, the Council of Graduate Schools has remained the only U.S. association dedicated solely to representing the interests of graduate education (CGS, 2004). The mission of the CGS is "to improve and advance graduate education," which it accomplishes "through advocacy in the federal policy arena, innovative research, and the development and dissemination of best practices" (CGS, 2004). The current membership of the CGS includes more than 450 universities in Canada and the United States—which award more than 95% of all doctorates and 70% of all master's degrees awarded annually in the U.S.—and many international institutions outside of North America, including institutions in Thailand, Egypt, and Australia.

The CGS mission statement presents its organizational purpose as:

> The Council of Graduate Schools (CGS) is dedicated to the improvement and advancement of graduate education. Its members are colleges and universities engaged in research, scholarship, and the preparation of candidates for advanced degrees. As the largest national association organized specifically to represent the interests of graduate education, CGS offers many opportunities for deans and graduate school personnel to exchange ideas and share information on major issues in graduate education. (J. Yopp, CGS, personal communication, May 13, 2004)

Among its many activities on behalf of its constituents, CGS monitors enacted and potential federal legislation affecting graduate-level education. A few of the many areas of focus for CGS' operations include student fellowships and scholarships and other financial aid considerations, research support, and, of particular interests for this research, international studies.

CGS provides information or testimony to individual members of Congress or their staff members to assist in the development of legislation and public policy. In collaboration with other national education organizations, CGS works to ensure that graduate education is represented as federal policy and legislation are developed. To members, the CGS staff provide thorough analyses of legislation and policies that could affect the graduate community. CGS has a very knowledgeable individual with regard to trade and international relations issues for higher education on its staff, Dr. Jonathan Yopp, whose contributions to this research will be explained in detail in the findings chapter. Since the vast majority of international students in the U.S. are studying at the graduate level, graduate and professional schools are, not surprisingly, more likely to be aware of and concerned about policies and legislation that might impact their international student populations. CGS serves its members by monitoring issues that might be of concern in this area, including trade policies.

Council of Independent Colleges (CIC)

The Council of Independent Colleges (CIC) was founded in 1956 and is an association of independent colleges and universities working together to support college and university leadership, advance institutional excellence, and enhance private higher education's contributions to society (CIC, 2004). CIC represents the interests of all small and mid-sized, independent, liberal arts colleges and universities in the United States, not by lobbying on behalf of its membership, but by providing operational support to them. Member institutions' campus leaders are invited to participate in CIC organized programs that are developed to assist institutions in improving their operations, including their campus's "educational programs, administrative and financial performance, and institutional visibility" (CIC, 2004).

CIC has a current membership of more than 530 independent colleges and universities, including liberal arts, comprehensive, and international institutions. According to the CIC, its membership has grown by 102 institutions over the past four years, with a retention rate of 98% since 1990. CIC lists one of its core operational goals as "Listening To Institutional Leaders," and notes that it accomplishes this goal of being responsive to the expressed needs and concerns of its constituents through multiple means. These include regular member surveys; developing task forces made up of member representatives, to plan conferences and workshops that directly address issues of particular interest to the members; placing presidents of its member campuses and executives from outside corporations/foundations on its Board of Directors, providing a check on the central staff and its direction; and bringing in outside experts to its central staff in Washington, DC, to provide expertise and new direction, with the goal of keeping CIC relevant to its members (CIC, 2004).

CIC represents a specific and particular sub-set of American higher education, small independent institutions, which often do not have the staffing or broad historic clout to actively engage issues not directly related to their operations. CIC provides information to its members and presents a collective "face" of these groups in Washington, to provide them with a stronger, unified "voice." CIC does not have a visible international policy initiative, but it has offered international exchange opportunities for the leaders of its member institutions. This practice, though a small part of its operations, has made broad international issues of interest to CIC, even though they do not pursue international policy issues in their operating agenda.

National Association of State Universities and Land Grant Colleges (NASULGC)

The National Association of State Universities and Land-Grant Colleges (NASULGC) was founded in 1887, making it, according to NASULGC, the nation's oldest higher education association. NASULGC is an association of public universities and university systems and land-grant institutions, with member campuses in all 50 states, as well as in the U.S. territories and in Washington, DC. NASULGC 's current structure was formed in 1963, when the American Association of Land-Grant Colleges and State Universities merged with the National Association of State Universities. Today, NASULGC is dedicated to supporting "excellence in teaching, research and public service" (NASULGC, 2003).

As of November 2004, the association's membership stood at 212 institutions, including 76 land-grant universities (36% of NASULGC's membership), of which 17 are the historically black public institutions, and 27 public higher education systems (12% of NASULGC's membership). In addition, tribal colleges became land-grant institutions in 1994, and 31 are represented in NASULGC through the membership of the American Indian Higher Education Consortium (AIHEC) (NASULGC, 2003).

NASULGC does have a government relations/international policy staff member, who keeps abreast of major legislative and other government developments affecting or regarding higher education. NASULGC does not, however, tend to lead an industry response toward international issues, often looking, as most of the other organizations do, to the American Council on Education (ACE) instead. As an organization focused on public, domestically oriented institutions, international issues are not primary or, in reality, even secondary, to the concerns of NASULGC's member institutions. It does have a staff member, Kerry Bolognese, who oversees NASULGC's Commission on International Programs, but that commission focuses on scholarships and international issues, not on broad international policy concerns. Dr. Bolognese and Dr. Mort Neufville, the Vice President of NASULGC, were aware of the GATS issue, however, from NASULGC's interactions with ACE and provided a very useful perspective on the GATS and its relevance to American higher education.

National Education Association (NEA)

Unlike the organizations described above, the National Education Association (NEA) is not primarily a higher education organization. Instead, NEA is a union and, according to its website, "the nation's largest professional employee organization and is committed to advancing the cause of public education" (NEA, 2004). NEA's mission statement describes the goals of NEA as: promoting "the cause of quality public education and advance the profession of education; expand the rights and further the interest of educational employees; and advocate human, civil, and economic rights for all" for the purpose of fulfilling 'the promise of a democratic society'" (NEA, 2004).

Founded in 1857 "to elevate the character and advance the interests of the profession of teaching and to promote the cause of popular education in the United States," "the NEA is a professional organization of educators, with 2.7 million members who "work at every level of education, from pre-school to university graduate programs. NEA has affiliate organizations in every state, as well as in more than 14,000 local communities across the United States" (NEA, 2004). It is with regard to the post-secondary arena of its operation that, "NEA represents approximately 120,000 higher education faculty and staff, primarily in public sector institutions. Approximately 60% of those are in community colleges" (Hendrickson, NEA, personal communication, November 8, 2004).

It is in light of its post-secondary operations that the GATS issue has become an issue about which NEA has established a prominent position. In fact, the NEA published a position paper on trade in educational services in early 2004, *Higher Education & International Trade Agreement: An examination of the threats and promises of globalization,* with the specific goal of explaining how the GATS is a "threat" to American higher education. Considering the size and influence of the NEA, this public position regarding the GATS is a particularly significant industry response to the evolving GATS issue for U.S. higher education.

The NEA has formulated its response to concerns about the GATS in conjunction with the European-based organization, Education International (EI). The NEA does staff an internationally oriented office (the Office of International Relations), which manages NEA's membership in EI, articulates NEA policy in international forums, and maintains communication with EI affiliated national education unions around the world. The office analyzes international educational experiences and incorporates relevant learning to NEA's strategic priorities (NEA, 2004).

According to the NEA's website, the Office of International Relations also monitors and works with the United Nations, intergovernmental agencies, and international non-governmental organizations on issues that affect education, the education profession, and trade union rights, among other concerns (NEA, 2004). In representing staff and faculty members, instead of institutions, as is the case with most of the other organizations included in this research, the NEA presents a specific and important perspective on the issue of trade with regard to jobs. It has an idealistic, perhaps, sense of the mission and purpose of education, both in the U.S. and around the world. Trade policies that include education at any level, then, are of interest to NEA, in that how an education "industry" expands or is regulated by trade would likely have an impact on its employees who make up the membership base of NEA. So, though it is not an integral higher education organization in terms of its accepted status as a voice for American higher education, NEA's perspective on the GATS and its relationship to American higher education should not be ignored in an examination of organizational responses to the U.S. government's position on education and the GATS.

The United States Department of Commerce (DOC), Office of Service Industries (OSI)

The Department of Commerce and Labor was created in 1903 and was renamed the Department of Commerce in 1913. Today, the DOC employs over 37,000 people at 10 bureau offices across the United States and in 86 countries around the world.

> "The commerce department provides information, technology services, and science that assist American business and society. It makes possible the weather reports heard every morning; it facilitates technology that Americans use daily in the workplace and at home; it supports the collection and development of statistical information essential for competitive business and our representative democracy; it helps American firms and consumers benefit from open and fair international markets:..." (DOC, 2004).

According to the DOC's website, the agency has three strategic goals:

- Provide the information and economic framework to enable the U.S. economy to operate efficiently and equitably, both nationally and globally;

- Provide the infrastructure for innovation with cutting-edge science and technology to enhance American competitiveness;
- Observe and manage the Earth's environment to promote sustainable growth (DOC, 2004)

Such varied organizations as the Census Bureau, the National Weather Service, the National Marine and Fisheries Service, and the International Trade Administration all fall under the umbrella of DOC programs. With regard to this research, the most significant program areas examining trade issues are the International Trade Administration (ITA) and, within the ITA, the Office of Service Industries.

The Office of Service Industries (OSI) focuses its efforts on three main areas of operations: trade policy, export development, and industry analysis. First, with regard to trade policy, the OSI supports and participates in bilateral and multilateral negotiations on services trade, including the GATS services agreement in the WTO and the development of new agreements on services in the recently negotiated Free Trade Area of the Americas (FTAA) and the Asia-Pacific Economic Cooperation (APEC), a forum for trade negotiations regarding the Pacific Rim (DOC, 2004). In addition, the OSI works with other U.S. agencies, including the USTR and the U.S. Department of Education, on implementing services trade agreements like those of the WTO and NAFTA. To ensure industry input in policy development, the Office of Service Industries overseas a Congressionally-mandated Industry Sector Advisory Committee for Services, which is jointly administered by the U.S. Department of Commerce and the Office of the U.S. Trade Representative. This committee for services includes a broad representative group from an array of services industries, including education.

Also, the OSI provides export development assistance and information for U.S. companies looking to expand into overseas markets. The Office oversees a trade promotion program of trade missions and industry conferences. It also provides help to American companies interested in developing particular export opportunities in specific overseas markets.

Finally, the deep and varied staff of the OSI provides in-depth industry analyses on key service industries. These analyses provide useful information on international trade and competitiveness in services to policy makers. By maintaining a broad staff of industry specialists who focus their efforts on specific service industries, including Education and Training Services, the OSI positions itself to "work closely with the private sector to provide export assistance and participate with other U.S. government agencies to improve foreign market access for U.S. companies" (DOC, 2004). With regard to education trade issues, the OSI Education and Training Services specialist provides the expertise needed to work with education industry representatives, other government agencies, and non-governmental organizations. The Department of Commerce, through its Office of Service Industries, maintains close relationships with the myriad groups actively examining these trade issues and provides leadership and opportunities for discussions on the issue.

CONCLUSIONS

These organizations and government agency, along with the USTR, which was described in detail in the previous chapter, form not only the core of recognized and respected individuals and organizations leading the dialogue on trade in higher education services in the United States but also the engaged periphery of organizations keeping tabs on the issue without engaging directly in any of the discussions or negotiations. Though beyond the scope of this research, a further peripheral ring would include campus officials and those representatives of organizations and business ventures that are not yet actively or even passively engaging this trade issue, but whose interests are likely to be affected by trade concerns in the future.

This issue of trade in higher education services is so new to even the best informed industry representatives, that despite the fact that their business is to stay abreast of broad policy issues that would be of concern to their constituents, it became apparent very early in this research that digging deeper into campus level involvement would result in little information for the effort. Individual industry members are not seeking information on this trade issue to any extent that would provide substantial value in investigating concerns about GATS on a campus level. Indeed, discussions with the groups listed above, communications with the organizations that responded to my initial query for information about their organization and GATS, and the complete lack of response from campus and for-profit industry representatives reinforces that this list constitutes the representative group of actors addressing this issue and supports the decision to suspend any research efforts to develop a "view from the campus" evaluation of this trade issue. Perhaps, if this issue becomes an established and enforced policy on the campus level, the future might see more campus officials actively engaging this issue. That is just not the case today, however, as the breadth of the American higher education industry accepts representation on this issue by the organizations outlined above.

Chapter Eight
Negotiating the Intersection of Trade and U.S. Higher Education

> . . I think there has been more change in the internal structure, the management, and the service delivery of higher education worldwide in the last 15 years than in the preceding several centuries. These changes in revenues and outputs are often unrecognized and undocumented and involve the inter-penetration of a public good with market behavior and a new balance between bureaucratic allocation and entrepreneurial activities. (Ward, 2002, p. 41)

The tensions described above by David Ward—between bureaucracy, the market, and the American higher education industry—are at the core of this research on higher education and the GATS. Chapters Eight and Nine present and examine the findings developed out of the extensive interviews with representatives of and analysis of documents from the organizations described in the previous chapter. With memberships that encompass the vast majority of U.S. higher education institutions, these organizations are positioned to represent the interests of American higher education with regard to broad policy concerns such as this issue of trade and trade policy development. Using data gathered from these organizations, it is possible to develop a comprehensive picture of how the traditional U.S. higher education "industry" is dealing with issues of trade and federal trade policies and what the major areas of concern are.

These findings are broken into observations of the higher education community's and the U.S. government's process of engagement on this issue (Chapter Eight) and specific issues of concern about GATS raised by the organizations themselves (Chapter Nine). Using themes that arose from the interviews, this chapter is broken into sub-sections regarding such major issue areas as: who represents higher education, how were they engaged in the trade policy formation, what were their specific areas of concern, and where will things go from here. This chapter presents observations of the environment around this trade policy formation and what the industry's response has been.

The questions used to gather this information are included as Appendix A, B, and C, and the responses to these questions generated an array of information including:

- who cares about this issue;
- when the issue came to light for each organization, if ever;
- if they do not pursue such issues themselves, to whom they look for leadership and representation on broad, international issues like this;
- what sort of input they have had from their constituents;
- how actively they have been involved with the development of the USTR proposal;
- who they believe would benefit and be negatively impacted the most strongly if higher education is included as a tradable service; and
- what their concerns are should higher education ultimately become an internationally defined industry, subject to sanctions and regulations from the WTO.

The following sections present observations of themes that arose from the data. From ignorance of the issue, to animosity among the actors, to an evolving understanding of where the most activity around trade in higher education services and the GATS will take place, the findings explained below provide insights into how policies develop and change within a government-industry relationship.

GENERAL IGNORANCE OF THE GATS ISSUE AMONG HIGHER EDUCATION

The first and broadest observation that became clear very early on in this research is that the higher education community/industry is not paying attention, en masse or even on a small scale, to this issue. By and large, the higher education community is simply not tracking this issue on the campus level, or, in most cases, at the lobbying level. This ignorance of trade liberalization is embedded in the larger, general ignorance of all international issues, excluding, perhaps, study abroad interests and, increasingly, visa concerns for international students and staff. When contacted about scheduling an interview and collecting any official (or, even, unofficial) documentation from organizations regarding their stance on the GATS, the majority of the organizations responded that they are not engaging this issue first-hand:

> We're trying to figure out here who should talk to you . . . (The person who had handled this issue for AAU was no longer there, and they had not decided whether to fill this open position.) (B. Toiv, AAU, personal communication, November 4, 2003)

> I cannot help you with this issue, as I have not been involved with it in any way. Speaking to me would be a waste of your time. The two higher education organizations in DC who have been active in this, that I know of, include the American Council on Education (ACE) and The Association of American Universities (AAU). (D. Baime, AACC, personal communication, October 29, 2003)

> . . . (W)e have not been involved in the GATS negotiations. Would like to be, and on rare occasions we do hear from our members that we should be, but time has always precluded involvement. We have a very small staff and a very big agenda, and we just can't do everything we'd like to do. I regret I am unable to provide you with any information on this matter. (V. Johnson, NAFSA, personal communication, November 12, 2004)

> If I may classify most of the issues we deal with in two ways. One, are the issues where member institutions say to us, this is troublesome to us, and they'll write their congresspersons and say, you know, this is awful, and NASULGC and the other members of the 6 (major presidential representative higher education organizations), you get on with this because it's pretty important to us. And then there is the other side that the members might not be quite familiar with them, and we would inform them and they say, well, okay we depend on you to take care of that, and I think this higher education initiative in GATS falls into this category, where it's just assumed that, oh well, it's not anything to worry about as long as you guys take care of it in Washington. And I think that's how I would classify that. (M. Neufville, NASULGC, personal communication, November 21, 2003)

> While GATS may eventually fall within the focus of COFHE, at the present time its emerging implications are much more likely to be

> tracked by ACE and by the government relations offices within our larger institutions rather than by COFHE. I can state quite simply that COFHE was not consulted in anyway about the USTR's decision to include higher education in their recent WTO proposal. COFHE's focus on access and affordability at the traditional undergraduate program level makes this issue something we watch only at a distance, at least until more definition of its implications to our work and our institutions emerges. (K. Dillon, COFHE, personal communication, November 13, 2003)

Ideally, such research about higher education would also include an examination of the campus response, but at this time, there really is no campus response. The issue is far outside the day-to-day operations of the campuses according to all of the interviewed higher education organizational representatives. Officials on the campus level do not have the capacity or desire to invest time in forming a position on trade concerns. The broad ignorance of the industry representatives merely reflects the ignorance of the campuses. And, as noted in the previous chapter, while input from the for-profit-sector would be highly informative about their concerns and influence in developing the trade position on education, they would not agree to participate in this research. For these reasons, the perspective from the campuses—non-profit and for-profit—has not been included in this research. Instead, this research sought to recognize those actors who do represent higher education individuals, institutions, and interests in such international policy matters, and to examine how they pursued a place at the table and why they believe they need to be there.

WHO TRULY REPRESENTS AMERICAN HIGHER EDUCATION?

> I think when we first went in, folks at USTR said 'well we've already talked to them', because they thought that what the NCITE group was doing represented us, so their first reaction was 'why are you bothering us?' (J. Eaton, CHEA, personal communication, May 13, 2004)

An unexpected finding that emerged from the data was that there is confusion and/or skepticism among the actors that those who claim to be speaking on behalf of higher education are, in fact, legitimate representatives of the vast U.S. higher education industry. One of the first and most intriguing questions posed by the USTR representative when interviewed was how could he and the USTR know for sure who represents the broad interests of higher education and why should he feel confident that the groups approaching the USTR for inclusion in the process are rightfully claiming a place at the table. Indeed, this question made sense, of course, when taking into account the miniscule access any one person or group of the USTR would have to the scope of the higher education industry, considering the breadth of industries—services, manufacturing, agriculture, etc.—that the USTR manages. Higher education, though an enormous service industry, is still just one of many important areas that fall within the scope of the USTR's responsibilities, so their asking the question "Who represents higher education?" seems a reasonable response to being asked how they are including the higher education industry in developing their position on higher education and the GATS.

> They (USTR) didn't understand very much about us any more than we understood very much about them, so it took awhile to kind of work through the understandings and based on that, I think that these people are reasonably convinced they have to connect with us. (J. Eaton, CHEA, personal communication, May 13, 2004)

From inside the world of higher education, studying it and working within it, one simply knows which organizations publish the most, are the most often cited, have the largest membership bases, and are the ones for which higher education professionals wish to work. Because of the visibility and quality of the organizations and their work, they are deemed the most credible representatives of the broad higher education industry. From outside, however, the hierarchy or differing levels of credibility among the organizations is much harder to discern. Why should the USTR not believe that NCITE is representing a broad perspective within higher education, if its leaders seem informed and engaged in a way that seems proactive and reasonable, while other organizations are late to the discussion?

In an odd contradiction, though the higher education industry in the United States is very large (4168 institutions [NCES, 2003]; $290 billion market size [Armstrong, 2003]), the number of membership organizations examining international issues in higher education is actually quite small.

> Most people are removed from it. It actually involves, and this is something that I hope your whole (book) will point out, is that there are no more than maybe 4–6 people in this whole country that can spend more than 10 minutes on this, and they happen to be, probably most of

> them, in this building. (M.P. Lenn, NCITE, personal communication, November 17, 2003)

This observation of the number of people in higher education who are paying attention to and are informed about this issue somewhat exaggerates the reality, by disregarding academic actors who are researching the GATS on campuses, as well as organizations that are not normally in the mix of international policy issues, such as AAUP and NEA. Regardless, that an industry of thousands of institutions, millions of employees and students, and billions of dollars in revenues could be subject to federal policies based, at best, on the input of maybe a dozen or fewer informed people seems improbable. But, this is the reality. In fact, because of the lack of broad interest in the issue, personal/professional connections had a remarkable effect on who had a seat at the table early on in the analysis of trade in higher education services. As noted by the representative of the Department of Commerce, "Marjorie (NCITE director) took the initiative and so she's benefited from that" (J. Moll, DOC, personal communication, November 21, 2003). Other organizations, organizations some might argue are more representative and respected than NCITE, had to find their way into the discourse before the initiatives developed further without their input.

When specifically asked to whom they look for leadership and information regarding an issue like trade policies affecting higher education, every organization except NCITE mentioned ACE and most mentioned CHEA. "Well, ACE is reflecting, I think, a community consensus. I mean, we traditionally talk through ACE when we have umbrella issues like that (trade)" (M. Neufville, NASULGC, personal communication, November 21, 2003). Others noted, "The two higher education organizations in DC who have been active in this, that I know of, include the American Council on Education and the Association of American Universities" (D. Baime, AACC, personal communication, October 29, 2003); "On the one hand I don't think Marjorie represents the full spectrum the way an ACE does, but I don't think ACE has taken the time to really understand it" (J. Moll, DOC, personal communication, November 21, 2003); and "While GATS may eventually fall within the focus of COFHE, at the present time its emerging implications are much more likely to be tracked by ACE . . ." (K. Dillon, COFHE, personal communication, November 13, 2003).

ACE also is well aware of its role as a kind of prognosticator for the higher education community, regarding broad issues that have the potential to become significant for its members.

> A national association has to be knowledgeable about the worldwide discussion that's swirling around it. We have to protect our members from imminent danger, and usually it's somewhere, we're in the trenches enough that you know, we see things coming or we know what the debates are. We don't have a good early warning system about GATS, and I don't think anybody does. On the other hand, weird things happen on the national front if we're not prepared. (M. Green, ACE, personal communication, November 19, 2003)

On the other hand, NCITE and its supporters seem protective and, perhaps, defensive about its place in the larger higher education community and its level of access to government agencies and officials.

> I feel like they (NCITE) are paying more attention than anyone else and I feel like Marjorie understands the issues better . . . So on the one hand I don't think Marjorie represents the full spectrum the way an ACE does, but I don't think ACE has taken the time to really understand it. They spent a lot of time with USTR over the last couple of years. If you look at the joint declaration that they (ACE and CHEA) wrote, I think they've come a long way. (J. Moll, DOC, personal communication, November 21, 2003)

When directly asked for a membership list or, at least, the number of members, NCITE would not or could not provide specific information about whom it represents. Instead, it reported being a membership organization with activities which "are supported by a wide range of educational institutions and organizations, including accrediting and certifying bodies, higher education associations (including testing organizations), and institutions of higher education interested in quality and mobility issues as higher education crosses borders" (M.P. Lenn, NCITE, personal communication, November 4, 2004): A broad and convincing statement, but one that is not, however, backed by concrete information about its membership and, by extension, how representative of the broad higher education industry its positions actually are.

There is an established, referred to as the "Big 6," made up of six organizations whose members are college and university presidents at public and private institutions of all sizes and demographic make-up. The Big 6 together represent over 90 percent of the institutions of higher education in the United States. These organizations meet regularly to maximize their individual operational strengths and minimize stretching their individual organization's capacities too far.

> It's really the 6 presidential associations: ACE, AAU, ASCU, NAICU, NASULGC, and AACC . . . the Big 6, what we call the presidential associations. And they have a group that . . . meet just about every two weeks for at least an hour or two in early morning, and then discuss all these issues and come to consensus of who should read what initiative, and they have also, what is it called, SOBs, that's not the traditional SOB, but I don't know how the name came about, but Sons of the Brethren, . . . and those are the chief legislative people who get together to form a certain legislative action, and then they will appoint people to carry out a task or agree on an institution. Usually they arrive at some consensus, and . . . it's circulated and then it's signed, everybody agreeing to whatever is presented, and if there is a dissenting voice, you might not sign it, but you agree not to oppose it, that's the usual tendency. So, that's how they operate, basically. . . . The 6 associations represent 90%, 90+ % of all higher education in the U.S., so we speak broadly . . . I would say . . . the top group, relating to issues of higher education would be the 6, because they represent the largest sector of higher education in the country. (R: And you said between those 6 it's 90% of the institutions?) 90 +. (M. Neufville, NASULGC, personal communication, November 21, 2003)

> . . . Our president, Peter Magrath, will work through their (ACE) president, David Ward, and the Big 6. . . . They have regular meetings and they . . . discuss issues where they reach consensus. . . . Because we do a lot of joint testimony, David Ward will go up the hill, and for example, take student visas, that's a big issue, and David Ward will represent the 6, go up to the hill, present testimony on behalf of the 6, you know, but that's been all worked out ahead of time, his statement and the principles he's representing. (M. Neufville, NASULGC, personal communication, November 21, 2003)

By all accounts of the membership organizations who responded to the question, "Who do you look to, for information or representation on issues like this one concerning trade?" ACE is the organization most often cited as the most respected regarding international concerns. ACE has positioned its operations to provide its presidential constituents with a comprehensive perspective and representation on international higher education concerns, particularly with regard to policy concerns. As this issue of including higher education in U.S. trade negotiations has evolved, ACE has been the most active on behalf of its membership and the numerous other higher education organizations that look to ACE for leadership on such issues. NCITE has also been thoroughly active and engaged on this issue, though the level of representation of this organization does remain unclear. In any event, these are the organizations, along with CHEA, which represents over 3000 institutions and agencies regarding accreditation and quality assurance concerns, that have produced the most research and have purposefully pursued a place in the trade policy developments.

Worthy of note, as well, are the stances taken by two organizations that represent not institutions but individuals employed in higher education. AAUP and NEA, as employee unions, represent faculty and staff across American higher education. Both have positive and influential reputations, and both have come out against including any education interests in the trade agreements.

When asked if or why their organization chose to engage this trade concern, all spoke of obligations to their members. Some noted that their members had more pressing concerns requiring the attention of their staffs, others wished they could be more involved but cannot spare the resources, while others were involving themselves in the process because their members expect them to predict and investigate issues that may be of concerns to them down the road. As one representative noted:

> The general answer is that, and this is purely my opinion, if you are a successful membership organization, you are half the time doing exactly what some of your members have asked you to do, as quickly and as well as you can possible do it. The other half of the time you are doing stuff that they have not yet asked you to do, but if you're good, it's stuff they will ask you two or three years from now, so you're helping them see a little bit beyond the horizon. And I think if you're not doing both of those, they'll go somewhere else. (R. Garth, CIC, personal communication, November 19, 2003)

An organization's credibility depends upon using its resources wisely and serving its constituents effectively. In balancing these concerns, many focus their efforts on specific areas, leaving others to specialize in different things. In a sense, this is like the cross-subsidizing that happens on campuses, where the larger departments create benefits that trickle down to smaller departments, allowing the whole to excel and function properly. From the comments of several of the research participants, it seems that organizational specialization may, in part, explain why most organizations are looking to a couple to investigate this trade issue. In this case of trade in higher education, ACE, CHEA, and, perhaps, NCITE are the organizations that have pursued in-depth representation on this trade issue, with the other organizations presuming that they will be thoroughly represented without having to directly concern themselves with this somewhat tangential trade concern. Whether because of apathy among their constituents, a lack of understanding of the trade issue, or the lack of staffing to cover this issue, there is no question very few organizations are examining this issue on behalf of their constituents. This trade issue is merely one of the many about which the higher education community simply looks to ACE for direction.

FACTIONS WITHIN THE HIGHER EDUCATION ASSOCIATION COMMUNITY

There is a notable and significant divide within the higher education community on the issue of whether to support policies promoting trade in higher education services. This divide has had a significant impact on how the USTR's policy was developed. On one side, the Center for Quality Assurance in International Education (CQAIE) and its National Committee on International Trade in Education (NCITE), has a dynamic leader in Marjorie Peace Lenn, who has been one of the most prominent figures in this debate. In addition, Jennifer Reason Moll a former employee of NCITE is now directing the international service concerns at the Department of Commerce (DOC). Both Dr. Lenn and Ms. Moll had the ear of the USTR's former Services director. NCITE and the DOC had all of its information and data in place to introduce higher education as a legitimate area for consideration to the Trade Representative's office and remained in an influential consulting role throughout the development of the stance on higher education that ultimately was presented to the WTO.

On the other side are the remaining organizations, many of whom fervently believe that the CQAIE/NCITE simply does not represent any broad interest of higher education, that it cannot claim any level of institutional membership that comes close to the broad memberships they have, and that CQAIE/NCITE has, to some real extent, misrepresented itself as speaking for the broad higher education community.

No one questions Marjorie Peace Lenn's knowledge of the issue or her capacity to speak intelligently and fervently about opening trade in higher education markets around the world; in fact, many note that she is the industry "expert" on this particular issue, even if her perspective is not in agreement with their own. What they do question is her having such an influential place at the table, since it remains unclear who, exactly, the members of her organization are and why their interests are more or, even, equally, valid as those represented by larger associations like ACE and CHEA.

> 'I'm not sure who anointed her the spokesman for higher education in this area,' says Sheldon E. Steinbach, vice president and general counsel of the American Council on Education. Even though Ms. Lenn's group does not represent a broad spectrum of colleges, he says, no other group in higher education was dealing with the issue, so 'she stepped into a vacuum.' (Foster, 2002, p. 3–4)

"Partly they got there first. And, we weren't aware or maybe we weren't minding the store well enough" (M. Green, ACE, personal communication, November 19, 2003). Not one of the other higher education NGOs included in this research has publicly allied itself with CQAIE/NCITE, though the Department of Commerce and the USTR's office both hold CQAIE/NCITE in high regard concerning their input in trade liberalization in higher education services.

> Well, what I saw was, I saw that, in my opinion, there was none of the willingness to fully engage the academic community. That it was more or less a hardening of positions of, independent and parallel evolution of what we would mean by internationalization. . . . (J. Yopp, CGS, personal communication, May 13, 2004)

There is a sense, illustrated in the above quote from CGS but present in many of the conversations with the higher education representatives, that the government and pro-GATS parties were not entirely respectful of the concerns of the academic community, and in the interviews with the government representatives, it did seem that they were somewhat patronizing toward the perspectives of the anti-GATS groups. Indeed, they seemed to be almost humoring the education community by engaging them in this dialogue. From their perspective, which is the perspective which will ultimately win out, the higher education community simply is not informed enough to think outside of their localized concerns. The higher education community's sense of not being fully respected in this process is not unfounded. NCITE, a higher education organization with a pro-GATS leaning, has been embraced more fully by the government trade representatives, simply because NCITE agrees with the government's position.

This divide within the higher education community seems to have devolved in some cases, into a level of personal animosity, where some individuals question others' intelligence, work ethic, or honesty, or mock what they see as bravado among certain actors. Though assured that their comments would be off the record/unattributed, the interviewees often spoke around their feelings about the other actors, though it was easy to read into their comments. Some of the telling comments included:

> They used to claim that they weren't consulted. Well, the USTR doesn't have time to call every association. They do a federal register notice for a purpose and if you have someone on your staff who is supposed to be handling that then they kind of need to handle it. So I didn't have a lot of sympathy for the claim that the government wasn't communicating enough. I mean they probably could have done more in the beginning to establish the communication earlier . . . (Anonymous, 2003)

> That is an assumption (the influence of the for-profits versus the nonprofits) and is a part of the rhetoric of those who wish to polarize the discussion. (Anonymous, 2003)

> I'm not criticizing X and Y, really; Y is actually quite intelligent. (Anonymous, 2003)

With backhanded compliments and begrudging acknowledgement of each other's rightful place in the dialogue, many of the people interviewed provided a window into the strained relationships between the actors. For the most part, however, it was not a slew of cryptic language that indicated this existing animosity. It was body language, facial expressions, and evasive answers that provided clues about and, often, simply made clear the level of distrust and disrespect between the two sides of what has become a polarized environment of international higher education interests.

> I don't think that there has been a proactive and effective engagement of the two sides of this debate, and I think there really are two sides at least, and there's some middle ground in there, and there are some middle opinions, and some hybrid opinions you might say. (J. Yopp, CGS, personal communication, May 13, 2004)

Some noted what they believe are factual errors in the information some organizations are using to argue against the inclusion of higher education in the GATS. These errors are interpreted as indicators of a lack of real understanding of the specifics of where higher education would or would not be affected by the GATS. "I was just looking at the ACE website before just because I thought I should take a look and I haven't looked at it in a long time, and I mean there are just some plain outright statements that are in error about the GATS and about the WTO. I mean, just simple things that are wrong like saying GATS members instead of saying WTO members. There was one sentence that said something like 'the United States proposed the inclusion or the inclusion of higher education with GATS in the year 2000'—NO" (Anonymous, 2003).

Though it is very likely that "middle opinions/hybrid opinions" will gain prominence in the ongoing discussion, trade the perception that many of those seeking influence have only a superficial understanding of the trade issues continues to influence the respect some of the actors have for others. Without shared respect for the breadth of perspectives that naturally exist regarding trade liberalization and education services, the dialogue among invested parties will likely remain at least somewhat tense and guarded. As this issue matures and evolves, however, and as the actors who were initially caught off guard by the GATS proposals become more familiar and comfortable with its nuances, it is likely the relationships among the representatives and interested parties will evolve and improve.

ASLEEP AT THE SWITCH

One of the most significant findings from this research is that the representatives of the "traditional" elements of American higher education were late in recognizing the importance of the issue of trade and, specifically, the inclusion of higher education as a tradable service industry in the GATS. Indeed, it was not until the December 2000 negotiating proposal on higher education was submitted by the U.S. Trade Representative to the World Trade Organization that two of the largest and most respected higher education organizations, the American Council on Education (ACE) and the Council for Higher Education Accreditation (CHEA), became aware of the need to become more active in the process of developing the final trade in services proposal with the USTR.

> The USTR really went out of its way to try to establish lines of communication with them because they weren't paying attention (J. Moll, DOC, personal communication, November 21, 2003)

"We were asleep at the switch," is how one representative described the delay in their grasping the significance of this issue and becoming involved. According to the U.S. Department of Commerce (DOC) representative, there were regular meetings and announcements in the *Federal Register* inviting the public's input on issues of the U.S. GATS proposal years before the December 2000 USTR negotiating proposal on higher education. The announcements often did not specify higher education as an element of the "services" being discussed, so those individuals within the higher education organizations that look for areas in which federal policies interact with higher education interests did not take particular note of these meetings. (This gap in recognizing higher education as a service industry is the cause of much of the discord between the government and pro-GATS actors and the majority of the higher education representatives.)

Still other organizations remain ignorant, either by choice or by circumstance, of trade issues involving higher education, many of which might have long-term repercussions for American higher education. As noted above, some groups are aware of the issue but simply do not have the staffing to invest in becoming more active on issues of trade (NAFTA, FTAA, etc.), while others do not recognize the relevance of an internationally-oriented issue and just do not see that it is relevant to the purposes of their particular organization (e.g., COFHE). Most representative organizations of higher education institutions do not engage internationally oriented issues directly, as the relevance of international concerns is minor for the operations of their members. Instead, they look to a couple of the biggest and best funded organizations to inform them when there are international concerns about which they should be aware. In such cases, most organizations look to ACE and CHEA, each of which articulate a commitment to represent its members well and express apprehension that they may miss something important:

> So that when we did get into the GATS game too late, our members didn't turn on us and say oh my God you were asleep at the switch, because it wasn't an immediate danger to them. But it could happen, and that worries me. Something will go on and we will find out months later, because the process is the way it is, and then it will have gone on. (M. Green, ACE, personal communication, May 13, 2004)

> At ACE, we pride ourselves in being aware of what's going on. We certainly weren't aware of what was happening until after . . . December 2000. I actually think I was probably the first one at ACE to become aware of the implications of it simply because one of our French colleagues called me and asked what in the world we were doing? And I asked about which thing. The concern was with GATS. It was at that point, needless to say, that we found out what was happening. (F. Hayward, ACE/CHEA, personal communication, November 18, 2003)

CHEA also did not get involved until after the December 2000 USTR submission to the WTO. This issue was actually brought to CHEA's attention by the AAU, who had heard concerns from institutions regarding intellectual property rights and the impending trade agreements. Once again, a thread of information led to a campus level concern, which lead to a major higher education NGO investing time and resources to learn more and become more engaged in the ongoing policy development.

After "waking up" to the issue of higher education's being included as a service industry within the WTO and, possibly, in the USTR's GATS offer for trade liberalization, ACE and CHEA jumped into the fray by devoting resources to learning more and establishing stronger connections with the USTR. Further, they sought information and input from their international counterparts, ultimately teaming up with Canadian and European peer organizations, to develop a fully realized response to the pressures of trade liberalization in higher education services that was "declared" in September 2001.

THE DECLARATION

The Joint Declaration on Higher Education and the General Agreement on Trade in Services (September 28, 2001) was the first statement by ACE and CHEA, in conjunction with the Association of Universities and Colleges of Canada and the European University Association, in response to the USTR's consideration of including higher education in its GATS offer. In it, these associations set forth a list of statements (some might say demands) recognizing the role and purpose of higher education and declaring how official policies on trade regulation conflict with the inherent value of higher education.

A summary list of the stated issues and concerns highlighted in the Declaration includes:

- the commodification of higher education
- individual governmental authority over its own higher education system
- fears over the imposition of outside higher education onto developing countries
- the importance of internationalization of higher education
- quality assurance concerns
- coordination of oversight for international higher education cooperation
- the significant differences between higher education and other service industries
- the increasingly grey area between public and private higher education

- a real cost/benefits analysis needs to be done
- a lack of transparency or openness regarding trade thus far must give way to better communication (AAUC, ACE, EUA, CHEA, 2001)

After the release of the Declaration, figurative lines in the sand were drawn and acknowledged, and the divisions within the higher education community and between government officials and higher education representatives were more distinct than at any other time regarding this issue.

> I was particularly interested in the Declaration . . . Most of which was a knee jerk reaction . . . With the United States, it's (the largely negative response to GATS by American higher education) mostly out of naiveté. Period. (M.P. Lenn, NCITE, personal communication, November 17, 2003)

Obviously, then, there was at least one organization in the higher education community that did not agree with the tone or stance taken by the authors of the Declaration.

The Declaration did, however, jumpstart further interactions between all of the interested groups and individuals. In a real sense, the Declaration was the tool ACE and CHEA used to open the door to the USTR's office and into the conversation on the GATS. Prior to the Declaration, ACE and CHEA were, perhaps, peripheral to the discussion on trade in higher education. By making such a public and comprehensive statement, on behalf of their combined membership of over 4,800 institutions and organizations, ACE and CHEA set themselves as the representatives of American higher education, deserving of influence and demanding that their concerns be addressed. Ultimately, they were included in the on-going dialogue between the USTR services office and the higher education industry at large, and both ACE and CHEA acknowledge that their concerns, as presented in the Declaration and in other arenas, have largely been included in the March 31, 2003 offer to the GATS. These developments were possible in no small part because of improvements in each side's ability to understand the concerns of the other.

THE 'LANGUAGE' BARRIER

There is a "language" barrier that is affecting how the involved actors interact. More accurately, it is a jargon barrier. The terms used by trade officials and economists in trade agreements are often unfamiliar to people in higher education. An example of language confusion noted by Judith

Eaton at CHEA (2004) is that, "to liberalize means to remove barriers, but liberalization requires government intervention and engagement, . . . which seems contradictory" (personal communication, November 20, 2003).

The gaps in understanding the specific language/jargon—on both sides of the GATS issue—exacerbate the tensions that already exist because of the philosophical divide between government officials and many of the higher education representatives regarding trade in education,

> We do try to give stuff to the trade representatives that could clarify (our position). Since they don't really understand higher education, they don't have a sense of what we do . . . And, since we don't really understand trade enough, we're not very good at predicting what information would prove most useful. It's enormously frustrating. (M. Green, ACE, personal communication, November 19, 2003)

The different focuses of the trade and higher education representatives explain much of the early tensions between the two sides. The lack of shared language/jargon prolonged the tension or, at least, further challenged the emerging relationship between the government officials and representatives of ACE and CHEA. In looking to NCITE for information, the USTR was in part simply turning to the higher education representative that also "spoke" the language of trade. The larger organizations, e.g. ACE and CHEA, then, have had to learn the terms and specifics on trade issues in order to contribute effectively to the debate and sound credible regarding their concerns.

The language of the GATS is also hard to understand and use appropriately without experience and context for of the terminology used in international agreements such as this. For example, by breaking down the tradable parts of higher education into four "Modes of Supply" and then assigning specific issues a random mode number (e.g., there is no obvious or useful reason to have Mode 1 be cross border supply, when cross border supply could easily be Mode 2, 3, or 4). Not only do those without training and experience in trade jargon have to learn the larger scope issues, such as the different kinds of education exports, but they also have to memorize assigned mode numbers and use the modes correctly in discussions and publications, as well.

The complexity of the GATS and the discussions around the USTR's position on trade in higher education services made it more apparent to ACE and CHEA that they had no true trade experts within their NGOs. Each sought to connect with outside trade lawyers for clarification and input on the prospective issues of the USTR's proposals for trade in education services for American higher education. Again, however, this need to learn about this trade in education issue at even a basic level slowed the ability of organizations like ACE and CHEA to participate thoughtfully and effectively in the dialogue that was developing to set the U.S. GATS offer. Ramping up to speed on GATS and higher education took time and required learning a whole new language, the language of trade. Now that at least a small but significant number of higher education representatives have invested in learning about trade, the dialogue is more balanced and informed on both sides.

BUILDING TRUST AMONG THE ACTORS

The lack of trust among the main groups influencing and involved in the development of the U.S. proposals and offer to the GATS was obvious during the data collection. This tension appears to be lessening, however, as the lines of communication among the government and higher education actors have been opened, and the dialogues are ongoing. Still, many of the actors involved believe they must vary their tactics and, in some cases, their language, to accomplish the myriad tasks they face in addressing an issue like international trade in higher education services.

> It's a pretty interesting observation (that the people on the very pro side think that the people on the very con side or the somewhat con side are selectively using points in their presentation of the information, and that there are inconsistencies depending on which audience people are seeking to impress) because well, I mean, I guess that anybody who is engaged in trying to convince people will always be somewhat selective. I would have said, predicted, that the pro-GATS and especially the trade people say we simply don't know what we're talking about and that we're using contentious rhetoric such as the commodification of higher education and it doesn't advance the discussion, and I come to the agree with that. I think we've got to stop talking about rhetoric and start talking about real things, although the difference in language is, you know, a sticking point. (M. Green, ACE, personal communication, May 13, 2004)

At the same time, the government officials want to be both receptive to the concerns of the higher education representatives while also remaining consistent with their position on trade across industries, so as to maintain credibility among industry and government representatives. ACE acknowledges the need to shift language depending upon their audience:

> We were trying to open lines of communication with the U.S. trade representatives, and we were trying to stir up a little conversation about the declaration, and so in a sense, the message in the declaration was not one that we were, not really our message to the USTR. Our message to them had to be let's sit down and talk, we need to work with you. So the language, we were kind of playing two angles at once, which are now converging, because we're beyond that. (M. Green, ACE, personal communication, November 19, 2003)

> I guess that anybody who is engaged in trying to convince people will always be somewhat selective (in the language they use). (M. Green, ACE, personal communication, May 13, 2004)

On and off the record, several of the actors interviewed mentioned this kind of lobbying technique of shifting the focus of their efforts and language depending on the end goal. Whether rallying support for a base cause or trying to be persuasive enough to create small shifts in policy, these actors all must balance their goals and use the appropriate methods to achieve them.

There is a sense on the part of the industry representatives from ACE and CHEA that they have had some positive influence on the USTR's perspective on the higher education industry.

> I mean they are persuaded that non-profit is different from for-profit, and I think they are persuaded they have a tiger by the tail because the authority to establish higher education institutions as to whom are they, to what are they really accountable, and you do not have a national system. So they're aware of that now. And they're aware of the complexity of the quality assurance operations. (J. Eaton, CHEA, personal communication, May 13, 2004)

Learning how to meet the "opponent" in these dialogues and present a convincing argument for compromise has been the most positive outcome for the higher education representatives of this on-going process of developing the U.S. GATS position. Still, it is likely that there are some elements that will never be reconciled to either side's satisfaction.

> What I would say is that it's a feeling, that if you enter into dialogue, there's an implicit agreement that there will then be some compromise and consensus. And, that there's a feeling, on the educational side, that the values that are represented can't be compromised. (J. Yopp, CGS, personal communication, May 13, 2004)

CONCLUSIONS

In presenting the challenges the higher education industry faced in trying to influence the development of trade policies regarding higher education services, it is easy to over-emphasize just how influential their input has been. Their efforts and engagement regarding trade policies since December 2000 have been important with regard to representing their constituents and meeting the defined responsibilities of their organizations. But, how important have they actually been in influencing policy formation within the USTR?

Analyzing the comments and attitude of the government representatives included in this research, it seems more accurate to conclude that the USTR chose to respect the authority of these organizations in their representation of the higher education industry but that they remain unconvinced that most, if not all, of the higher education concerns are truly legitimate. In fact, there appeared to be an almost amused attitude toward the energetic opposition presented by such groups as ACE and CHEA.

In interviews, the USTR presented trade in higher education as more of an inevitability than an area of continued negotiation, and that their efforts to include the industry representatives who expressed opposition to the idea of treating higher education as a tradable good were more for being inclusive in the process than actually seeking to use any new information to inform their position. They noted that most of the specific exclusions listed in the March 31, 2003, offer were redundant, since the pre-amble to the GATS contains a broad statement of regulatory autonomy for all members nations in all industries.

> *Recognizing* the right of Members to regulate, and to introduce new regulations, on the supply of services within their territories in order to meet national policy objectives and, given asymmetries existing with respect to the degree of development of services regulations in different countries, the particular need of developing countries to exercise this right; . . . (WTO, 2003)

With this statement, the WTO seems to be acknowledging that trade in services, in particular, are significant enough to national interests that Member nations might need to re-evaluate their commitments and the extent of their commitments in service industries regularly. With such a statement, it appears that the USTR has a wide berth in determining what is and is not ultimately liberalized through the GATS offer, allowing for an ambiguity that should allow higher education flexibility in responding to trade liberalization.

The USTR representatives also acknowledged that higher education is too sizeable an industry in the U.S. to be ignored in any agreement on trade in services, but also noted that in the larger scheme of the USTR's offer to the GATS, higher education is a very small industry of concern. So, their willingness to include industry representatives in the dialogue about the evolving GATS offer was more as a courtesy to the industry than an effort to gather useful information for forming the offer itself.

The following chapter presents the residual issues raised by the industry representatives and the ways in which they may or may not have been incorporated in the March 31, 2003, offer to the GATS. Many, if not most, of the concerns are addressed in some way in the offer, though some fundamental divides, most notably the need to include higher education in trade agreements at all, remain. In fact, the process of involving themselves and pushing to have their concerns addressed by the government continues to motivate higher education industry representatives, regardless of whether the trade office is being entirely candid in its willingness to incorporate industry concerns into its trade agreement offers or whether their efforts will result in any true change in the direction of trade in higher education services.

Chapter Nine

The Associations' Perceptions and Concerns about Free Trade

This chapter presents the most frequently raised and/or most significant issues and concerns about trade liberalization of higher education through the GATS that emerged from the collected data. An overarching theme that arose throughout the research is that higher education is being 'threatened' by trade. The National Education Association, for example, even produced an analysis of the trade issue entitled: *Higher Education & International Trade: An Examination of the Threats and Promises of Globalization* (2004), which focuses significantly more on threats than promises. Recognizing the pervasive sense of having to respond to the 'threat' of trade helps frame the major themes that arose from the research.

This chapter explores the array of specific issues that concern the participants, including: the necessity of including higher education in trade agreements, the benefits of free trade in higher education, increased federal government involvement in higher education, the diversity of American higher education, the blurring of distinctions between public and private, accreditation and quality assurance concerns, the rising influence of the for-profit sector, the increasing prominence of the professions, the differing issues of U.S. interests abroad and foreign interests in the U.S., and specific concerns about the terms and conditions of the GATS. As this issue of trade regulations involving higher education is relatively new to the higher education industry and has not even reached a campus-level discourse, it is likely that the list of issues, complaints, and concerns will expand even beyond the issues explained below.

WHY INCLUDE HIGHER EDUCATION IN THE GATS NEGOTIATIONS AT ALL?

The size and economic value of all post-secondary education in the United States places it among the nation's largest and most lucrative industries, service or otherwise, for-profit and not-for-profit. Because of its value, according to a USTR representative, there was simply no reasonable option not to consider higher education as it developed a position on broad issues regarding trade in services. As noted in the earlier chapter on the USTR and its position on trade in education services, education has been considered an important tradable service for decades.

> Education has been included as a service sector from the beginning, that is, from the late 1970s and 1980s when the U.S. initiated its efforts to get other countries to focus on service industries as part of the negotiations. Service industries, which at that time accounted for about 70 percent of U.S. non-agricultural employment (and now accounts for 80 percent), urged that the U.S. Government provide services with treatment equal to that accorded to agricultural and industrial goods in trade agreements. (B. Ascher, personal communication, November 10, 2003)

Further, the noted barriers to providers of higher education services abroad include:

> . . . national legislation and policies that inhibit foreign education providers from obtaining national licenses; qualifications authorities that have difficulty recognizing foreign educational credentials; telecommunications laws that restrict the use of national satellites and receiving dishes; foreign-exchange controls that limit direct investment by foreign education providers, place minimum capital investment requirements on foreign-owned firms, and assess prohibitively high taxes on all revenue made by foreign entities; limitations on foreign ownership; and disregard for international agreements concerning intellectual property rights. (Moll, 2002, p. 5)

With the idea of providing greater access to foreign markets for American providers, the USTR and the DOC very purposefully have pushed for liberalization in trade in higher education in order to reduce and, ultimately, remove barriers that inhibit the ability of U.S. education exporters to maximize their opportunities abroad.

How to include education in a trade agreement on services, however, has not always been clear to either government or industry representatives. Should primary and secondary education be included in the U.S. proposal (as it is in just a few other nations' proposals)? Should any agreements focus on for-profit or trade schools? Should traditional higher education be included? Ultimately, the U.S. did not include primary or secondary education in its GATS initial offer, but it did include trade, certificate, and most other levels of tertiary education in its offer. Many of the representatives of higher education remain skeptical of the intentions of the USTR as well as the arguments for including higher education services in any trade agreements.

Several representatives question, in interviews, articles, and press releases, the basic necessity of including higher education in any trade in services agreements.

> I do need to know exactly what the problem is which we are attempting to solve (through trade negotiations including higher education). For example, career colleges, which do not give degrees but perhaps give diplomas or certificates in very special training areas, may well have problems that can be addressed through trade discussions. I do understand that problem. That is not, however, a problem for not-for-profit higher education. Nondegree training is quite different from the products of higher education. Therefore, if training, in a very specific vocational and professional way, has problems in international delivery, then that should be the problem addressed. (Ward, 2002)

This theme of which 'product' of higher education is being aided by including the entire higher education industry in an international trade agreement also extends to the differences between for-profit and not-for-profit higher education.

> . . . And, I guess what struck us was that the issues which were laid out as issues that were causing problems for the for-profit sector didn't seem to us to be issues that warrant a major inclusion. Issues, for example, (like) the repatriation of profits, I mean those are issues that can be dealt with either bilaterally or multilaterally in terms of banking and other kinds of regulations . . . (F. Hayward, ACE/CHEA, personal communication, November 18, 2003)

Though beyond the scope of this study, an examination of concerns like the repatriation of profits and other issues more in line with multinational corporations than universities would provide an interesting context for understanding the differences between the interests of for-profit versus not-for-profit higher education. For the purpose of this research, which is specifically examining how the traditional (not-for-profit) higher education industry has responded to the emerging issue of trade, simply understanding the desire to maximize profits in an open market is enough to frame the concerns of the for-profit higher education sector.

When asked which elements of higher education were of the greatest concern to the trade representatives as they were developing this stance on trade in higher education services, individuals within the USTR's office acknowledged that the for-profit industry, which is more in line with non-education service industries, such as finance or telecommunications, that are normally associated with trade, was the focus of their attention to higher education.

The pro-GATS side of this debate has yet to present a convincing rationale to show how this inclusion of higher education in the GATS would benefit the largest segment of American higher education, the traditional non-profit community/industry.

> I think the misunderstandings that exist between higher-education institutions and their governments over the inclusion of educational services in the GATS negotiations do need further deliberation. I think we do need better information and more transparency about the international delivery of higher education. . . . (H)owever, I am not at all convinced that I understand what the problem is that GATS will fix. (Ward, 2002)

This statement by the president of the most influential representative higher education association suggests that the GATS could lead not to a solution to broad trade concerns but, instead, to increasingly complicated regulations and broad negative ramifications for students and institutions of higher education. This skepticism is at the heart of the suspicions regarding trade liberalization and higher education in the U.S. and is in contrast to those who believe that the potential benefits of including higher education in service trade liberalization outweigh any anticipated cons.

POTENTIAL BENEFITS OF LIBERALIZING TRADE IN HIGHER EDUCATION SERVICES

Though this research uncovered a preponderance of negative perspectives on including higher education in any agreements on trade in services, there are those—many of whom are actually in a position to truly affect policy development—who believe strongly in the positive benefits of trade in education services. Some of the benefits would include the expansion of opportunities for students to access the highest quality higher education available and the increased ability of foreign providers to fill voids left by domestic providers. Other beneficiaries of free trade in higher education, besides students, are the providers of these international enterprises.

According to Jennifer Moll (2002), of the Department of Commerce's Office of Service Industries, "international trade liberalization also enhances the array of export opportunities available to U.S. education and training providers by increasing their access to overseas markets." As the purpose of the DOC and the USTR is, by-and-large, to promote the welfare of American business interests, it is completely logical that their efforts seek to promote the U.S. education entrepreneurial interests through trade agreements. The non-profit sector, however, has largely not sought to expand its interests in a for-profit fashion abroad and remains alienated from and wary of policies that group their sector's interests with those of the for-profits.

Nonetheless, of the groups and individuals who participated in this research, very few articulated support for the GATS based on the potential benefits outlined above. On the contrary, the sense of the GATS as a 'threat' to higher education was the pervasive theme of the data collection. It appears that these benefits are either not perceived to be significant enough to outweigh the perceived negative ramifications or are, perhaps, not well understood.

FEDERAL GOVERNMENT INVOLVEMENT IN HIGHER EDUCATION

> When trade issues are connected to the delivery of higher education at a time of extensive and often market driven changes, there will obviously be great suspicion and anxiety about a new set of changes that are not fully understood. In particular, we are puzzled when government entities would like to be less involved in our lives domestically, but now want in a sense to re-enter our lives internationally. I think there is a paradox there that we need to understand. (Ward, 2002)

On both sides, numerous interviewees acknowledged that this trade issue brings the federal government into the realm of higher education in a way that is new and unchartered. In most regards, the states regulate and control higher education, setting standards and requirements for operating within their borders. Inclusion in federal foreign policy transfers some level of control over higher education from the states to the federal government, without, by-and-large, the acquiescence of the states.

> Because the minute you get into sphere of trade you move from an individual institutional or state level to the national level. What would that mean if agreements were made that had binding effects on the states? (F. Hayward, ACE/CHEA, personal communication, November 18, 2003)

> The states control higher education, it's not the federal government that controls them, so there is as long as you have a legislature, a Congress, you are never, ever going to be able to control higher education, because the Congress doesn't usurp the states' rights, and the administration has said that states have certain rights to be protected. (K. Bolognese, NASULGC, personal communication, November 21, 2003)

That the states maintain primary governmental authority over higher education is true, but the willingness of Congress to protect states' autonomy regarding higher education over the perceived benefits of free trade certainly cannot be assumed. Conservative tenets like protecting states' rights and free trade come into conflict in a case like this, and determining which interest is more pressing for lawmakers will undoubtedly determine where their priorities will lie. Within the higher education community, however, the possible incursion of the federal government in the operations of higher education is seen overwhelmingly as a negative.

"American university presidents were very much opposed to putting higher education under GATS," (F. Hayward, ACE/CHEA, personal communication, November 18, 2003). "There's nothing that makes a president perk up more than more federal bureaucracy looking over his shoulders," (K. Bolognese, NASULGC, personal communication, November 21, 2003). The autonomy that has been historically and famously characteristic of American higher education makes intervention by the federal government suspect. In this case, with an issue about which few at the campus level have any familiarity, the suspicions about the government's motives, and the possible ramifications of their actions, are exacerbated.

It is also possible that this animosity toward government taking a closer interest in higher education as an industry is merely a by-product of a growing discontent with government intervention of any kind.

> I do think that this process does highlight something, which we all know as Americans, which is a complete, utter disdain for government. (M.P. Lenn, NCITE, personal communication, November 17, 2003)

The majority of the industry representatives who participated in this research, however, did not express overt disdain for the government as much as skepticism that the government could know enough or care enough about higher education to act in a way that was supportive of the breadth and diversity of the American higher education system (industry).

DECENTRALIZED DIVERSITY OF AMERICAN HIGHER EDUCATION

Massive size, decentralization, and diversity are elements of U.S. higher education that make it challenging to imagine that any blanket trade policy for all service industries could respect the full array of unique institutions in the industry. In particular, as noted above, different branches of government are responsible for different aspects of the U.S. education system, including the higher education system, and the myriad other forms of post-secondary education and training, complicating the equation of what adds up to the whole of American higher education

> Certainly here (in the U.S.), our system of higher education is somewhat complicated because it is so decentralized. You have a federal government role, a state government role, a local government role at the community college and technical college level, and private colleges, public colleges, for-profit colleges, and everybody co-exists and gets along and it works fairly well. (Stroup, 2002, p. 149)

The "complicated" nature of American higher education is what makes it unique and serves to provide students of all interests and backgrounds some place in the system to obtain the education they seek. Concerns about the GATS and trade liberalization and how such forces would impact American higher education often involve fear of forced conformity and subjugation of differences to a single, federally determined model of behavior.

> One of the fundamental reasons why we object to the GATS thing, overlooking higher education, is the diversity of institutions in the United States. You have, you know, smaller . . . liberal arts colleges, you know, very expensive, but you have the large public research institutions, you have lesser expensive smaller institutions, so that's quite a mix trying to shoehorn into a cookie-cutter approach. (M. Neufville, NASULGC, personal communication, November 21, 2003)

Perhaps due to ignorance of the exact nature of the USTR's offer on trade in higher education services, or, conversely, through an astute sense of where trade liberalization in education services will likely impact institutions, the representatives of many higher education associations articulated concerns that the federal government is not respecting the diversity of the higher education system as it includes it in trade agreements. By applying a single standard for complying to trade agreement policies, the USTR's offer to the GATS does not distinguish between the different kinds and purposes of institutions and gives a sense of being ignorant of the diversity of the higher education system in the U.S. and the fact that this diversity is largely why the system as a whole is considered to be successful.

> Well, the other thing is that it also jeopardizes the cross-subsidies that institutions practice so that business and computer sciences (exist along with other, less popular departments) . . . and there's demand for it then they teach a lot of that, they get revenue, and they subsidize the other programs if they're being deprived of that, but that's a bit of a fine point that a lot of people just wouldn't think about until they understood how institutions work. (M. Green, ACE, personal communication, November 19, 2003)

Within this diversity of higher education, traditional public and private institutions have co-existed and served the vast majority of all enrolled students well. Even within these two sub-sectors, public and private, are a full range of institutions—doctoral granting and community college public institutions; private research universities and small liberal arts colleges, among many others. As sources of funding for higher education continue to evolve, the distinction between public and private institutions within the broad higher education community will be increasingly hard to recognize.

DISTINCTION BETWEEN PUBLIC AND PRIVATE INSTITUTIONS BLURRING

"There are all kinds of assurances that public and private non-profit institutions will not be subject to GATS rules" (F. Hayward, ACE/CHEA, personal communication, November 18, 2003), but the possibility of differential treatment for public and private higher education is a major concern and issue uncovered through this research. What is public and private higher education is increasingly unclear in American higher education, with large amounts of federal funding going to private institutions and many public institutions receiving less and less of their operating budgets from their state legislatures. Worries about the sources of needed funding have largely been issues for students, faculty, and administrators of the institutions themselves, particularly when examining financial aid concerns or the source for research funding. With this introduction of trade regulations and the possibility of competitive open markets in educational services, the issue of what is public and what is private higher education becomes an international business and political concern.

In particular, as noted in Chapter Five, Article 1.3 (b and c) states:

> For the purposes of this Agreement: . . . (b) "services" includes any service in any sector except services supplied in the exercise of governmental authority; and (c) "a service supplied in the exercise of governmental authority" means any service which is supplied neither on a commercial basis, nor in competition with one or more service suppliers. (WTO, 2004)

Under Article 1.3, then, one can conceive of an interpretation of the GATS through which public institutions would not be subject to being sued under GATS terms while private institutions would. In order to make this public/private distinction, of course, one would need to be able to distinguish between public and private institutions.

Because of the specific language of Article 1.3, the GATS can be interpreted as requiring clear definitions for what is public and what would be subject to the terms of the agreement.

> Because some on the GATS side will say, 'well we never meant to compromise the right of a government to provide' education for the common good, that education is a common good, and that there is something in the language in GATS with its study that is when it is a government. But on the other hand, there's language in there that, you know, (. . .) the government can't do something that would compete. Well, education competes with the private sector of education, and that there are, if there are tax benefits, then they're going to, probably file for the business side, saying that you're subsidizing this, and we're not being subsidized, we're, you know. So, this again is unclear and calls for dialogue. (J. Yopp, CGS, personal communication, May 13, 2004)

Within the U.S. system, however, the terms are not as easily applied to the realities of the institutions. Even proponents of the USTR's position on the GATS and higher education services acknowledge the reasonableness of the underlying confusion on the part of higher education representatives regarding what is public and in the government authority, what makes for competition, and how the U.S. system would fall within the interpretation of the GATS. "I do think that the 'exercise in government authority clause,' I do think that it is vague . . . There're so many entrepreneurial programs and joint ventures. It's just very difficult for me to see a distinct separation" (J. Moll, DOC, personal communication, November 21, 2003).

It is this vagueness in defining what in the U.S. system is public and what is private that is causing the most concern about keeping higher education out of the GATS agreement on trade in services.

> Close observers of the issue (of GATS) generally concede that providers of higher education—even public sector higher education—are in substantial competition with each other, both in terms of degree provision and in terms of other functions of institutions of higher education—expert consultation for example. (NEA, 2004)

The implications of this merging of public and private higher education funding, output, and identities, could have potentially significant ramifications on countries that are already scaling back their support for public education, particularly in the developing world but in the U.S. as well.

> I think the deregulation, if the receiving countries don't have the infrastructure to deal with it, then I think it has the potential to weaken public, national higher education. You know, I think the dangers are so hard to predict in the U.S. This Article 1.3 "Who's In and Who's Out" that could be a real mess. I mean there is no purely public institution. So what does this mean? (M. Green, ACE, personal communication, November 19, 2003)

Ultimately, there is no consensus within the higher education community on the likelihood that a distinction between public and private higher education would have any bearing on whether the GATS is or is not a significant issue for American colleges and universities. Even government representatives within the USTR and Department of Commerce speak of the nebulous nature of such distinctions and the current lack of clarity on how to apply the regulations developed in trade agreements. While the perhaps knee-jerk reaction against all government involvement in defining and regulating higher education has led to immediate opposition to including higher education services in the GATS, not all of the associations that have come out publicly against including higher education are convinced that the public/private issue can be sorted out with the information available thus far.

> I think it's fuzzy. I, people disagree with me, I think we made too much of it . . . The way it's been presented is this: that if higher education is in GATS, any authority that it would have vis-à-vis colleges and universities would be confined to public institutions and not private institutions, because they would have to look to the states to some extent, and the argument that-and they see . . . I don't know if they still do, but they used to-that you're going to split the higher ed community between the publics and the privates. And I don't know that that's what would happen. It's not clear to me, because that whole issue of what's an arm of the government, isn't clear to me. And public doesn't mean you are, and private doesn't mean you aren't, it's more complicated. (J. Eaton, CHEA, personal communication, November 20, 2003)

Whether public institutions are protected from the GATS because they operated under the auspices of the government or are subject to the GATS and privatizations concerns because they operate in competition with other higher education providers remains a debatable issue and one that will continue to stall negotiations about trade in higher education services.

ACCREDITATION AND QUALITY ASSURANCE CONCERNS

Accreditation, the process of evaluating and establishing the markers for quality in higher education, is an area that might be dramatically impacted by trade liberalization in higher education. It is also, perhaps, the most complicated to understand in the context of trade. The process of earning accredited status requires an institution to ask for a team of volunteer faculty/administrators from peer institutions to examine their operations against a regionally developed set of criteria, to determine whether their operations meet an acceptable basic standard. Accreditation processes are somewhat bare-boned and relatively conspicuous.

> In reality accreditation is relatively inexpensive in that most of it is done on a voluntary basis. So people who go to the institutions as part of visiting teams are in general not paid. Their expenses are covered but they're not paid a fee. With a very small staff you can accredit a large number of organizations simply because the review is done by peers on a voluntary basis. (F. Hayward, ACE/CHEA, personal communication, November 18, 2003)

It is because of this streamlined process, with regard to clarity of execution and minimal institutional or systematic expense, and the validity provided by its peer to peer structure, that accreditation has been able to become an acceptable norm and standard in American higher education.

Accreditation in the United States is regional, not national, and the standards used to determine whether an institution is accredited evolve over time. Accreditation is also voluntary and entirely non-governmental, though, accreditation is required to access government funding for institutions and their students. This recognition by the government of the value of accreditation gives accreditation in the United States something more than credibility; it establishes accreditation as a signal of quality or, more accurately, a lack of accreditation as a signal of inferior quality. Accreditation, then, is a de facto requirement for any degree-granting institution operating in the United States, and this presents an interesting concern on at least two fronts: for foreign institutions looking to open campuses in the U.S. with U.S. accreditation and for U.S.-based regional accreditation agencies who might be asked to accredit an institution of a foreign trading partner.

If foreign institutions were to open campuses in the U.S., it is reasonable to anticipate that they would seek accreditation on par with domestic institutions. Some measure would have to exist to make this possible. As noted above, the current accreditation system in the U.S. is not tied to a single or clearly defined set of standards, and this ambiguity might make even basic accreditation impossible within a GATS-regulated higher education marketplace.

> As a practical matter, accreditation excludes some providers from offering higher education services, and it involves a somewhat subjective application of a constantly evolving set of regional standards. The GATS transparency rule requires a clear statement of any regulations that might prevent a provider from offering services in a particular country, and the market access rule requires the removal of such barriers. Therefore, by its nature, accreditation could run afoul of these rules, and any GATS commitments the United States makes on higher education will need to include a specific exception addressing accreditation. (Flower, AAUP, 2003, p. 69)

American accreditation, by establishing standards and expectations of quality, may be something that foreign institutions seek to attach to their own institutions. Non-U.S. institutions could utilize the measures of transparency and market access to affiliate themselves fully with the American higher education system. They could also challenge the accreditation system altogether, protesting the legitimacy of accreditation through the GATS dispute settlement process, possibly leading to the elimination of accreditation all together.

> Well, technically, they could be open and not be accredited . . . they could be accredited if they fit into the standards. No one is preventing them in that way, if they fit the standards, they can be accredited . . . And it almost becomes impossible to maintain quality, or regulate it. (M. Neufville, NASULGC, personal communication, November 21, 2003)

Instead of threatening American higher education accreditation, however, some argue that conforming to accreditation would force foreign providers to Americanize their institutions.

> It was the Japanese government that wanted to purchase certain institutions (in the U.S.). Now those have been (transformed) into the U.S. image because they wanted accreditation. And therein lies the coarse part of the picture: that if you do want to have students and interrelate, then you end up being U.S. higher education. So that which is foreign in origin may not look very foreign by the time the accreditors are back. (M.P. Lenn, NCITE, personal communication, November 17, 2003)

Accreditation, undoubtedly a defining element of American higher education, could either force a certain level of conformity or encourage important basic standard for all providers. Its impact on foreign providers in the U.S. is debatable, since competition among all institutions might force conformity. Even without accreditation concerns, American students seeking higher education could effectively force providers to offer educational options of comparable quality.

The U.S. accreditation system might also be called upon to provide accreditation to foreign institutions in their home countries. This would open those institutions to U.S. financial benefits as well as provide a marketing tool that they could use to 'sell' their education and degrees. Prior to concerns about the GATS, the North American Free Trade Agreement (NAFTA) provided at least one challenge to limiting accreditation to American institutions.

> Similarly when I was involved with accreditation, it (the impact of the GATS) was equally of concern to many of the accreditors. Their worry grew out of the experience of one of the accreditors with NAFTA where a . . . non-American university wanted to be accredited by this particular accreditor and then that accrediting association said, in essence, we don't do accreditation outside the United States. And they argued that under NAFTA they needed to be treated the same way as anyone else. In the end that institution dropped its bid but it wasn't

> entirely clear what would've happened. And the implications for that potentially are profound. (F. Hayward, ACE/CHEA, personal communication, November 18, 2003)

The implications may be profound, not just with regard to the mechanisms of accreditation but also with regard to the underlying purpose and goals of accreditation in assuring quality.

> It's totally inappropriate that quality assurance issues be included (in a GATS offer), because I think that quality assurance accreditation right now functions best at a national level . . . I think that it makes no sense that you can have a trade agreement, and deal with the very, very difficult values and questions and judgments as a part of accreditation and quality assurance in any country, and get anywhere, so I see it as the potential to create some kind of rigid mechanism about how bureaucracies ought to function, success for quality assurance is much more textured . . . (J. Eaton, CHEA, personal communication, November 20, 2003)

Higher education serves cultural purposes for individual nations by encapsulating national histories, providing venues for cultural research and examination, and ensuring some continuity within significant historic institutions. Globalization and the development of multinational education corporations are testing this historic norm by taking education across borders and cultures.

> . . . (O)ne of the motivating factors here is some consistency about quality across countries, and that is one of the issues, but where I'm coming from is a more technical (position), that GATS really doesn't talk about it explicitly. (J. Eaton, CHEA, personal communication, November 20, 2003)

Accreditation seeks to evaluate the quality of education provided by an institution, and quality is a highly subjective. If the accreditation process is to be respectful of the cultural elements of higher education, it may be impossible to develop a cross-national accreditation system. On the contrary, accreditation in this regard seems anathema to international homogenization.

Regional accreditation norms might be established among nations that share borders and cultural histories, however, and the success of these standards in protecting national identities while promoting international continuity concerning quality will likely determine whether a broad international accreditation standard will be possible in the future.

> Well, I mean, Europe's talking about European, in essence, meta-accreditation; . . . Latin America is talking about a regional quality assurance initiative; . . . often all the Gulf states talk (. . .), about a regional initiative. So, if this starts happening, then over time that's where we'll move, but we've got to build in all that. (J. Eaton, CHEA, personal communication, November 20, 2003)

In Europe, in particular, the Lisbon Convention (1997) and Bologna Declaration (1999) are examples of efforts taken to promote the transferability of education qualifications across borders. By providing a structure and shared definitions and expectations, these kinds of regional agreements help shape the outcomes of trade liberalization in a way that can be supported by providers and the students, faculty, and staff of the campuses.

Accreditation leaders in American higher education remain skeptical about the GATS and how well their interests are protected by the USTR's offer. The current position of the USTR does not provide an indication that accreditation and quality assurance concerns have influenced the direction of the USTR's position on trade in higher education services. In its current form, the GATS does not provided specific information about baseline quality in education or how to protect students from "diploma mills," which have been known to appear even in well-developed education environments like the U.S. This issue of quality assurance and how to promote and protect it, then, will likely remain a contentious one between the traditional higher education segment and the USTR.

NON-PROFITS VERSUS FOR-PROFITS

Another issue that came up repeatedly in the data was the likelihood that the for-profit sector of higher education was the primary force behind, as well as the likely beneficiaries of, the USTR's including higher education in its offer to the GATS. Since the for-profit institutions are not represented in this research through primary sources, the perspectives represented here are, to some extent, one-sided. NCITE, which claims to represent for-profit interests, and government representatives, who overtly acknowledge being concerned about the business interests of the for-profit sector of higher education were interviewed in the course of this research. ["There is no question the people that the trade representative office listens to tend to be private corporations," (F. Hayward, ACE/CHEA, personal communication, November 18, 2003).]

According to the USTR, the for-profits brought the issue of including higher education in the U.S. offer to the GATS in order to support their efforts in expanding overseas. Their concerns ranged from being able to sell their educational products and materials overseas without being hit with tariffs to repatriation of their profits without penalties.

> Well, I think that the issue was important to the for-profit sector for some time and it really is/was the for-profit sector that put it on the radar screen of the trade representative's office. Some had difficulties in getting their material into various countries without having to pay duty on it. Taking out fees for let's say examinations, with kinds of restrictions on the currency, affected their ability to do that. So there were certainly some concerns. (F. Hayward, ACE/CHEA, personal communication, November 18, 2003)

The traditional higher education institutions, however, were not facing the same concerns about their operations, and, as noted above by David Ward of ACE, they began to question whether the issues facing the for-profit sector of higher education truly warranted including all of higher education in their offer to the GATS. Other associations, like CHEA and CIC, noted that though they have no first-hand knowledge of the influence of the for-profits on the trade representative's policy development, the issues being addressed by the USTR's offer support the concerns of the for-profits and may, in fact, be somewhat contrary to the position of the traditional elements of American higher education.

Domestically, the rise of the for-profit institution has challenged the financial stability of many traditional public and private institutions. In fact, the overwhelmingly negative response to trade in higher education services may stem in part from the appearance that for-profits are gaining leverage on traditional higher education in yet another area.

> Well, they (Association of Catholic Colleges and Universities members) are threatened primarily by the for-profits, I don't know whether anyone has really done the arithmetic of why it's possible for them to make a profit when it is so hard to finance private education, otherwise. And I think it has to be bulk, good volume, a good deal of distance education, perhaps less quality control, and a sharp focus on technical competencies that people can acquire quickly without really going into university studies in any traditional sense of the word. I think that. So the primary concern of our schools along those lines is with for-profits as such, and they see the for-profits, or proprietors as we call them in this building, as really being the at the cutting edge of the international (arena), because they can exploit the identity of school. (M. Hellwig, ACCU, personal communication, November 17, 2003)

In one instance, when asked who would benefit most from trade liberalization in education services, one of the representatives responded by referring to "the proprietary institutions who smell money" (R. Hendrickson, NEA, personal communication, November 8, 2004). Beyond profit-oriented distinctions, there appear to be animosities developing between traditional higher education and the for-profit sector.

This issue of trade liberalization brings the divisions between the sectors further to the fore, even if traditional American higher education is, itself, evolving toward some "for-profit" ways. As with the blurring distinction between public and private institutions, the boundaries between the not-for-profits and the for-profits are also slipping, as more not-for-profit institutions—public and private—develop profit-oriented operations.

> Many of the not-for-profits state organizations nonetheless have a separate entity that does distance education or does other kinds of /provides other kinds of educational services with the idea of at least breaking even and probably making a profit. So, I think it's more like to be a particular kind of case that causes grief that people haven't thought about that ends up in some kind of suit. (F. Hayward, ACE/CHEA, personal communication, November 18, 2003)

If the not-for-profit status proves to be significant in determining an institution's susceptibility to GATS regulations, institutions will have to develop credible explanations for these profit-making areas within their non-profit campuses. Their representatives are already rationalizing why these profit-oriented segments of their institutions are not, in actuality, for-profit.

> I wouldn't want to classify it as for-profit. I would say it's a self-supporting activity . . . And I think universities are getting more and more engaged in self-supporting activities because of budget stresses, both out-of-state and federal loans. And I firmly believe that universities are being forced into that position. I take, for example, the food lab cultural sciences, and the business area. Most of those programs rely heavily on support from outside the state funding mechanism. Most of those programs are supported maybe I would say a third by state budgets, so they have to rely on their counties, the private sector, or business activities that could generate income. And it's really disturbing to see the way we are moving, but it's a reality, and campuses and departments, colleges and the units are being judged by their ability to generate external sources of funding. And you might see on any given promotion intended document that external resources generated, how

> much. (M. Neufville, NASULGC, personal communication, November 21, 2003)

All of this equivocating, however, tends to imply that there is something wrong with being a for-profit higher education institution or provider. This research, however, does not seek to take a position on the value or worthiness of for-profit higher education. It merely seeks to examine how a specific trade policy impacts traditional American higher education with. Through the course of the research, however, the mild animosity of the non-profit sector toward the for-profit sector was readily apparent and, perhaps, influential in their generally negative attitude about trade in higher education services.

PROMINENCE OF THE PROFESSIONS

According to NCITE, CHEA, and an examination of the literature, the globalization of the professions was among the initial instigators for expanding trade in higher education services. Primarily, the ideal and, to some extent, necessity of establishing mutually recognized standards for the professions ["Issues of mutual recognition in the professions," (M.P. Lenn, NCITE, personal communication, November 17, 2003)] including medicine, engineering, and architecture, among other professions, were among the driving forces behind increased globalization in higher education as a whole and the call for cross-border quality assurance guidelines.

Professional education, including business, medicine, and engineering, as well as many of the hard sciences are disciplines that are necessarily similar regardless of the country in which they are practiced.

> I think that the professions, which would be engineering, education, medicine, architecture, are easier to find equivalencies, in their education, in their degree structure and they're presentation. I believe that, and certification. And I think that most people would agree with that. I mean, basically, if you think about training a nurse anesthesiologist, which is covered by the NAFTA thing, there's not a lot of variation that's going to go on. I mean, you're going to use certain drugs, and you're going have to, or you'll kill your patients. The same with the principles of engineering, I mean when you're a civil engineer and you're building bridges, you're going to be finding very great agreement in physical and engineering principles. I mean it's just like in mathematics. I've given papers with mathematicians and brought together people in Austria, in a conference, and they were from, I don't know, maybe 9

> or 10 countries, speaking different languages and so on, but there was no problem with everyone coming to common ground because they were based upon mathematical principles. (J. Yopp, CGS, personal communication, May 13, 2004)

With the professions, trade concerns center more on the movement of individuals—students and faculty—than on institutions, and, even more specifically, on the ability to practice the profession after receiving the professional education in a foreign country. In one example, a graduate of Oxford University in the United Kingdom and the law school at Vanderbilt University, was refused permission to take the Bar exam in the state of Tennessee due to a state law which forbade admission to the Bar for anyone who received their undergraduate education from an institution without recognized accreditation (which, in this case, was originally deemed to include foreign institutions.)

> . . . (T)he state of Tennessee mandated that only students who have graduated from a regionally accredited undergraduate program may take the Bar. In my capacity as vice-president of the Council on Postsecondary Accreditation I had to make a call to the state of Tennessee's Bar Association to say that you have a candidate whose undergraduate degree is from Oxford University, which has nothing to do with U.S. accreditation, and his law school education at Vanderbilt who wants to take your exam, and we are going to have to insist that you do something logical about this. You know, which they did. (M.P. Lenn, NCITE, personal communication, November 17, 2003)

Without government or international mandates requiring such acceptance of international degrees, there is no current mechanism in place to ease the transfer of credentials across borders.

The GATS is one mechanism through which this could occur, though the professions were pushing this goal well before regulations through the GATS became a possible reality for education.

> I think that when you get outside of GATS, I think it's easier to talk about internationalizing professions, and it's certainly easier to talk about within professions internationally . . . engineering is distinct from social work. (J. Eaton, CHEA, personal communication, November 20, 2003)

Trade agreements and policies are complicated and require some level of familiarity with the processes and law of international trade to feel comfortable with the implications of trade in education. By looking at the professions and providing the professions as example of how education crosses borders, the issues of barriers to trade in education become, perhaps, a bit easier to comprehend. Still, most of the higher education representatives who did mention issues of professional education noted that the focus on the professions detracts from understanding the impact of trade on other realms of education.

"When you go by cost-effectiveness for getting people trained for professions, you slice out the liberal arts, and treating it (education) as a commercial exchange deals a great deal with cost-effectiveness for getting people trained . . ." (M. Hellwig, personal communication, November 17, 2003). In addition to ignoring the implications for the liberal arts, trade policies that are developed around the professions and practical education also do not take into account the cultural elements of education and their impact on the domestic environment.

> . . . (I)t is when you get into the other disciplines where you got a more, a stronger cultural component, and you've got more of a creative and behavior component that you're going to have the interaction with culture. . . . So I think that, that given that, but I don't agree that these professions are not concerned about the need to preserve cultural, you know, see that's where we differ. And that's what I meant by this bridging issues. So they're not going to have one engineering, and they're not going to do it in one way, there's going to be preservation of cultural diversity, and there's going to be this recognition. (J. Yopp, CGS, personal communication, May 13, 2004)

This argument, that trade policies ignore culture and the specific norms and values of individual countries by resulting in homogenized educational products, is shared by most of anti-GATS element in American and international higher education. The level of concern about the ramifications of trade on the domestic higher education climate differs, too, depending on whether the focus is on the providers or on the recipients of the education being exported.

U.S. INTERESTS ABROAD VERSUS FOREIGN INROADS IN THE U.S. MARKET

> The United States has a strong interest in exports of education services. U.S. education is in great demand overseas, particularly for business,

> computer and information technology, engineering, English language and other subjects. It is the fifth or sixth leading U.S. service export. (B. Ascher, USTR, personal communication, November 10, 2003)

The export of higher education occurs in four ways, the four Modes of Supply described in the GATS and explained in Chapter Five, though some are better understood than others. The two most obvious ways to export higher education would be bringing the education overseas—either through the actual movement of educational supplies, such as books or cds or other materials, or through opening campuses abroad. The third mechanism, which in some ways seems more like importing than exporting, brings the overseas consumer or worker to the United States to receive their education. In the fourth case, a foreign instructor earns his/her living by teaching abroad. In all cases, foreign money is being used to consume a U.S.-produced product, with the proceeds going to U.S.-based providers. The implications of each mode of exporting higher education, however, differ, with the mode of opening a campus or providing an entire curriculum on foreign soil becoming more varied and, to an increasing extent, more controversial.

Attitudes toward the provision of American higher education opportunities abroad range from whole-hearted support to real apprehension. Those in favor of trade look to the opportunities to maximize the profits of American education providers and bring educational resources to environments that can benefit from them. Those who object to unregulated trade in education are concerned about neo-colonial infiltration of the education systems of foreign countries, benefiting the bottom-line of the providers who exploit the reputation of the supposed superiority of American higher education in countries that cannot meet the internal demand for education. Critics also note concerns about the potential for increased 'brain drain' concerns, as the larger number of graduates saturate the local economy and seek their fortunes elsewhere, particularly graduates whose coursework was unsuited to the local employment market.

The more positive perspective is represented in the USTR's position of including higher education services in its GATS offer and in the Department of Commerce's support for the GATS initiative. The representatives of the traditional higher education industry are articulating the more negative position regarding trade and its effect on receiving countries, particularly regarding the appropriateness of exporting the American model of higher education and whether the curricula relate to the home job market for the overseas consumers. ("The profitable business courses would cause some ecological imbalances (in the developing world)," (M. Green, ACE, personal communication, November 19, 2003).

The implications for American higher education institutions, however, is less about whether the provision of American higher education is fair to the overseas consumer than whether foreign providers could threaten the stability of American institutions and the market for higher education in the U.S. On the one side, from the literature, Philip Altbach (Spring 2003) presents a case against the likelihood that foreign providers will attempt to make inroads into the United States higher education system for three main reasons: 1) the diversity and breadth of the U.S. system of higher education already meets the needs of even the most obscure niche markets for education 2) Americans believe American higher education is superior to that offered anywhere else in the world and are unlikely consumers of foreign higher education for fear of quality or less prestige; and 3) the attempt to develop an institution in the U.S. is prohibitively expensive and would deter foreign providers from even attempting to operate in the U.S.

On the other side of this issue is an argument that the diversity of the U.S. system, in fact, would ultimately attract foreign providers.

> I think we're very arrogant if we think it won't affect our market. Look at automobiles. I think it is a very differentiated market for a certain number of people. One of the most important things is what is the reputation of the institution? What's the quality of the service provided? That's the most important thing. But for a lot of people, if it's a credible, at a cost they can afford, if it teaches them what they need to know then that's . . . the issue and I think that will be increasingly in the cases, let's say certification for certain kinds of software. In order to do certain kinds of Microsoft repairs and consultation, you'll need to be certified. There may be cheaper ways of getting that certification or they may be people. There's no reason why there can't be people in Japan who develop programs that are much more efficient in helping to teach people in a shorter time to learn what they need to know. (F. Hayward, ACE/CHEA, personal communication, November 18, 2003)

There have been examples of foreign providers seeking to expand in the United States, and the results have largely been mixed.

According to NCITE (2003), when the Open University of the United Kingdom opened their operations in the United State, the accreditation process became a significant hindrance to the institution's success. Ultimately, the United States Open University found it impossible to attract the necessary numbers of students, largely because their lack of accreditation restricted its students' access to federal financial aid and to employer tuition reimbursement, both of which require attendance at an accredited institution. U.S. Open University had to close in 2002, having spent $20 million getting established, but losing money after finding their programs under-enrolled and their tuition revenues unable to sustain their operations, in large part due to their lacking accreditation (Arnone, 2002).

On the other hand, accreditation and Americanization has kept several Japanese higher education initiatives operating in the U.S., like those of Teikyo University (now the founding element of the education multinational corporation Teikyo Group), which bought or became affiliated with four American campuses Post College (now Post University) in Connecticut, Regis College in Massachusetts, Salem College in West Virginia, and Westmar College in Iowa (sold in 1995), three of which are still operating.

The aborted effort of the U.S. Open University in 2002, and the homogenization through accreditation of the Teikyo education initiatives operating in the U.S. show the challenges currently facing foreign institutions looking to operate in the United States under the current norms. There is no current indication, however, that efforts to expand into the U.S. have ended. On the contrary, even after their failed attempt to operate independently in the U.S., the Open University did not give up on operating within the United States, however, as they entered into a partnership with the New School University in New York in 2003 to "develop distance-education programs and expand both institutions' markets in North America an Europe," "focusing on "a joint management-development programs consisting on five online courses" (Carnevale, 2003, P. A28). Such an effort indicated a belief that the U.S. market is ready for foreign providers, and with the GATS's potential to provide a level playing field for foreign providers, the ability of foreign institutions—either through developing physical campuses or through distance education—to compete with domestic ones may, in fact, stimulate greater foreign expansion into the U.S. domestic market.

SPECIFIC CONCERNS ABOUT THE TERMS OF THE GATS

Outside of these broad concerns about the implications of free trade on the traditional higher education sector, participants also spoke about specific issues regarding the GATS structure and requirements. In trying to demystify the GATS for themselves and their constituents, the representatives have to understand both the environment of free trade as well as the details and particular requirements, terminology, and structures of the GATS. As those who were looking closely into the implications of the GATS on higher education became more comfortable with the understanding of the GATS, the following issues arose as specific areas requiring attention.

Fast Track Negotiations

Fast-track negotiations, which allow for trade agreements to be negotiated without any input from Congress, are among the many policies re-introduced by the Bush administration regarding the passage of trade and other multilateral agreements. By law, Congress must approve all formal international treaties, including trade agreements, but fast-track negotiations limit Congressional input to a yes or no vote on the final version of the agreement/treaty (NEA, 2004). All negotiations and policy development occur in secret and rapidly, making it nearly impossible for interested outside actors to engage in any lobbying for change. By the time they learn of the specific details of any agreement, its progress toward finalization is nearly complete.

> With the fast track legislation it becomes even more difficult to do anything about it because what higher education is used to doing when there are issues is to respond. One of the issues that the ACE fights about regularly is making funding available for loans and scholarships, for example. And that's a regular issue on the agenda either to get the amount increased or to prevent some bill that would put restrictions on who's eligible. We can go and we can lobby about that piece of legislation. Sometimes you win and sometimes you lose. But with fast track the only way to win is to vote no for the whole trade bill. And that's very difficult to do. I think it would make it probably much more difficult to do anything once a rule is passed. I guess the other thing that is related is the secrecy of the whole process. I mean, as you are aware, most of the negotiations are done in secret. The offers are a secret. And there are people who try to find these and leak them. But if you are not aware of what's being discussed then you don't see it until it's in print and that's too late. (F. Hayward, ACE/CHEA, personal communication, November 18, 2003)

The fast-track status of trade agreements has made it nearly impossible for the higher education industry, which is already too short-staffed to follow most international concerns, to remain informed of impending trade issues that might impact their constituents. This "secretive" element of the trade negotiations remains worrisome to many of the industry representatives who participated in this research.

Progressive Liberalization

> . . . There is a clause a basic principle to GATS and that is the thing called progressive liberalization. So if you exempted, for example, the

> scholarships in the state of California or Wisconsin for citizens at the beginning, would those in ten years be expected to disappear? It's hard to know. Our view was what is to be gained from the U.S. signing on to this and what are the potential losses. And there were so many things that we couldn't see, that we were concerned. (F. Hayward, ACE/CHEA, personal communication, November 18, 2003)

As noted in Chapter Five, the concept of progressive liberalization is one of continued expansion of free trade within the GATS. The goal would be to regularly re-examine official restrictions or issues not included in trade agreements and slowly remove all barriers to trade. In the case of the USTR's GATS proposal offer of free trade liberalization of higher education services, current exclusions, like admission policies or financial aid regulations, might be considered for liberalization in the near future. In fact, by making any offer to the GATS, the USTR is almost guaranteeing the eventual liberalization of those areas, as committing to the GATS is equivalent to accepting the ideal of progressive liberalization.

> I think the whole notion of protecting scholarships and fellowships . . . is somewhat at risk by progressive notion and progressive liberalization. So I think that's a potential worry as well. (F. Hayward, ACE/CHEA, personal communication, November 18, 2003)

Dispute Settlement Process

So we really have to work that out, so what could happen is that there could wind up being, you know, 20 years down the road trade disputes, and the . . . institutions are sort of hung out to dry by the feds, with just the . . . legal and financial responsibility of the institutions to prepare things to defend themselves even though the real actor in trade court is governments. (M. Green, ACE, personal communication, November 19, 2003)

This concern, as stated by ACE, perfectly sums up the concerns raised by a few of the participants in this research. Related to the concerns about increased federal involvement in higher education raised earlier, within the GATS structure, a dispute regarding a trade concerns also involves governments arguing in a WTO forum. The government would then call upon the institution to explain and defend the policy being questioned, so that the government could defend their practice to the WTO. No one outside of ACE mentioned this concern, though that is likely due to a complete lack of familiarity with the specifics of the dispute settlement process. It is reasonable to suppose that education unions, such as AAUP and NEA, as well as individual campuses would object strenuously to being subject to this process. This issue (as with the entire GATS initiative for most of American higher education) simply has not shown on their radar as of yet.

Use of Higher Education as a Pawn within the Trade Negotiations

Many individuals included in this research, within the government and the higher education industry, noted on and off the record that some of the posturing around higher education's status within the GATS is to position the overall trade agreement process to benefit the overall goals of the USTR. It may not be a specific priority of the U.S. government to expand avenues for trade in higher education services; but it may well be of interest to a trading partner who might produce something to which the U.S. government would want easier access. In this scenario, higher education becomes a negotiating pawn, something to be used to achieve another, more pressing end for the USTR.

> They might end up having to do education trade offs in terms of other things. As you know, as the current realm has recently demonstrated, if we want something in one area, and the idea this last time that we were going to be more generous in dealing with subsidies for agriculture in exchange for other kinds of agreements. And they (developing countries) are feeling, I think rightly, that they have agreed to all kinds of things which have been to the advantage of the industrialized nations but not received very little in benefit. (F. Hayward, ACE/CHEA, personal communication, November 18, 2003)

Ultimately, each nation will need to examine its priorities in balancing economic expansion versus cultural protection and promotion to determine whether and how to involve its domestic higher education environment in international trade policies.

> In the end, no matter what the rules say, you've got to put something on the table which somebody else wants to trade with you. So I think, it may be the kinds of rules and regulations that are put into force will not have a lot of appeal. I know that in Europe they have been thinking about various ways to exclude higher education if they can't stop it. And one of them is to invoke a kind of cultural provision. (F. Hayward, ACE/CHEA, personal communication, November 18, 2003)

If a reasonable balance between trade and culture is not possible, either because other nations are unwilling to engage in trade in education or because cultural norms outweigh economic pressures, the whole issue of the implications for trade becomes moot, at least within the GATS environment.

CONCLUSIONS

The higher education industry will continue to have to skim the multiple sources for information on even tangential trade-related issues that may or may not directly affect their operations. The higher education NGOs simply do not have the funding or personnel to stay on top of the policies being developed through international and federal organizations. They are forced to pick among the issues and hope that they are not caught unaware of something that somehow becomes an issue to their members. In some cases, it is a member who brings an issue to an association's attention, notifying the association that this is important to its membership. In other cases, the NGOs try to remain ahead of the curve and provide advance information to its members about issues that may become relevant on their campuses.

Over time and through numerous experiences trying to be all things to their constituents, the associations have informally accepted a division of labor regarding the issues they follow. They also look to each other to keep them abreast of the concerns that fall within the area of expertise of an individual association. In most cases, it is the size and funding of an association that determines their position in the information chain of higher education associations. ACE and CHEA, representing 1,800 and 3,000+ colleges and universities, respectively, encompass the vast majority of higher education. This comprehensive membership base gives them credibility in speaking on behalf of higher education and places them in positions of leadership among other higher education associations. ACE in particular, has had the historic role of being the consensus building association, as well as having the greatest capacity to anticipate and address concerns before their constituents and peer associations are affected. ACE is the umbrella organization under which many if not most of the other 200 higher education associations receive cover regarding major policy issues that are of concern to all (Burd, 2005).

A distillation of the whole gamut of concerns raised by the participants in this research and in the broad literature on trade in higher education reduces the whole into an obvious theoretical area emerging in higher education, that of the commodification of higher education. Economic and market concerns arose repeatedly during the course of the data collection illustrating the antipathy of the higher education community—here, again, as represented by these large associations—toward the movement away from viewing higher education as a public good and cultural actor to a private good and investment in an individual and his/her ability to maximize returns of their educational investment. The following chapter presents an exploration of theory on the commodification of higher education and its significance in understanding the context of trade liberalization of higher education services.

Chapter Ten

Understanding Trade Concerns through Commodification Theory

> Higher education is increasingly being seen as a commercial product to be bought and sold like any other commodity. Higher education commercialization has now reached the global marketplace. (Altbach, Spring 2001)

While the previous two chapters presented themes and broad concerns that emerged from the data, this chapter will present one theory of higher education that emerged from the evidence gathered through this study—the commodification of higher education. Analyzing the evidence to find any collective themes provided the opportunity to use the data itself to determine which, if any, relevant theories would explain the phenomena uncovered through this research. These findings share commonalities that point toward one particular theory—the commodification of higher education. Applying commodification theory to the issues raised in this study completes the circular nature of the inductive approach: the issues point toward theory; the theory explains and further develops the context of the issues; and the findings support and provide evidence of the theory.

This chapter will first define commodification as the theory being used to reintroduce and provide context for the major issues that arose through the data collection and analysis. The next section presents instances within the data collection in which concerns about commodification are specifically discussed. Finally, the issue of the commodification of higher education is presented in the broadest context of higher education, in order to situate the trade debate into the wide framework of American higher education.

DEFINING COMMODIFICATION IN THE CONTEXT OF HIGHER EDUCATION

> Commodify: To turn into or treat as a commodity; make commercial (Commodity: An article of trade of commerce)
>
> Merriam-Webster Dictionary (dictionary.com), 2005

> [According to Marx] . . . in the system of commodity production, where goods and services are produced for sale, a given commodity has two values, the value of its utility, (what I can do with this commodity) and its value for exchange, or how much money I can get for it. This fact of capitalist economics means that there is a tendency on the part of producers to think about the appearance of a product separately from its substantive use. (Shumar, 1997, p. 15)

Commodification is the transformation of something (in this case, the service of education) into a product that is bought and sold. Theorists (including Bok, 2003; Giroux, 2001; Aronowitz, 2000; Pusser, 2002; Gould, 2003; Slaughter and Leslie, 1997; and Etzkowitz and Leydesdorff, 1997) use terms like capitalization, corporatization, marketization, and commercialization largely interchangeably, to describe this same phenomena of market-driven pressures that have transformed education from operating for the public good to operating in a competitive industry, with institutions and other providers competing for financial gains. The Marxist definition of commodification, as presented by Shumar, is particularly applicable here, as it articulates most accurately an important theme that arose throughout this research on trade—that economics and corporate thinking have invaded the way society relates to education. Shumar uses his definition of commodification to situate education among other service products that are subject to the marketplace, such as tourism, engineering, and construction.

RELATING THE DATA TO THEORY

The themes that arose from this study are described in detail in the previous chapter, and include:

- concerns over why higher education would be of interest to the USTR and the WTO,
- the potential benefits of trade liberalization for higher education,
- the implications of increased federal government involvement in higher education,

- the blurring line between public and private higher education,
- accreditation and quality control issues,
- the growing significance of the for-profit sector,
- the prominence of the professions in promoting trade interests, and
- the difference between U.S. interests abroad and foreign interests in the U.S.

Concerns about the commodification of higher education arose repeatedly during the data collection, even in interviews at higher education associations that were not engaging the issue of trade directly. For those associations leading the industry in opposition to trade in higher education services, the commodification of higher education was often cited as the main culprit exposing higher education to government intervention. Those organizations and government agencies that are on the other side of the debate, promoting trade in higher education services, complained that the simplification of the issue into one of commodification undermined legitimate issues deserving of debate and negotiation. The repeated observation of the commodification of higher education ultimately emerged as more than a simple finding of the research; it provides an explanation for the emergence of higher education as a tradable service industry.

In this study on trade policy development and higher education, a shared concern among the many participants was that American higher education is being treated as a singular industry facing commercial competition, requiring purposeful strategies to remain viable.

Commodification and Trade: From the Data

Bok (2003) proposes that the commodification/commercialization of higher education is a liberal concern within the academy, where left leaning professors believe "academic ideals are routinely compromised for the sake of money" (p. 16). It is at this intersection of money and education that the issue of the commodification of education becomes contentious in the higher education community. Throughout the data collection for this research, concerns about commodification arose repeatedly.

In many cases, the term 'commodification' was used pejoratively by those who were against including higher education in the GATS, meaning the devaluing of higher education from service for the public good to a service like any other, whose profitability was the overarching concern of providers and regulators. In other cases, particularly among the pro-GATS participants, the term commodification was seen as purposefully divisive without having any real meaning or legitimate cause for concern underlying it. And, in one important instance, the two perspectives came together in recognition of the perceptions of each side toward the other.

> I would have said, predicted, that the pro-GATS and especially the trade people say we simply don't know what we're talking about and that we're using contemperate rhetoric such as 'the commodification of higher education' and it doesn't advance the discussion. (M. Green, ACE, November 19, 2003)

As noted in the previous chapters, the differing perspectives on this issue of trade remain somewhat contentious, but each side, at least with regard to those actually engaging the debate, recognizes the stance of the other and the content of their concerns, even if they do not agree.

There is also a gap in understanding what the educational products in higher education are and how far into an institution's operations they fall. To some, testing and book publication and other more overt and palpable educational products are, perhaps, logical issues for trade concern. ["Well, and an awful lot of this is trade in products, like testing instruments and stuff and books and stuff like that. And those are all for-profit, mostly for-profit entities" (J. Eaton, CHEA, personal communication, May 13, 2004.)] These kinds of educational instruments are historically recognized and understood commodities—products you can touch and physically exchange. The recognition of the education itself as a commodity, however, remains a more contentious issue.

> We don't look upon education as a commodity. It is unique. . . . (I)t (broad free trade in higher education) will destroy the diversity, the diversity of educational systems, by homogenizing them and commercializing them, and we call it commodification, making commodities. Because when they're commercialized and they're homogenized to the least common denominator based upon cost efficiency and returns to stockholders, you lose the diversity of institutions, and who wants to teach differently and give different perspectives, and this is how innovation curves. So, if GATS and WTO continue on that line, it's going to compromise innovation, which is the very nature of research component of education, especially of graduate education. (J. Yopp, CGS, personal communication, May 14, 2004)

Others balked at the shifting momentum toward commercial higher education and its appeal to those seeking educational products to further their personal and professional goals, fearing that the inherent value of higher education as venue for the transmission of culture and knowledge on all subjects will be diminished by a greater focus on education as training or job preparation.

> They (ACCU members) are very concerned about treating higher education as a piece of merchandise, as a commercial commodity, because it undercuts the liberal arts. When you go by cost-effectiveness for getting people trained for professions, you slice out the liberal arts, and treating it as a commercial exchange, deals a great deal with cost-effectiveness for getting people trained. It also, I think, undercuts the kind of concerns we hope to inculcate in students in Catholic universities, the kind of concern to the common good, in public welfare, and commercial competition is not a primary concern. (M. Hellwig, ACCU, personal communication, November 17, 2003)

If the GATS requires a certain level of competition in any industry to include (or, at least a lack of competition to exclude) that industry in trade agreements, any proposal that includes higher education services presumes to define higher education as a commodity. Those who balk at the commodification of higher education, as both terminology and execution, know they need to present a different concept to the USTR in order to slow the progression to full trade liberalization in higher education services.

> (W)hat we need to do at ACE, . . . we can't just go to the U.S. trade reps office and say we object to the commodification of higher education . . . but here's what we want, and we have to (have an alternate perspective to offer). . . . (M. Green, ACE, personal communication, November 19, 2003)

This sort of the dialogue between the government agencies and the higher education representatives, where higher education is facing increasing intervention on the part of government and must explain and defend its position more regularly, is relatively new to institutions and their representatives. The following sections define and explain the theory of commodification that is being used to contextualize the evidence generated through this study and are followed by an examination of the evidence as it relates to commodification.

COMMODIFICATION THEORY AND THE SIGNIFICANCE OF THE GATS

The terms of the GATS—presented in greater detail in Chapter Five but important in the context of understanding commodification, as well—help illustrate how higher education can be exported and traded abroad. The ability to be traded is a defining characteristic of any commodity, so the inclusion of higher education services in major trade agreements like the GATS further establishes higher education as a commodity. In the terminology of the GATS, the four modes of supply for exporting higher education are: cross-border supply (using technology to send higher education tools overseas); consumption abroad (students studying abroad); commercial presence (opening a campus abroad); and presence of natural persons (national personnel going abroad to provide the service). There are competitive aspects within each of these modes of supply, even among the most traditional elements of U.S. higher education, supporting the perspective of education as a commodity.

By far the largest mode of supply for exporting American higher education, especially for the non-profit institutions, is the enrollment of foreign students, at the undergraduate and graduate levels. As noted earlier, foreign student enrollments now account for over $13 billion in export revenues for the U.S. (IIE, 2004). This figure does not include the revenues from the other three modes of export supply and, therefore, severely underestimates the economic value of trade in higher education services (Knight, 2003, Barrow, 2003):

> The official statistics on trade in higher education services, which include those of government agencies and international organizations such as the United Nations, simply do not include those areas of trade in higher education where the greatest future growth is likely to occur over the next decade. The official statistics do not capture fees paid by students enrolled in most forms of electronic or distance education (cross-border supply), the fees paid by students receiving instruction in their home countries from foreign providers (commercial presence), or those being instructed in their home country by visiting foreign teachers or trainers (presence of individuals) (WTO, 1998b, 7). The official trade statistics also do not capture the international trade in higher education services conducted by for-profit educational institutions . . .

> or by corporate education and training facilities in foreign countries (commercial presence), because these activities are recorded by their host countries as part of the gross "domestic" product, rather than as foreign trade (WTO, 1998b, 1). (Barrow, 2003, p. 241–2)

The true monetary value of trade in higher education services for the U.S. cannot be determined without including information on the revenue generated by numerous methods of export other than foreign students enrollments in the U.S., though it can be assumed to be significantly greater than the $13 billion figure of foreign enrollments in U.S. institutions.

Again, as noted earlier, higher education is the fifth largest service industry in the United States (ACE, 2003; NCITE, 2003; Ascher, 2003), and the importance of the industry to improving the trade balance of the U.S. with its foreign trade partners should not be underestimated. It is reasonable to expect that, as the three modes of supply not calculated in the value of traded higher education become more mainstream and readily analyzed, the true value of trade in higher education services will merely increase the pressures to expand opportunities and remove barriers to trade.

The current expansion of U.S. education opportunities overseas, capitalizing on the burgeoning demand for American education, supports the idea that by engaging in the marketplace for education, higher education simply is a commodity, with consumers seeking the best value from competing providers, who seek to maximize their revenues. From this perspective, then, commodification is moving away from being a debated question of whether society can accept higher education's being treated as a service commodity. Instead, commodification simply appears to be the appropriate term to describe the phenomena happening in higher education operations and expansion today.

Traditional higher education in the U.S., therefore, is in a position of having to convince the government that free trade in higher education services would do more harm than good. Several findings outlined in Chapter Nine, as well as the general debate surrounding free trade in higher education services, can be explained by examining them in the context of theory regarding the commodification of higher education, as the commodification of higher education explains both the rationale for promoting free trade agreements and the negativity felt by many toward trade liberalization and the GATS. The arguments in support of trade liberalization fully integrate the idea of commodification, higher education as an industry that trades a service for a price within a market, without reservation. The promise of liberalization outweighs any perceived threats, and, moreover, the competition in the education market would ensure quality and reasonable costs, both benefits to the education consumer in the U.S. and abroad.

Other issues related to and explained by commodification include concerns about the rising influence of the for-profit sector and the blurred boundaries that separate public from private higher education. For-profit higher education, by definition, embraces a commodified notion of education, through which the educational products being offered are marketed specifically to bring in revenues to corporate shareholders. For-profit higher education is $15.4 billion growth industry in the United States (Blumenstyck, 1 January 2005), approximately 5% of the entire U.S. higher education industry, and the dense competition among all forms of higher education in the U.S. has propelled many for-profit providers to seek markets abroad. The USTR recognizes the revenue potential for these American corporations and sees no problem in seeking remedies to current barriers blocking overseas expansion for higher education services. By approaching higher education as a profitable commodity, providers and government trade negotiators are able to justify efforts to open markets for exporting educational services.

On the anti-trade side of the debate, concerns over the influence of the for-profit sector are fortified by the notion that the commodification of higher education services has made trade liberalization attractive. That the USTR would choose to support the position of the for-profits over the objections of the overwhelming majority of American higher education supports the perception that the government no longer recognizes the public good and non-monetary value of higher education. In this case, the for-profits benefits from this shifting position on the role of higher education in society. This shift has also dramatically influenced the funding of public higher education and the perceived commodification of even the most traditional sectors of American higher education.

Public expenditures on higher education in the U.S. and abroad have been diminishing for decades, and the climate for funding higher education remains unfavorable in 2005. Decreased public funding has led to increased levels of privatization on public campuses, often through the development of 'self-supporting' (for-profit) programs. Even segments of traditional higher education are being developed and marketed specifically to maximize revenues, further collapsing the boundaries between for-profit and non-profit, public and private higher education. Commodification theory explains these findings by showing that once education is priced, bought, and sold with the goal of appealing and competing in a market, it has been distilled to a basic educational product, regardless of provider. Trade liberalization also distills the issue to this basic level, ignoring in large measure the historic place and cultural significance of education, and promotes leaving the success or failure of education enterprises to the market

Outside of these specific issues discovered through the research, it is reasonable to situate the entire issue of the GATS within an examination of commodification, since trade, by definition, requires a product and a marketplace in which to buy, sell, or barter that product. Regardless of the protections put in place to appease the traditional segments of American higher education, the USTR has already adapted its position on higher education to an international marketplace that by definition treats higher education as a product in which one compares products and prices and invests significant resources. To better understand the debate over the interpretation of higher education as a commodity, one needs to examine the elements of higher education that are bought and sold, bartered, or otherwise are openly subject to market forces

Commodification across the Higher Education Industry

Some argue that the commodification of higher education, the recognition on the part of campuses that they needed to be actively competing against other campuses for students and their tuition dollars, began in the 1970s, in response to fears of diminishing enrollments and the financial impact this would have on campuses. First, institutions sought a broader base of 'consumer' for their educational 'product,' increasing the visibility and importance of previously peripheral or, even, non-existent areas of operations like public relations, institutional marketing, and enrollment management (Shumar, 1997; Gould, 2003). Institutions also sought to develop new degree and certification programs, to bring new demographics to their institutions, such as older students and those seeking professional development or work-specific credentialing. On the student enrollment side of the operations equation, once institutions began actively competing against each other for students and designing curricular innovations simply to increase enrollments and revenues, their mission had to be seen as moving away from simply serving a public good to serving a self-interest related to the market for higher education.

In addition, on the faculty and staff side of the institutional equation, the attitude toward the labor of colleges and universities also began to change. Faculty were pressed to become more efficient and productive through teaching more, developing projects to attract outside sources of funding, and expecting less financial support from their institutions. The size of the administration, or management sector, of institutions also began to explode at this time, indicating a commitment to manage the operations of institutions as businesses, with corporate philosophies and techniques used to streamline operations and minimize costs (Shumar, 1997; Slaughter and Leslie, 1997).

Finally, as a cost cutting measure, entire areas of institutional operations were transferred to outside vendors who won contracts through competitive bidding. Bookstores, dining halls, buildings and grounds maintenance, campus safety, among other campus operations, were being developed and enhanced to attract students while often simultaneously being 'outsourced' or contracted to outside operators, who would provide the service at a cost, ideally, less than the cost of the institution's supporting that operation internally (Barrow, 2003; Gould, 2003). In this, institutions were, themselves, commodifying elements of their operations and looking for ways to pay less for the service they needed. This focus on the bottom-line and cost cutting was and remains another symptom of the broader movement of higher education toward using business modeling in its operations (Gould, 2003; Drucker, 1997).

After the financial scares of the 1970s, the technologically driven 1990s also promoted its own examples of education as a commodity.

> All of us in the academic world were familiar in the 1990s with the attempts at commercialization of education through distance learning and through, again, the corporate models. And a lot of investment went into that. Even universities had wings that would commercialize and establish this. Those ventures largely failed; . . . to use the commercial term, the customer didn't accept it. (J. Yopp, CGS, personal communication, May 13, 2004)

With such prestigious traditional institutions as Columbia, Stanford, Cornell, and NYU, along with consortium ventures like Unext.com, entering into distance education and pouring huge sums of money into the initiatives, the 1990s were a time of great hope for the expansion of corporate-institutional links and profiting from educational products. Instead,

> Amid a flurry of press releases and mostly breathless media coverage, the dot-edus built their businesses in a hurry, only to find themselves staring down a stark reality: the students never showed up. "University presidents and administrators were talked into this by computer companies and journalists," says (Andrew) Feenberg (research chair in philosophy of technology at Simon Fraser University). But like many other would-be Internet entrepreneurs, the dot-edus discovered that building an Internet business turned out to be considerably more complicated than buying a few million dollars' worth of hardware and software,

> hiring pricey consultants, and waiting for the money to pour in. (Wright, 2005, p. 4)

These are specific examples of methods of commodification within the operations of higher education institutions and provide some commonly understood elements of higher education to illustrate how something that seemed integral to education could become something more likely to be managed through market forces. What these example highlight further is the fact that higher education is evolving—in what it looks like, who provides it, who the students are, how they pay for their courses, where they take their classes, who teaches—and there is no evidence that shows a slowing of this evolution any time in the future.

With this history in mind, trade liberalization and the expansion of opportunities for higher education providers in the international market for education is a reasonable extension of the commodification process already in place. It is simply one response to the changes affecting higher education, in this case, to the desire to take advantage of increasingly broad markets for American educational products. The market offers opportunities for those who seek a place in it, and trade liberalization seeks to open markets to higher education providers, affecting providers and consumers of international higher education opportunities.

HIGHER EDUCATION AS A PUBLIC GOOD OR SERVICE INDUSTRY?

In order to appreciate the debate surrounding the idea of the commodification of higher education, one has first to address the modern and controversial idea that education is a service to be traded in the international market for higher education services and then examine the issue of whether trade will force changes onto the traditional sector of American higher education that are negative and unwelcome. For an industry that has survived relatively unchanged for centuries, change is often unwelcome and imposed change is something to fight.

At a most basic level, regarding higher education as a commodity is an idea in conflict with traditional perspectives on the purpose of higher education.

According to J.R. Wheeler, as noted by Lucas (1994), the purpose of higher education is:

> . . . to preserve and transmit liberal culture; to share useful knowledge with the populace at large; to serve as an agent of beneficial social

> change in a burgeoning industrial and commercial order; and to serve as a center for disinterested inquiry and the production of new knowledge through research and scholarly writing. (p. 186)

Jacques Barzun's presents a somewhat tongue in cheek description of the purpose of the university in *The American University* (1968):

> The universities are expected, among other things, to turn out scientists and engineers, foster international understanding, provide a home for the arts, satisfy divergent tastes in architecture and sexual mores, cure cancer, recast the penal code, and train equally for the professions and for a life of cultured contentment in the Coming Age of Leisure. (p. 2)

He describes the tensions between the vocational, social, and idealistic missions of higher education and notes: " . . . an institution can serve several purposes. In all endeavors there is product and by-product; and makers of college plans are full of notions about what their colleges will do to and for those who entrust themselves to it" (p. 213). Barzun goes on to criticize the educational product being provided by the expanding higher education industry for diminishing any expected level of quality in order to meet the demands of massification, the rapid increase in the numbers and percentage of the college age cohort attending college. From massification to globalization, this argument that the expansion of higher education to meet the demand of the education 'market' will diminish quality translates perfectly to today (Altbach, 2004), with both eras shunning the 'commodification' of higher education as a product designed to compel consumption.

In large part, the ideal vision of American higher education as serving the public good remains the perspective held by much of higher education and by the majority of participants in this research. This ideal interpretation of higher education shuns the concept that higher education might be considered a knowledge product (Altbach, 2001); instead, it holds education to be an ideal of social service. Barzun's ideas are also evident in the data collected in this research, where those opposed to trade in higher education services see the whole process of likening higher education to financial services, insurance, or any other profit-oriented industry as a devaluation of the inherent ideals of higher education. The frustration, then, of those who believe higher education is being transformed into a market-driven industry, instead of an agent for promoting and enhancing society and humanity, has formed the basis for scorning the commodification of higher education.

Whether higher education is, in fact, a 'product' or tradable commodity is open to an individual interpretation of whether higher education is something whose value is based on supply and demand forces in the market for education services. Though individuals usually pay to attend higher education institutions in the U.S., are institutions selling students their educational service or are they selling access to educational opportunities, and is there really a difference? Through the course of this research, it became apparent that how one answers this series of questions depends on their perspective on and relationship to higher education.

TWO PERSPECTIVES ON THE COMMODIFICATION OF HIGHER EDUCATION

Those who focus on the financial opportunities available because of the burgeoning demand around the world for American higher education balk at the idea that commodification represents a transformation of higher education from a social ideal and tool for improvement to a mechanism for personal and corporate profit-making. Instead, they believe expansion of education is good, and if it provides profits at the same time, everyone wins. On the other side are those who believe the transnational expansion of institutional providers of education removes local control and input from education, taking away the credibility of education as an agent for social and cultural value protection and enhancement. In this perspective, the commodification of higher education, or interpretation of higher education as a product to bring profits to the provider, devalues all higher education to some degree and ought to be discouraged and fought by those who believe in the traditional ideals of higher education.

Commodification, however, remains a term and process that is laden with pejorative interpretation by those who use it to oppose the promotion of higher education as a product and by those who see it as a way to rally support away from those who are promoting the financial opportunities for higher education providers outside of mainstream American higher education. In large part, one's perspective on commodification with regard to education appears largely related to the constituents and interests being represented and is largely subjective. How higher education relates to the market is open to interpretation; and that interpretation is a fundamental difference between those who reject the notion of higher education as a commodity and those who believe the potential for profitability of and opportunities for expanding higher education are the most important considerations. To the latter, using the term commodification stigmatizes what should be seen as beneficial to higher education.

The commodification of higher education is not necessarily a purposeful change with respect to how higher education is produced as much as it is an internal interpretation of how higher education is perceived by external actors. For the purpose of this research, which has examined the traditional non-profit sector of higher education in America, issues of commodification encompass concerns many higher education NGOs have regarding the influence outsiders, those not working within institutions, have on how higher education is developing and what higher education should be.

> 'There is strong pressure to make education more technical, like training,' says Andrew Feenberg, research chair in philosophy of technology at Vancouver's Simon Fraser University. 'That pressure comes from both the corporate world, (sic) and from students themselves, who are very career oriented.' The result: a growing commoditization of the curriculum and a tendency for schools to market education as a product. (Wright, 2005, p. 2)

In this example, students are considered outsiders, since they are looking at higher education as an object that they can use for personal gain. Outsiders, such as corporations and student consumers of education, have profound influence on the way education is provided, particularly as their financial inputs are increasingly vital to institutional viability. By adjusting their operations in order to generate student enrollments or corporate funding for research, institutions place themselves at the whim of such outsiders who then determine what the actual value of the institution's educational product is by deciding whether or not to 'consume' it.

WHO BENEFITS FROM SITUATING HIGHER EDUCATION IN THE MARKET ECONOMY?

As noted throughout the last few chapters, treating higher education as a commodity benefits those whose main relationship to higher education is financial—for-profit institutions; businesses who serve higher education institutions; the government receiving taxes from the revenues of expanding U.S. interests abroad; any organization, business, or institution whose relationship with higher education is concerned with maximizing profits. As noted throughout the evidence presented in the previous chapters, there is no group that would specifically acknowledge believing education to be a commodity, but the actions of many involved in this trade debate indicate otherwise.

Those who wish to promote trade in higher education services are seeking markets for higher education, and the focus on markets immediately places higher education within the context of a commodity. In the U.S., students do, in fact, often choose between comparable educational 'products' and 'buy' one over the other based on price or some other determination of value. The consumer attitude of students may be feeding an institutional commodification, where campus leaders interpret their own operations and institutional obligations through the lens of positioning their campus' 'product' to be more desirable than another campus.' Without directly acknowledging this shift, the campuses may be contributing to the perception of a competitive market for higher education.

The system in the U.S. may be commodifying itself separately from or alongside the interference of outside interests, though this broad observation is beyond the scope of this research. It does, however, inform the complexity of this commodification debate and the impossibility of ultimately defining the beneficiaries of the commodification of higher education. Perhaps students benefit; perhaps the most agile institutions benefit; perhaps the economy benefits; perhaps only those who stand to profit from a competitive educational market benefit. The debate over the beneficiaries of commodification will continue as American higher education evolves to meet the needs of its various constituencies.

CONCLUSIONS

The commodification of the higher education industry in the United States represents a force that is acting against traditional higher education, which is facing rapid changes in the relationships between its constituents (faculty, staff, students, trustees) and the government. Trade proponents believe that these are permanent changes to the landscape of American higher education, and that the non-profit sector is both somewhat ignorant of the changes and ill equipped to deal with them. The reluctance of traditional higher education—as represented in this research by large non-governmental membership associations that encompass the vast majority of non-profit U.S. institutions—to acknowledge or adjust to these changes does not reflect, necessarily, their being out of touch with the reality of higher education today. It does, however, reflect the difficulty the traditional higher education sector is having interpreting and reacting to these changes. Commodification theory provides a highly useful framework for understanding the changing environment in which the issues of trade in higher education services raised in this research are developing today.

Commodification of higher education is not a theory that suggests that the end is nigh for traditional American higher education. Higher education is a powerfully influential sector in the United States, with many institutions revered as among the best elements of the American culture. The most respected institutions in the U.S. are non-profit, traditional ones. The most competitive institutions are also within the pool of non-profit, traditional higher education. The institutions are more than relevant; they are influential and enduring. Instead, the theory provides a reasonable explanation for some significant changes that are taking place within traditional higher education and along its margins, where new forms of higher education—corporate universities, distance education, for-profit segments on non-profit institutions—operate.

With regard to trade, commodification also helps explain the different philosophies held and tensions between the factions within the higher education industry, providing insight into what can be expected in future developments regarding trade and other international market initiatives. Traditional higher education in the U.S. is facing challenges; not ones that will cripple the system, but ones that will force the industry to re-examine how it operates and why and develop effective responses to the new challenges posed by international market considerations and competition from non-traditional providers.

Chapter Eleven
Conclusions

> Education is the foundation for all other services and for the production of manufactured and agricultural goods as well. Worldwide dissemination of education can help raise the standard of living and the quality of life. Ultimately all countries can benefit. (Papovitch, 2002, p. 33)

Trade concerns have exposed the dissonance in the relationship between the traditional higher education sector, industry, and government. This examination of trade liberalization and its potential to dramatically affect higher education has provided significant insights into the process of informing policy formation. In the end, it tells a story of an industry that is not in a good position to engage proactively in the creation of or the debate around trade policies regarding higher education for three main reasons: trade issues are complex and outside of the normal area of operations of the industry; factions in the community of higher education associations that formed around the trade issue have created an environment in which there is no unified voice recognized by the involved government agencies that represents broad industry concerns; and the majority of the higher education industry—from representative associations to campus leaders and trustees to faculty, staff, and students—are largely ignorant of the issue and not demanding a place in the debate.

In addition, the relationships between government agency representatives and the higher education associations have been affected by the higher education representatives' lack of power to demand recognition of their concerns. Instead, the government agencies appear to perceive the stance taken by associations like ACE, CHEA, and NEA as unnecessary and, even, naïve. Though both sides, the government and the associations, appear to have reached a more respectful position toward each other, the power in this policy debate will always reside with the USTR, and the higher education industry must continue to look for avenues through which they can convince the USTR that their position is right. This debate will undoubtedly continue well into the future, particularly since the worldwide GATS negotiations have stalled and are still open.

This chapter summarizes the wide range of industry issues and concerns presented in earlier chapters, offers suggestions for changing how each side approaches the other, policy recommendation and ideas about how this ongoing negotiation process might prove more fruitful for both sides of the issue, and provides predictions on the future of trade liberalization related to American higher education services. It concludes with suggestions about potential areas of research that would complement and extend the information gathered through this book

FROM THE DATA: CONFLICT AND COOPERATION

This book focuses exclusively on the perceptions of the traditional sector of higher education in the United States—as represented by higher education membership associations—to the potential ramifications of free trade in higher education. Trade liberalization in higher education services is a relatively new issue confronting the higher education community (industry) both around the world and in the United States. Though those who develop trade policy for the federal government hold that higher education has always been included in the trade in services agenda, the higher education industry seems largely to have been caught off guard by the current developments, namely the inclusion of higher education in the USTR's GATS proposals and, ultimately, its initial offer. Now that they are no longer 'asleep at the switch,' the associations that represent higher education are looking to engage the issue, and the government agencies involved, in order to influence the direction that the new trade policies will take. It is where government policies intersect the self-interest of the higher education industry that trade issues have generated both conflict and burgeoning cooperation.

The areas of conflict include whose interests are being promoted through trade (for-profits), which elements of higher education are being valued above others (for–profit), and what protections are to be included in trade agreements that ensure the institution-level autonomy that is a defining element of American higher education. The tensions around trade are not limited to the interactions between government and higher education representatives, however. The higher education industry has divided into two factions, those who support trade liberalization in higher education services (a small, but influential minority) and those who oppose it.

Generally, those who oppose trade in higher education services are the groups that represent the traditional higher education sector—non-profit, often liberal arts-oriented, serving the vast majority of enrolled students in the U.S. Those who support the new trade initiatives tend to represent the new wave of higher education providers—for-profit education institutions and *edupreneurs* (Lipps, 2000), education corporations and market-oriented providers who develop educational products for consumption by consumers concerned with the price and the practical application of the coursework they buy. One organization, NCITE, claims to represent institutions from both the traditional and for-profit realms, but the membership of and sources of funding for NCITE cannot be confirmed. NCITE has become a polarizing agent in its approach to influencing international policies regarding higher education, as it has used its access to influential policy developers seemingly without attempting to form a coalition among the more representative associations and without having the credibility to speak legitimately for the interests of the broadest segment of American higher education. It appears to stand alone in the higher education community in its unqualified support for free trade in higher education services. It may be possible, however, to credit NCITE with creating an environment where those opposed to free trade began cooperating to counter NCITE's influence.

The emerging cooperation appears to exist on two levels. First, the traditional elements of the higher education community—including public state and land grant institutions, private four-year research universities, independent colleges, community colleges, and religiously affiliated institutions—have sought leadership in this discourse through the American Council on Education (ACE), which represents the presidents of 1,800 colleges and universities but is also recognized as the industry leader in investigating international policy concerns for the broad American higher education system. Associations who do not share membership bases with ACE not only look to ACE for information but also for leadership on issues that are beyond the smaller associations' scope and ability to engage on their own. The Council for Higher Education Accreditation (CHEA) serves a similar role as ACE in this regard, but with a much smaller issue focus, quality assurance and accreditation concerns. Between ACE and CHEA, however, the traditional segments of American higher education have representatives examining and investigating issue areas, like trade, that seem far removed from the day to day operations on the campus level but which could have long term implications for institutions.

The second area of cooperation is developing between the two main government agencies involved in developing the U.S. position on trade in higher education services—the Office of the United State's Trade Representative and the Department of Commerce—and the ACE and CHEA, as representatives for the larger higher education representative community. Since ACE and CHEA became aware of the emerging policy development after the December 2000 USTR proposal to the WTO on higher education, ACE and CHEA have sought opportunities to prove the validity of their status as legitimate representatives of the higher education industry and of the concerns they were bringing to the table. At the same time, the USTR has been purposeful in including these two major associations in on-going conversations about how to structure the USTR's offer on higher education to the GATS.

In addition, the president of ACE, David Ward, has been invited to sit on the Department of Commerce's Industry Sector Advisory Committee for Services, on which Marjorie Peace Lenn, the president of NCITE also sits. Having ACE at the table—particularly given the fact that NCITE, representing the other side of the debate, is actively involved—will enable a more thorough and representative examination of the issues by having these two conflicting perspectives equally represented. Finally, individuals like Jonathan Yopp, Director of Federal Relations at the Council of Graduate Schools and member of the NCITE board, may serve as bridges between the two sides, as he recognizes the important of transnational educational opportunities but also holds a personal perspective that is concerned with protecting the cultural identity of higher education. He promotes searching for a compromise position that protects national autonomy and the vital role education plays as a cultural medium while allowing international investments in education that can benefit the entrepreneur and student alike. It is likely that this kind of approach will move the debate into new areas in the future.

A SUMMARY OF THE PROS AND CONS OF TRADE IN HIGHER EDUCATION SERVICES

The information gathered during this study exposed an array of opinions, pro and con, about the implications of trade liberalization for American higher education. Those who support trade liberalization in higher education services see it as an opportunity for American providers of education services to tap into markets for their services overseas. The removal of trade barriers, such as visas restricting the hiring of foreigners, accreditation requirements, and taxation on imported educational materials, could eliminate the obstacles keeping multinational education providers from expanding operations abroad. Higher education is a multi-billion dollar international market, and the United States retains a comparative advantage in higher education, as foreign students continue to look to America's colleges and universities as among the best in the world and worthy of the costs to enroll. Exporting American higher education abroad, according to proponents, would merely increase the numbers of students served by American higher education interests and would allow those American multinationals to compete with institutions from Australia and the United Kingdom that have already developed extensive networks within their regions and beyond.

Opponents anticipate more detrimental outcomes should higher education be included in an international agreement on trade. They are critical of the federal government's taking a significant position on a legally binding element of higher education, which has historically been the purview of the states in terms of regulations and requirements. Many see this initiative as yet another example of the government's encroaching on the autonomy that has historically been a defining element of American higher education.

The diversity of the American system of higher education also seems to be threatened by trade liberalization, according to many opposed to including higher education in the GATS negotiations. They believe that there could never be a blanket system of regulations, like that of trade liberalization within the WTO, that could adequately represent the interests of the many different institution types in the United States. On the contrary, they feel the initiatives are deliberately developed to promote the interests of the for-profit sector over those of the much larger, broadly diverse, and more domestically significant not-for-profit sector.

Finally, accreditation and quality assurance concerns bridge the pro and con sides of the debate. Proponents believe that the spread of the western (U.S.) model of higher education would lead of other nations' improving their own accreditation standards, perhaps in accord with those in the U.S., resulting in improved higher education services around the world. Opponents, however, support the contention that accreditation issues are specifically pertinent to an individual nation's culture and educational norms and cannot simply be replicated effectively in different countries. Both the supporters and opponents of free trade regulations in higher education believe that accreditation and quality assurances lead to a certain level of conformity to set standards. Proponents see this conformity as being one mechanism for building confidence in the quality of new programs and institutions. Opponents, however, recognize this assimilation as something likely to be challenged through the dispute resolution process of the WTO, with the possible outcome of severely curtailing a nation's ability to set its own standards for higher education accreditation.

The positions have become polarized, in part because it is a very small community of bureaucrats and policy analysts who are actually knowledgeable enough to have an opinion about the issue. As noted in Chapter Eight, there are perhaps only a half dozen individuals in American higher education who are actively following this issue enough to formulate an educated opinion. Further, they feared differential treatment between the public and private institutions would expose the difficulty of distinguishing between public and private higher education, perhaps leading to differential treatment between these sub-sectors of the traditional non-profit sector of American higher education.

Concerns over the complexity and ambiguities of the GATS have led to skepticism that protections offered today will be valid in the future. Determining whether higher education is a protected industry not subject to trade regulations remains a nebulous issue. Progressive liberalization and the idea that higher education may be used as a pawn to gain leverage in trade negotiations have left many of the higher education representatives with a sense that higher education could be vulnerable to sweeping trade regulations in the future, regardless of any assurances to the contrary today.

This book explores both the environment in which government agencies and higher education representatives are engaging each other around the issue of trade in higher education services and the common perspectives and concerns shared by the participants. The data collected during this study also offers some insight into future issues that are likely to arise in light of the current impasse facing the GATS and of the impending implications of trade in higher education services on both the state level and on the campus level. Higher education leaders are not trade experts; and the trade experts know very little about higher education. Finding common language and interests with which to base the conversations around the pros and cons of trade in higher education services remains a significant challenge.

RECOMMENDATIONS FOR IMPROVING FUTURE NEGOTIATIONS

In analyzing the information gathered through this study, it is clear that each side of this trade issue could benefit from new strategies to respond to the positions and concerns of the other. Higher education should present a more unified and cohesive front in any negotiations with the government and to ensure that their constituents' interests are being served. On the government side changing their mode of operations might add credibility to their processes as well as help the USTR anticipate challenges that might come from higher education issues in the future. The following are four recommendations for action to address several of the key findings.

Bring in an Expert

The traditional higher education sector needs an in-house expert on trade and globalization, perhaps within ACE, the flagship higher education association. Having this issue remain on the perimeter of an already marginalized area of work—international issues—left the associations exposed to criticisms of being naïve and misinformed about this trade issue. The association representatives spoke of being asleep at the switch, challenged by the jargon of trade, confused about the minute details of the GATS structure, and concerned that the for-profit sector was more familiar with the issues of trade and more influential in the policy development than they were. Having an expert on staff at one of the major associations would be an important step in overcoming these problems.

By hiring or contracting with someone whose interests are to inform and advise a higher education association specifically, the industry would be in a position to anticipate and act proactively regarding issues of international trade and globalization. It could also begin to provide a unified response by having this person be the contact person for other associations, as well. This person could seek to maintain regular contact with important people within the USTR and across government, to remain well informed on issues that could impact higher education. This internal expert could attend international trade conferences, making the interests of the American higher education industry better known and informed. Having an insider with well-developed knowledge and connections regarding this trade issue would position the traditional higher education sector as a more formidable presence in the on-going debate about trade and higher education. It would enable the traditional higher education sector to match the expertise the pro-GATS actors already have.

Reach out to Potential Allies

The higher education associations should seek allies whose influence might be useful as the full weight of the trade issue comes to bear on American higher education. They should make purposeful connections with state higher education agencies, informing them of the potential impact of federal initiatives on historically state regulated higher education. The states have congressional representation and may be able to call upon Congress to push back against the USTR when necessary. Other potential allies are campus officials and trustees, who could provide support and, perhaps, influential networking that might also carry weight in negotiations with the USTR. Certainly, informing constituents and generating broader, well-informed support for their efforts regarding trade would serve the higher education associations well by substantiating their position as representatives of a broad constituency.

Accept that Trade is Coming and be Prepared

The time may have come when all elements of higher education must accept that some form of regulated global trade is inevitable, and instead of fighting against it, the associations should arm themselves with information and suggestions for alternatives to the government's position. Whether concerned about the influx of international operators into the U.S. market, the effects of progressive liberalization on protections guaranteed today, or the impact of imported higher education on the welfare of developing countries, the higher education associations with reservations about the GATS need to continue investing the time and efforts to be completely informed about and engaged in the on-going developments at the federal and international levels. Their efforts to promote their position would be well-served by negotiating from a position that recognizes the reality of the situation and presents alternative options within that reality.

The USTR should take the Higher Education Associations more Seriously

Though negotiating from the position of relative power, the USTR would benefit in the long run by taking the issues brought up by ACE and CHEA as seriously as any other input they receive about the issue of trade liberalization and higher education. Higher education is a unique industry. It is not a homogenous entity that can be regulated by any singular policy. The complexity and diversity of the U.S. systems of higher education is likely to complicate any effort to cage it into a uniform trade agreement. Expecting that there will not be any substantial disputes about higher education, as the USTR seems to be doing now, seems short sighted and dangerous in the long run.

Issues of accreditation, in particular, are very specific to the cultural, social, and professional norms of the environment in which an institution operates. Decentralized diversity is one aspect of the U.S. higher education system that makes it so effective in serving students of all kinds and interests and is what makes the system as respected as it is. Any policies from the federal government that impinge upon the flexibility of the U.S. accreditation bodies could undermine this diversity and would likely run into extensive resistance across the American system of higher education. The USTR and other government agencies engaging this issue of trade, such as the DOC, would find their own positions much better understood, developed, and supported with greater and more meaningful exchanges with the representatives of the traditional non-profit sector of American higher education.

All of these recommendations involve improved communication and the broader distribution of information across all sectors that should be interested in this issue of trade in higher education services, even if those sectors are unaware that they should be interested. These recommendations also call for the higher education industry to invest in developing an expertise in this issue of international trade in higher education services and the nuances of how globalization might affect higher education in the near future. The onus is clearly on higher education to become even better informed and more aggressively engaged in monitoring and affecting international trade policies and their implications for American higher education.

PREDICTIONS OF FUTURE ISSUES REGARDING TRADE IN HIGHER EDUCATION SERVICES

This section presents some ideas about possible issues that are looming regarding the push toward free trade in higher education services. These ideas emerged from the data collection but were not broadly substantiated to a degree that would give them credibility as findings. Instead, the following three points are informed hunches about the direction this trade issue will take in the near future.

Among the future issues gleaned from this research is the real possibility that this specific research question about the GATS might become moot in light of the numerous bilateral and multilateral trade agreements being negotiated by the USTR. In addition, there appears to be a burgeoning interest in issues of trade in higher education at the state level, since states have long had primary regulatory authority over higher education and might find this authority threatened by the terms and conditions of legally binding international treaties regarding higher education. And, finally, it seem inevitable that trade issues will reach the campus-level, once the implications of operating in an environment regulated by somewhat invisible trade protections trickle down through the representative associations to the campuses themselves. Each of these potential issues are presented below not as proven concerns supported by extensive data but as educated and informed predictions about what the future might hold for American interests in trade in higher education services.

The GATS will be Overshadowed by Bilateral and Regional Trade Agreements

In two off-the-record interviews with a representative from the USTR, the question of what the future holds for the GATS led to discussions about trade agreements being developed outside of the auspices of the WTO and GATS. In the fall of 2003, the WTO's meeting in Cancun was halted without progress on many major issues, including the GATS, due to protests from delegations from developing nations and from other opponents to the WTO. The atmosphere at the USTR regarding the future of the GATS is that it is all on hold and that the U.S. is seeking trade agreements in other forms. The USTR did not seem concerned that their interests may be stymied by delays within the GATS timeline, since developing the U.S. offer for liberalization of service industries through the GATS has been particularly complicated, certainly more complicated than the bilateral and multilateral/regional agreements they have been developing simultaneously and outside of the GATS.

One main benefit of the bilateral and regional forms of trade agreements from the USTR's perspective is that the structure is less labor intensive to construct and manage. With regional trade agreements like the North American Free Trade Agreement and the Free Trade Agreement of the Americas, identifying which industries are included is based on the offer purposefully excluding specific industries (opt out model), as opposed to listing only those industries that are included (opt in), which is the GATS structure. With the opt out model, the nations draw up their offers to their trading partners, listing only those industries that are *not* being offered for inclusion in the agreement. According to the USTR representative, these excluded industry lists are much smaller and less complicated to develop than their listing of included industries in their GATS offer. With the GATS opt out structure, the USTR has had to investigate each domestic service industry individually to determine whether and how to include it; a much more time consuming and involved process. Though the opt out model benefits the USTR in terms of its own efforts, it poses legitimate new challenges for the industries, however.

The GATS negotiations are set to a master schedule, and all proposals and offers from WTO members to the GATS are made available to the public. It was through the publication of the U.S. negotiating proposal regarding higher education, in fact, that ACE, CHEA, and other higher education associations first realized that trade liberalization was an issue about which they needed to be aware. Other trade agreements not negotiated under the auspices of the WTO, however, currently fall under the fast track authority of the executive branch and have no mandated public release. Anyone interested in following the progress of bilateral or regional agreements would need to be proactive and invest their own time and resources in following the USTR's call for input on ongoing trade negotiations (NEA, 2004).

In the U.S. higher education industry, even the most internationally engaged associations do not have the resources or staff to follow the numerous bilateral agreements being negotiated.

> If we had the staff, I'd cover it (the rise of bilateral agreements). But we just don't have the staff. I mean, we watch for things, and we have a little bit of help. But what I'm looking for is more is there some great zinger in a bilateral agreement that could turn around and bite us down the road in another agreement (J. Eaton, CHEA, personal communication, May 13, 2004).

> We don't know what's going on in the bilateral trade agreements. I'm not even sure what we would do; well we'd probably have to hire a trade lawyer to track what's going on in trade agreement, bilateral trade agreements. And then I'm not sure what we would do with that information. (M. Green, ACE, personal communication, May 13, 2004)

Even the most influential higher education associations, like ACE and CHEA, are able to commit only a small subset of their operations to international concerns, making it nearly impossible to find the resources necessary to examine the breadth of international issues that are related to higher education. None of these generalist associations (as opposed to an organization like NCITE, which exists solely to follow international trade activities) have the personnel or financial resources to invest in a time-consuming commitment to following the minutiae of the many trade agreements being simultaneously negotiated.

New bilateral and regional trade agreements will likely include provisions specifically detailing the terms for trade in higher education services. Because of the arguments presented by the USTR in its negotiating proposals, any U.S. trade agreement will likely protect some elements of higher education, at least initially. It cannot be guaranteed, however, that there are to be exceptions made for regulating higher education services; and the domestic U.S. higher education industry may need to prepare for some challenges from foreign countries whose companies believe they are not being treated fairly in their ability to compete with U.S. providers.

Bilateral and similar agreements also supersede any broad international commitments made through the GATS, according to the USTR representative, so these agreements may be potentially more important to track and understand than the GATS. They are also more likely to become a reality than the GATS because of the relative ease of negotiating between smaller participating countries. It seems inevitable that higher education will have to face a challenge to its operations through a bilateral trade agreement before any real effort to follow the numerous trade agreements may emerge, but the lack of funding and personnel necessary to follow such varied and various agreements would continue to be a barrier to staying ahead of the issue. The issues and concerns that came out through this research on the GATS regarding free trade in higher education would also apply to other trade agreements, so the findings of this research are transferable to the new arena of bilateral, regional, and multilateral trade agreements.

States will become More Engaged in Trade Issues around Higher Education

Since it has largely been in the purview of the states to regulate, fund, and monitor higher education, this issue of free trade in higher education services should inevitably become a cause for concern at the state level. Currently, there are no structures in place for including states in federal trade negotiations, even regarding issues that would significantly impact state operations and interests, like higher education. If, as presumed, higher education is ultimately treated as a tradable service under the GATS, it becomes subject to the terms and conditions of federally negotiated international trade laws. States' interests for maintaining autonomy over their educational systems, whether presented through Congress or through individual governors and legislatures, would, under such conditions, necessitate a confrontation and set of negotiations between the individual states and the USTR.

The National Conference of State Legislatures (NCSL) has taken an aggressive stance against sweeping trade agreements, in order to protect the autonomy of State and local governments. In a letter sent to (now former) Ambassador Robert Zoellick of the USTR, the NCSL stressed their support for both international trade liberalization and the historic autonomy of the states:

> The National Conference of State Legislatures believes that international agreements that liberalize the world trading and investment system are essential to American prosperity but that they must first be harmonized with traditional American law and values of constitutional federalism. Great care must be exercised to protect state laws and authority from unjustified challenges that will predictably result from the broad language of trade agreements. (NCSL, March 24, 2003).

This letter anticipated the March 31, 2003, consolidated offer on trade in services to the GATS and actually stipulated points that were of particular concern for the NCSL:

> - Local monopolies—
>   Will GATS affect state authority to grant or re-regulate local monopolies?
> - Coverage of public services—
>   Are public services (e.g. municipal power or water agencies) covered by GATS?
> - Domestic regulation—
>   Will GATS affect domestic regulation generally, even in sectors where the United States has yet to make a specific commitment?
> - Specific commitments—
>   Will sector commitments by the United States affect state and local authority over services that are traditionally regulated by states or provided by local governments (e.g. health facilities, insurance, licensing of attorneys and other professionals, sewerage, water and electricity)?
>
> . . . NCSL would welcome the opportunity to consult with the USTR staff on the above questions and study the pending GATS proposals before they are tabled. (NCSL, March 24, 2003)

The USTR did not seek broad input from the states, however, until after the March 31, 2003, Consolidated Offer to the GATS was tabled. It was the letter that arrived in April 2003, however, that brought higher education concerns to the NCSL.

In April 2003, the USTR sent a letter to the states' governors, by way of the National Governors Association, seeking state input and ideas on the potential impact of international trade in higher education on individual state's interests. Many of those letters, in turn, were forwarded to the National Conference of State Legislatures, to investigate how the USTR was handling their proposal to the GATS with regard to service industries that are of particular concern at the state level. With regard to higher education, the letter from the USTR stated:

> Nothing in the proposed U.S. offer or WTO obligations will interfere with the ability of individual U.S. institutions to maintain autonomy in admissions policies, in setting tuition rates, and in the development of curricula or course content. Educational and training entities will need to comply with requirements of the jurisdiction in which the facility is established, and with requirements of certain non-governmental organizations relevant to the specific fields of study, as appropriate. (Padilla, April 14, 2003).

According to Jeremy Meadows, the contact in Washington, DC for the NCSL Standing Committee for Economic Development, Trade, and Cultural Affairs, this focus on higher education by the USTR was of real concern to the NCSL and its constituents.

> A lot of our concerns with GATS is related to, for instance, if you take higher education, the fact that the federal government might be out there negotiating what is historically and predominantly a state-regulated service, and when you're talking about public education at least, a state financed service, without us at the table (J. Meadows, personal communication, November 21, 2003).

Finally, the USTR, in a letter directed to the state governors, asked the governors "to voluntarily commit his or her state to be covered under the government procurement provision of new and recently negotiated free trade agreements" (NCSL, January 19, 2005), setting off greater interest in the impact of trade agreements on state autonomy (J. Meadows, personal communication, November 21, 2003). In September 2003, the NCSL replied on behalf of the states' governors and joined with the Council of State Governments, the U.S. Conference of Mayors, and the National League of Cities to reiterate concerns that trade policies were being developed in conflict with the U.S. Constitution. In particular, the letter tresses the need for:

> . . . an improved consultation process (which) would include requesting authority from the appropriate state or local authority before a state or local rule, regulations, or statute is listed in a trade agreement or offer. In general, we prefer a system that relies upon affirmative consent from affected state and local entities, rather than a negative opt-out. (NCSL, September 23, 2003)

The concern then, and now, is that the structure of trade agreements does not require greater input from the states nor transparency within the development of the U.S. positions of trade. The NCSL does not appear to trust that the USTR is capable to representing the state and local interests in the trade agreements.

There has been an existing tension between the USTR and the NCSL over the unilateral way the USTR appears to be managing its policy development, particularly regarding issues where states' rights seem to be overlooked.

> We completely understand that USTR is a small agency, that they have a massive agenda, they are stretched way thin, and that they have a lot

> of work to do with very few resources, but nonetheless, we do not agree that the way to streamline the process and to simplify the process is to contact the governor or to contact the single . . . trade promotion authority in a state, in order to discuss some of these relatively complex public policy issues. Higher education policy is not set in the governor's office. The budget is voted through the legislature. Tuition levels are considered and debated and university budgets are developed in the legislature. So, the legislatures have to be consulted. And that's one of our ongoing issues, is the consultation, you know, not just do the states have to be at the table, but you have to bear in mind that the governors may not be the end all be all authority. And that's one of our issues with the higher education. (J. Meadows, personal communication, November 21, 2003)

From this interview and from the documents made available by the NCSL, which contained information that complemented the concerns raised by many of the industry representatives, it became even more evident that states will likely demand autonomy over their higher education systems and will need to be satisfied that their rights are being protected within any international trade agreements being made. It will most likely require a complaint about conducting business in a state that has policies that are not in compliance with the GATS (or the smaller, bilateral/regional-type agreements) to truly involve the states and their legislatures, but this is an easily conceivable situation should free trade in higher education services become a legally-binding reality, either through the GATS or another form of U.S. trade agreement.

Campus Leaders will join the Debate

Finally, it seems inevitable that this issue will eventually become a concern at the campus level. Perhaps some campus leaders do or will support free trade, as they seek to expand their self-supporting or profit-making arms into overseas markets. With domestic institutions like Cornell University's Medical School, the Wharton School of Business of the University of Pennsylvania, and the University of Maryland already operating satellite campuses overseas, one can imagine numerous additional scenarios in which successful domestic nonprofit institutions would seek opportunities abroad, to benefit their domestic students' ability to study abroad and to reach a broad international student base. Such institutions would undoubtedly welcome the removal of barriers to their foreign operations, at least at an operational level.

Other campus leaders may object to the ability of federally directed international trade laws to set policies for their own campuses. Since there remains a good deal of ambiguity about what areas of higher education operations would ultimately be included and regulated by the GATS, it is possible to imagine challenges to a wide array of operational norms of individual campuses—from admission and financial aid policies, to charging different tuition levels for domestic and foreign students, to institutional credential requirements for hiring faculty and staff, to allowing states to subsidize higher education thereby creating an unfair environment in which to compete and resulting in demands for privatization of parts, if not the whole, of public institutions (NEA, 2004). The current lack of interest that appears to exist on the campus level is not surprising given the remoteness of the issue from immediate issues and operations. It is conceivable, however, that a challenge under the GATS or another trade agreement would bring the issue to the campus and would lead to industry-wide activity around understanding and influencing trade policy even further.

Getting information to and feedback from campuses about impending free trade agreements seems imperative and inevitable. As campus leaders, faculty, staff, and students gain more information and perspective on this issue and the full range of benefits and repercussions to free trade, there will undoubtedly be an entirely new wave of activity around this issue.

Each of the projected issues outlined above came directly from the data collection in this research as likely results of the evolving policies on trade. In addition, each is deserving of future research regarding globalization and trade in education services. Along with these three areas, there are others that, while not coming directly out of the data collected in this research, would provide significant insights into the complexities of trade in education and the polarized responses that have resulted from including higher education in broad international trade policy agreements.

SUGGESTIONS FOR FUTURE RESEARCH

Future research possibilities regarding trade in higher education seem endless given the relative obscurity the issue still has within international higher education research, let alone within general higher education research. From the data and the findings outlined in the previous chapters, two useful questions to ask regarding ideas for future research include where the GATS will go and what will follow it. In addition to the supposed future issues raised above, all of which would make for important research topics, two additional areas deserving in-depth research arose out of the findings detailed in the previous chapters—1) the value of research into the for-profit higher education industry and its push toward international expansion and 2) the ability to compare the trade agreement terms to alternative models from the European Union for creating international agreements around education that do not treat education as a tradable service industry.

The For-Profit Perspective

The most significant limitation of this research is also the area that would provide the most useful future insights in this issue. By the accounts given from those involved in the development of the USTR's proposal on higher education, the for-profit sector was instrumental in pushing the issue in its dealings with the USTR. No for-profit institution or association would agree to participate in this research, leaving a significant void in understanding the complete picture of this issue of trade in higher education services. The for-profit perspective would complement and complete this research on the traditional, non-profit sector.

The for-profit sector of American higher education is growing rapidly, facing increased scrutiny, leading the charge toward improving broad international trade opportunities for the entire industry. Their significance and influence on this trade policy issue is reason enough to conduct in-depth research into their operations. Indeed, understanding the business models of the diverse for-profit sector, the motivating factors that point toward multinational expansion, and the challenges this expansion poses to traditional higher education both in the U.S. and abroad are vital to situating the significance of the for-profit sector in the overall higher education industry. For example, a case study of the Sylvan International University's decision to sell off its K-12 Sylvan Learning Centers business in order to focus on opening multiple campuses abroad, as Laureate Education, Inc., would provide an important window into the business of education, how an entrepreneurial effort domestically could lead to multinational expansion, and the market for American education abroad.

The Apollo Group, Inc., among the 100 fastest growing corporations in the United States, is a part of the Fortune 500 (Fortune, 2004), and owns the University of Phoenix, the largest private higher education institution in the United States. Any research into the Apollo Group would undoubtedly be an important contribution toward better understanding the for-profit sector and how it compares to the non-profit sector in the U.S.

Further research into the importance of the for-profit sector in the domestic economy would shed light on its ability to influence the direction of trade policies on education and would provide an insightful complement to the research included here. Though currently only five percent of the domestic market for higher education, the for-profit sector in American higher education is a newly powerful, influential, and lucrative ($15.4 billion) industry, and there is a growing sense that it threatens the foundations of the traditional, not-for-profit sector. Further research could confirm or refute the accuracy of the perceptions regarding for-profit higher education, in this case with regard to its influence within the international trade policy arena.

Lisbon, Sorbonne, and Bologna: Alternative Models from the EU

This section, though not specifically related to the GATS issue, offers alternatives to free trade agreements as the mechanism for cross-national higher education. The European Union (EU), which at first appeared to embrace including higher education in the GATS, has since rescinded its initial proposals to include higher education in its offer to the GATS. Concerns about the cultural implications of free trade in higher education led to a broad EU re-examination of the best modes for promoting internationalization among its students and institutions while protecting national and institutional autonomy from the conformity wrought by globalization. The current focus of the EU regarding the globalization (or, at least "regionalization") of higher education has, instead, focused on forging cooperation among its member nations, to develop policies that promote the benefits and minimize the detriments of broad 'trade-like' international exchanges among its institutions and their constituents.

Being able to offer a reasonable alternative would strengthen the credibility of the higher education representatives working with the USTR on trade issues. Future research directly comparing and contrasting the terms and conditions of the GATS and the following European initiatives—the Lisbon Convention, Sorbonne Declaration, and Bologna Declaration—would benefit the higher education community, in particular, by illustrating the benefits or detriments of one model over the other, to add additional perspective to the debate.

The Council of Europe/UNESCO Lisbon Convention of 1997, followed by the EU's Sorbonne Declaration in 1998 and Bologna Declaration of 1999 provide alternative models for international cooperation around higher education to that being posed by the GATS. The specifics of these three international agreements could be useful as a more palatable structure in which to promote free trade in higher education services than the seemingly more heavy handed and less culturally respectful GATS.

First, the Lisbon Convention (the Convention on the Recognition of Qualifications concerning Higher Education) established several principles of transferability within international higher education that highlight the need for a mutually respectful and beneficial protocol to recognize degrees and credentialing across borders. By acknowledging the importance of open information and transparency across higher education systems, the

Convention promotes the movement of students, graduates, and scholars across borders, effectively promoting the export of education services. At the same time, the Convention requires signatories to presume compatibility of degrees unless it can prove significant differences in the qualifications of the foreign and signatory's systems. This standard promotes respect for the autonomy of nations in constructing educational foundations that suit the needs of that country without requiring conformity to a single external educational model. Cross-border recognition of degrees is merely one element contained within the broad GATS ideal of trade liberalization, but as outlined in the Lisbon Convention, can be managed in a way that promotes movement across borders without taxing the domestic systems for producing the education most appropriate for that country and its economy.

The four largest exporting nations of higher education, the United States, the United Kingdom, Australia, and Canada, are all signatories to the Lisbon Convention. All signatories recognize, at least, the impending need to recognize and promote the value of international study.

> Since the Convention was agreed in 1997, the requirement for quality has become more explicit. This is reflected in the UNESCO / Council of Europe Code of Good Practice in Transnational Education, a subsidiary text to the Convention: Academic quality and standards of transnational education programmes should be at least comparable to those of the awarding institution as well as to those of the receiving country. (Nyborg, 2003)

According to Nyborg, 2003, the great diversity of education systems in the European region reflects its cultural, social, political, religious and economic diversity, an exceptional asset which should be fully respected. The Lisbon Convention was developed to do just this.

The Sorbonne and Bologna Declarations further sought to create a system in which domestic higher education was respected and valued while simultaneously opening the system to all EU students. The Sorbonne agreement clarifies its purpose in stating: "The countries signing this Declaration undertake to encourage changes in the architecture of their higher education systems to facilitate mutual recognition of qualifications, while continuing to uphold the benefits of their specific national features. . . . (The Sorbonne Declaration, 24–25 May 1998). The Sorbonne Declaration introduced the phrase "The European area of higher education," which became the ideal around which new trade agreements will be developed.

From the Sorbonne Declaration emerged the Bologna Declaration, which has 29 signatory nations across Europe and promotes the ideal of "A

Europe of Knowledge" (Bologna Declaration, 1999) and the independent value of higher education for each member country of the Declaration. Bologna states: "The importance of education and educational co-operation in the development and strengthening of stable, peaceful and democratic societies is universally acknowledged as paramount, . . ." (Bologna Declaration, 1999). The most significant statement made by Bologna, however, was its directive to establish a European Higher Education Area, with comparable degrees, transferable credit systems, ease of mobility for all members of the higher education community (faculty, staff, students), standardization of some form of quality assurance, and maintaining "the necessary European dimensions" to their higher education systems to ensure that higher education remains tied to its cultural bases regardless of how far it may extend (Bologna Declaration, 1999).

The progressive development of the Lisbon Convention and Sorbonne and Bologna Declarations represents the possibility for promoting educational exchange and innovation in an environment that remains respectful of the cultural and social significance of education to individual nations. One can imagine that in-depth research into these multinational agreements could provide insights into ways in which trade policies could be adapted to promote entrepreneurial growth in exported higher education, to meet a burgeoning demand that domestic providers are unable to meet, and to preserve those elements of higher education that are culturally sensitive and significant to the home nation. Ensuring cultural and domestic autonomy in a forum that simultaneously seeks an internationally consistent standard for some elements of higher education may be the best answer to the question of how to manage globalization's influence on higher education.

IN CLOSING

The Bologna Declaration provides the most compelling explanation for the compulsion to promote and export one's higher education opportunities in stating:

> We must in particular look at the objective of increasing the international competitiveness of the European system of higher education. The vitality and efficiency of any civilisation can be measured by the appeal that its culture has for other countries. We need to ensure that the European higher education system acquires a world-wide degree of attraction equal to our extraordinary cultural and scientific traditions. (Bologna Declaration, 1999)

This same compulsion, to present to the world the very best that ones higher education system has to offer, also explains the tensions that surround trade in American higher education services.

The GATS represents more than the current international policy initiative of debate. For American higher education, the GATS represents the first overt federally-led initiative to place higher education within the confines of international regulations, not as an incidental outcome of a broader initiative but as a specific policy goal. To some, these regulations are, in fact, liberating, offering the opportunity to pursue economic investments abroad without fear of facing barriers to trade imposed by foreign government on their operation. To others, the regulations are an indication of a slippery slope, where education continues to be moved away from its historic role as a service to its community toward its status as a lucrative and competitive service industry. The tensions between these perspectives formed the basis of this research.

From the pro-GATS perspective of the government representatives and at least one representative of a higher education organization, the markets decide what will succeed, and any effort on the part of American providers to export their product into a foreign market should be promoted, leaving the foreign market to decide whether the educational product will find success with the student consumers abroad. If it offends or proves unworthy of the expenditure, the provider will not succeed. If it meets a need, the provider and consumer both benefit, and the skills developed, in turn, benefit the economy into which the education consumer will eventually seek work. This seems to be a perfectly reasonable, if idealistic, capitalist examination and outcome of the globalization of the higher education industry.

From the perspective of the domestic not-for-profit higher education industry, which balks even at being called an industry and which appears decidedly opposed to the GATS, any regulations that impinge on their ability to remain autonomous in their operations, curriculum, and philosophies are counter to the freedom from most federal, and certainly any international, regulations that higher education has historically enjoyed. That the government would interested in promoting trade in and the significance of the market for higher education has merely strengthened the sense in the anti-GATS sector that higher education is no longer valued as a public good but, instead, has been transformed in the minds of those creating policy into a lucrative and valuable knowledge product or commodity.

Much of the research in Chapters Seven, Eight, and Nine, detailing the various areas of concern regarding trade in higher education, stems from this idea that those on the outside—government agency representatives, the for-profit sector, lobbyists—have actually had greater influence of the position of the USTR's position on trade in higher education services than the traditional American higher education industry has had. This, in fact, is an accurate observation. The higher education industry has not been the most influential in or had much impact on the development of the USTR's offer for trade liberalization in services to the GATS.

So What?

Which leads to the most important question of all—so what? Why does it matter who has the ear of the trade representative in helping develop the offer to the GATS? What is the big concern about free trade, when, by most accounts, the domestic implications of the GATS will not likely be significant? At the end of developing and analyzing this study, it is not clear that trade liberalization is an inherently terrible thing for American higher education. Assuming that foreign providers do attempt to infiltrate the U.S. higher education "market," which remains a relatively large assumption given the significant failures of past attempts, perhaps their presence would provide useful competition. There are many mediocre higher education institutions in the U.S., surviving because of a lack of local competition or ambivalence on the part of students to seeking better opportunities. Those kinds of education markets might be better off with some competition from outside providers. By encouraging competition in a competitive U.S. market, the GATS has as real a potential for spurring improvements to the market as it does for hurting the higher education system as the public knows it.

In addition, the GATS may prove to be an important turning point in government–higher education relations, without actually resulting in implemented trade policies. This may be the era to which future researchers look to find the issue that brought the federal government and international agencies into the operations of American higher education. The GATS certainly has provided a useful target for an array of globalization fans and foes, and will undoubtedly be the catalyst for many examinations of globalization and the international market for exported higher education services.

It would not be unreasonable to predict that the GATS will likely amount to nothing of any broad significance after all. Bilateral and regional agreements may take precedence over the GATS both in terms of their ease of use as a tool for promoting free trade and with regard to the authority of the agreement itself. Any terms and conditions of the GATS will be secondary to those of regional and/or bilateral agreements, taking some of the sting out of the GATS but also providing greater cause for concern about the ability of the higher education to influence policy development around trade. Trade as an issue is here to stay, however, whether through the GATS or the many other trade agreement possibilities.

Currently, the small community of analysts familiar with trade concerns is primarily focused on the GATS, because it is the most public of the international agreements and because they have to pick where to focus their international efforts, which are a tiny part of their overall responsibilities. These representatives have earned a place in the industry discussions with the USTR about the GATS after several years of patient discourse on both sides. None of the industry representatives had the personnel or budget to invest in following the myriad bilateral and regional agreements being developed and know to be concerned about what they do not know. It seems highly likely that it will be one of the more obscure agreements that ultimately will test the responsiveness of the higher education industry to trade regulations and concerns.

In the meantime, the GATS will remain the more glamorous concern, while smaller agreements may quietly establish trade in higher education services as a norm in the face of little to no interference by either the industry or interested outsiders. The USTR's GATS offer regarding higher education has startled the industry into awareness of the government's interest in its industry, but the industry has yet to develop a preemptive strategy for catching possible elements that might impact higher education in the numerous bilateral and regional trade agreements currently being developed. Traditional American higher education may simply lack the time and resources to affect any change in the overall position of the government on trade issues, and if it is not the GATS that shakes up the world of American higher education, it will likely be one of many other trade agreements currently being negotiated. The consequences of this shift are certainly fodder for follow-up research.

Regardless of the final results of the GATS negotiations, however, the exercise in responding to the GATS has provided many in the traditional sector of American higher education with at least a rudimentary understanding of the implications of free trade and the knowledge that more information and attention is needed in order to remain relevant in the globalized higher education arena. As the issue filters down through more representative associations, into the state legislatures, and onto the campuses, the current association leaders in the traditional higher education sector will have established enough credibility among their peers and their contacts in government to provide useful and important guidance on how to respond. This research merely touches upon one aspect of what is to come in the evolution of international higher education through globalization and trade in higher education services.

Appendix A

Questions asked of Higher Education Association Representatives

- What is the mission of your organization?
- Who are your members (constituents)?
- What are the primary areas of concern/concentration for your organization; for your area of your organization?
- How does your organization develop its positions on policy issues?
- What is your organization's position on the USTR's proposal to the WTO to liberalize trade in higher education services through the GATS?
- How much feedback have you received from your constituents about this issue?
- What (if any) are your constituents' stated concerns regarding trade liberalization of higher education through GATS?
- What are your organization's overt, stated concerns regarding trade liberalization of higher education through GATS?
- How has your position on this trade issue been developed in relation to your constituents' input and concerns?
- What efforts have you undertaken on behalf of your constituents regarding the U.S. policy on higher education and GATS?
- What would you like to see happen with regard to the USTR's position on higher education trade and GATS?
- From your experience and perspective, how effective do you think your organization's efforts can/will be in bringing about your ideal outcomes of this trade issue?
- What will you do next in your efforts to influence this issue of trade in higher education services?
- What other sources of information—people, organizations, publications, etc.—would you recommend for me to use to become better informed about these issues?

Appendix B
Questions Asked of USTR Officials

- What is the mission of the service-industry relations segment of the USTR?
- With the sheer breadth of services covered under GATS, how did higher education become an area of your considering for liberalization through GATS?
- How did the USTR formulate the higher education piece of its GATS proposal; whom did you consult in and out of higher education; and what are your primary goals?
- What do you see as the positive benefits of liberalizing trade in higher education services?
- What do you see as the areas of greatest concern for the DOC/USTR in liberalizing trade in higher education services? How would you anticipate off-setting these concerns?
- How are you responding to external critiques from representative higher education organizations like ACE, CHEA, and AAUP, that trade issues are exacerbating public/private divisions, favoring for-profit higher education, diminishing institutional autonomy, and the increased commodification of education?
- How representative do you feel these organizations are and are some more credible for your purposes than others?
- Will you look to higher education institutions and organization to assist in formulating your ideas and policies as these issues evolve? Why or why not?
- What do you anticipate will be the short-term and long-term effects of this kind of international trade policy change on American higher education?
- Where do you anticipate trade in higher education will go from here?
- What other sources of information—people, organizations, publications, etc.—would you recommend for me to use to become better informed about these issues?

Appendix C

Questions Asked of the Department of Commerce Representative

- What is the mission of the international services segment of the DOC?
- With the sheer breadth of services covered under GATS, how did higher education become an area of your considering for liberalization through GATS?
- How did you influence the higher education piece of the USTR's GATS proposal; whom did you consult in and out of higher education; and what were your primary goals?
- What do you see as the positive benefits of liberalizing trade in higher education services?
- What do you see as the areas of greatest concern for the DOC/USTR in liberalizing trade in higher education services? How would you anticipate off-setting these concerns?
- How are you responding to external critiques from representative higher education organizations like ACE, CHEA, and AAUP, that trade issues are exacerbating public/private divisions, favoring for-profit higher education, diminishing institutional autonomy, and the increased commodification of education, among other issues?
- How representative do you feel these organizations are and are some more credible for your purposes than others?
- Will you look to higher education institutions and organization to assist in formulating your ideas and policies as these issues evolve? Why or why not?
- What do you anticipate will be the short-term and long-term effects of this kind of international trade policy change on American higher education?
- Where do you anticipate trade in higher education will go from here?

- What other sources of information—people, organizations, publications, etc.—would you recommend for me to use to become better informed about these issues?

Appendix D
Questions asked of the National Conference of State Legislatures Representative

- What is the mission of the NCSL regarding trade?
- How did the NCSL become aware of the GATS? What are the general concerns of the NCSL about the GATS?
- With the sheer breadth of services covered under the GATS, how has higher education become an area of concern for the NCSL?
- What do you see as the positive benefits—at the state and local level—of liberalizing trade in higher education services?
- What do you see as the areas of greatest concern for states and localities in liberalizing trade in higher education services? How would you anticipate off-setting these concerns?
- Who do you look to for information on higher education concerns? With the GATS in particular? Why?
- Will you look to higher education institutions—perhaps public institutions in particular—and organizations to assist in formulating your ideas and policies as these issues evolve? Why or why not?
- What do you anticipate will be the short-term and long-term effects of this kind of international trade policy change on higher education at the state level?
- What will your efforts be from here on out regarding international trade liberalization in service industries like higher education?
- What other sources of information—people, organizations, publications, etc.—would you recommend for me to use to become better informed about these issues?

Bibliography

Alexiadou, N., & Brock, C. (Eds.). (1999). *Education as a commodity.* Saxmundham, Suffolk, UK: John Catt Educational Ltd.

Altbach, P. G. (1991). University reform. In P. G. Altbach (Ed.), *International higher education: An encyclopedia* (pp. 261–274). New York: Garland Press.

Altbach, P. G. (1998a). *Comparative higher education: Knowledge, the university, and development.* Hong Kong: Comparative Education Research Center, University of Hong Kong.

Altbach, P. G. (1998b). The foreign student dilemma. In P. G. Altbach (Ed.), *Comparative higher education* (pp. 225–245). Hong Kong: Comparative Education Research Center, University of Hong Kong.

Altbach, P. G. (1998c). Higher education, democracy, and development: Implications for new industrialized countries. In P. G. Altbach (Ed.), *Comparative higher education* (pp. 249–274). Hong Kong: Comparative Education Research Center, University of Hong Kong.

Altbach, P. G. (1998d). Patterns in higher education development. In P. G. Altbach, R. O. Berdahl & P. J. Gumport (Eds.), *American higher education in the 21st century* (pp. 15–37). Baltimore: Johns Hopkins University Press.

Altbach, P. G. (1998e). The university as center and periphery. In P. G. Altbach (Ed.), *Comparative higher education* (pp. 29–54). Hong Kong: Comparative Education Research Center, University of Hong Kong.

Altbach, P. G. (Spring 2001). *Higher education and the WTO: Globalization run amok.* Retrieved January 30, 2005, from http://www.bc.edu/bc_org/avp/soe/cihe/newsletter/news23/text001.htm

Altbach, P. G. (2001b). Internationalization and exchanges in a globalized university. *Journal of Studies in International Education, 5*(1), 5–25.

Altbach, P. G. (2002). Globalization and the university: Myths and realities in an unequal world. *Current Issues in Catholic Higher Education, 23*(Winter), 5–25.

Altbach, P. G. (2002, September 5). Say no to global trade in education. *The Japan Times,* p. 19.

Altbach, P. G. (Fall 2002). Farewell to the common good: Knowledge and education as international commodities. *International Educator, XI,* 13–17.

Altbach, P.G. (Spring 2003). Why the United States will not be a market for foreign higher education products: A case against GATS. Retrieved November 11, 2004, from http://www.bc.edu/bc_org/avp/soe/cihe/newsletter/news31/text003.htm

Altbach, P. G. (2004). Higher education crosses borders: Can the United States remain the top destination for foreign students. *Change, 36*(2), 18–24.

Altbach, P. G., Berdahl, R. O., & Gumport, P. J. (1998). Introduction. In P. G. Altbach, R. O. Berdahl & P. J. Gumport (Eds.), *American higher education in the 21st century* (pp. 1–11). Baltimore: The Johns Hopkins University Press.

Altbach, P. G., Berdahl, R. O., & Gumport, P. J. (Eds.). (1999). *American higher education in the 21st century: Social, political, and economic challenges.* Baltimore: Johns Hopkins University Press.

Altbach, P. G., & Davis, T. M. (1999). Global challenge and national response: Notes for an international dialogue on higher education. In P. G. Altbach & P. M. Peterson (Eds.), *Higher education in the 21st century: Global challenge and national response* (Vol. 23, pp. 3–10). Annapolis Junction, MD: IIE Books.

Altbach, P. G., & Peterson, P. M. (Eds.). (1999). *Higher education in the 21st century: Global challenge and national response* (Vol. 23). Annapolis Junction, MD: IIE Books.

American Association of University Professors. (2004). Legislative Action Alert—March 18, 2004: "Advisory Board" For International Studies Proposed. Retrieved November 21, 2003, from http://www.aaup.org/govrel/ActionCenter/31804alert.htm

American Council on Education. (1995). *Educating Americans for a world in flux: Ten ground rules for internationalizing higher education.* Washington, DC: American Council on Education.

American Council on Education (ACE). (2002). *An overview of higher education and GATS.* Retrieved March 17, 2003, from www.acenet.edu/programs/international/gats/overview.cfm

American Council on Education (ACE). (March 2003). *Adverse consequences to the traditional U.S. higher education services sector resulting from the U.S. offer in WTO services negotiations.* Retrieved November 21, 2003, from http://www.acenet.edu/washington/letters/2003/03march/Zoellick.Attach.cfm

American Council on Education (ACE). (2004). *U.S. update on GATS: January 2004.* Retrieved March 20, 2004, from http://www.acenet.edu/programs/international/gats/2004-update.cfm

Arenson, K. W. (November 18, 2002). No decline found in number of students going overseas or coming to the U.S. *The New York Times.* Retrieved March 11, 2003, from http://www.nytimes.com

Armstrong, D. (2003). *The A-list: Head of the class.* Retrieved February 16, 2005, from http://www.forbes.com/global/2003/0414/048_print.html

Arnone, M. (2002) United States Open U. to Close After Spending $20-Million. *The Chronicle of Higher Education, 48*(23), A44.

Aronowitz, S. (2000). *The knowledge factory.* Boston: Beacon Press.

Aronowitz, S., & Gautney, H. (Eds.). (2003). *Implicating empire: Globalization & resistance in the 21st century world order.* New York: Basic Books.

AUCC, ACE, EUA, & CHEA. (September 28, 2001). *Joint declaration on higher education and the General Agreement on Trade in Services*. Retrieved November 11, 2003, from http://www.aucc.ca/_pdf/english/statements/2001/gats_10_25_e.pdf

Bagi Abdel Ghani Babiker, A. (2002). Higher education, globalization and quality assurance in the Arab states. In S. Uvalic´-Trumbic´ (Ed.), *Globalization and the market in higher education* (pp. 105–112). Paris: UNESCO.

Barblan, A. (2002). The international provision of higher education: Do universities need GATS? *Higher Education Management and Policy, 14*(3), 77–92.

Barrow, C. W. (2003). Globalization, trade liberalization, and the higher education industry. In S. Aronowitz & H. Gautney (Eds.), *Implicating empire: Globalization & resistance in the 21st century world order* (pp. 229–254). New York: Basic Books.

Barrow, C. W., Didou-Aupetit, S., & Mallea, J. (2003). *Globalisation, trade liberalisation, and higher education in North America: The emergence of a new market under NAFTA?* Dordrecht, The Netherlands: Kluwer Academic Publishers.

Barzun, J. (1968). *The American university: How it runs, Where it is going*. New York: Harper Colophon Books.

Beck, U. (2000). *What is globalization?* (P. Camiller, Trans.). Cambridge, UK: Polity Press.

Bergan, S. (2002). The European higher education area and recognition of qualifications in the context of globalization. In S. Uvalic´-Trumbic´ (Ed.), *Globalization and the market in higher education* (pp. 61–72). Paris: UNESCO.

Blumenstyk, G. (2003). Spanning the globe: Higher-education companies take their turf battles overseas. *The Chronicle of Higher Education, 49*(42), A21.

Blumenstyk, G. (2005). For-profit education: Online courses fuel growth. *The Chronicle of Higher Education, 51*(18), A11.

Bok, D. (2003). *Universities in the marketplace*. Princeton: Princeton University Press.

Breton, G., & Lambert, M. (Eds.). (2003). *Universities and globalization: Private linkages, public trust*. Paris: UNESCO Publishing.

Brock, C. (1999). Introduction. In N. Alexiadou & C. Brock (Eds.), *Education as a commodity* (pp. 7–8). Saxmundham, Suffolk, UK: John Catt Educational Ltd.

Brock-Utne, B., & Garbo, G. (Eds.). (1999). *Globalization—on whose terms? Report No. 5*. Olso: University of Oslo, Institute for Educational Research.

Brubacher, J. S., & Rudy, W. (1997). *Higher education in transition: A history of American colleges and universities* (4th ed.). New Brunswick, N.J.: Transaction Publishers.

Brubacher, J. S., & Rudy, W. (1997). Distinguishing features of American higher education. In *Higher education in transition: A history of American colleges and universities* (4th ed., pp. 423–442). New Brunswick, NJ: Transaction Press.

Brubacher, J. S., & Rudy, W. (1997). The university transformed. In *Higher education in transition: A history of American colleges and universities* (4th ed., pp. 399–411). New Brunswick, NJ: Transaction Press.

Brubacher, J. S., & Rudy, W. (1997). American Higher Education at the Dawn of a New Millennium. In *Higher education in transition: A history of American colleges and universities* (4th ed., pp. 412–422).

Buchbinder, H. (1993). The market oriented university and the changing role of knowledge. *Higher Education,* 26(October), pp. 331–348.

Burd, S. (2005). College lobbyists' dilemma: Collaboration or resistance? *The Chronicle of Higher Education, 51*(22), A17.

Callan, H. (1998). Internationalization in Europe. In P. Scott (Ed.), *The globalization of higher education* (pp. 44–57). Buckingham, UK: Open University Press.

Carnavale, D. (2003). New School and Open U. to collaborate. *The Chronicle of Higher Education, 49*(22), A28.

Carnoy, M., & Rhoten, D. (2002). What does globalization mean for educational change? A comparative approach. *Comparative Education Review, 46*(1), 1–9.

Center for Quality Assurance in International Education (CQAIE). (2003). A change agent organization. Retrieved October 15, 2003, from http://www.cqaie.org

CHEA. (2003a). *CHEA at a glance.* Retrieved October 15, 2003, from www.chea.org

CHEA. (2003b). *CHEA principles.* Retrieved October 15, 2003, from www.chea.org

CHEA. (2003c). *CHEA purposes.* Retrieved October 15, 2003, from www.chea.org

CHEA. (2003d). International quality review and enhancing the international public good of higher education *(Draft).*

Coombs, P. (1985). *World crisis in education.* New York: Oxford University Press.

Council of Independent Colleges. (2004). About CIC. Retrieved October 15, 2004, from http://www.cic.org/about/index.asp

Croxford, L. (2001). Global university education: Some cultural considerations. *Higher Education in Europe, 26*(1), 53–60.

Currie, J., & Newson, J. (Eds.). (1998). *Universities and globalization: Critical perspectives.* Thousand Oaks, CA: SAGE Publications, Inc.

Daniel, J. S. (2002). Quality assurance, accreditation and the recognition of qualifications in higher education in an international perspective. In S. Uvalić-Trumbić (Ed.), *Globalization and the market in higher education* (pp. 11–20). Paris: UNESCO.

David, P. (1997, October 2). Universities: Inside the knowledge factory. *The Economist.*

de Wit, H. (2001). *Internationalization of higher education in the United States of America and Europe.* Westport, CT: Greenwood Press.

DeAngelis, R. (1998). The last decade of higher education reform in Australia and France. In J. Currie & J. Newson (Eds.), *Universities and globalization: Critical perspectives* (pp. 123–140). Thousand Oaks, CA: SAGE Publications, Inc.

Denzin, N.K. & Lincoln, Y.S. (Eds.) (1994). Handbook of qualitative research. Thousand Oaks, CA: SAGE Publications.

Deupree, J. L., Johnson, M. E., & Lenn, M. P. (Eds.). (2002). *OECD/U.S. Forum on Trade in Educational Services: Conference Proceedings.* Washington, DC: The Center for Quality Assurance in International Education.

Dey, E. L., & Hurtado, S. (1998). Students, colleges, and society: Considering the interconnections. In P. G. Altbach, R. O. Berdahl & P. J. Gumport (Eds.), *American higher education in the 21st century* (pp. 298–322). Baltimore: The Johns Hopkins University Press.

Eaton, J.S. (2003). *Accreditation and recognition in the United States.* Paper presented at the OECD/Norway Forum on Trade in Educational Services: Managing the

Internationalisation of Post-Secondary Education. Trondheim, Norway. Retrieved February 17, 2005, from http://www.flyspesialisten.no/vfs_trd/ufd/7QAUS.pdf

Etzkowitz, H. (1997). The entrepreneurial university and the emergence of democratic corporatism. In H. Etzkowitz & L. Leydesdorff (Eds.), *Universities and the global knowledge economy: A triple helix of university-industry-government relations* (pp. 141–154). London: Pinter.

Etzkowitz, H., & Leydesdorff, L. (Eds.). (1997). *Universities and the global knowledge economy: A triple helix of university-industry-government relations.* London: Pinter.

Etzkowitz, H., Webster, A., & Healey, P. (Eds.). (1998). *Capitalizing knowledge: New intersections of industry and academia.* Albany, NY: State University of New York Press.

Etzkowitz, H., Webster, A., & Healey, P. (1998). Introduction. In H. Etzkowitz, A. Webster & P. Healey (Eds.), *Capitalizing knowledge: New intersections of industry and academia* (pp. 1–20). Albany, NY: State University of New York Press.

Flower, R. (May 22, 2003). *GATS and higher education: Faculty perspectives.* Paper presented at the Assuring the Integrity of Higher Education in the Global Marketplace Conference, Washington, DC

Flower, R. (2003). Education as commodity. *Academe, 89*(4), 69.

Foster, A. (January 18, 2002). Colleges, fighting U.S. Trade proposal, say it favors for-profit distance education. *The Chronicle of Higher Education,* 33.

Friedman, T. L. (1999). *The Lexus and the olive tree: Understanding globalization.* New York: Anchor Books.

Froment, E. (2001, November 9). Help make trade rules or get stung at the market. *The Times Higher Education Supplement,* 12.

Giroux, H. A. (2001). Introduction: Critical education or training: Beyond the Commodification of higher education. In H. A. Giroux & K. Myrsiades (Eds.), *Beyond the corporate university: Culture and pedagogy in the new millennium* (pp. 1–14). Lanham, MD: Rowman & Littlefield Publishers, Inc.

Giroux, H. A., & Myrsiades, K. (Eds.). (2001). *Beyond the corporate university: Culture and pedagogy in the new millennium.* Lanham, MD: Rowman & Littlefield Publishers, Inc.

Gnanam, A. (2002). Globalization and its impact on quality assurance, accreditation and the recognition of qualifications: A view from Asia and the Pacific. In S. Uvalic´-Trumbic´ (Ed.), *Globalization and the market in higher education* (pp. 95–104). Paris: UNESCO.

Goodwin, C. D., & Nacht, M. (1991). *Missing the boat: The failure to internationalize American higher education.* Cambridge, UK: Cambridge University Press.

Gould, E. (2003). *The university in a corporate culture.* New Haven, CT: Yale University Press.

Green, A. (1997). *Education, globalization and the nation-state.* New York: St. Martin's Press.

Haskins, C. (1965). *The rise of universities.* Ithaca: Cornell University Press.

Hirsch, W. Z., & Weber, L. E. (Eds.). (2002). *As the walls of academia are tumbling down*. London: Economica.

Institute for International Education. (2004). Open Doors 2004: International Students in the U.S. Retrieved February 21, 2005, from http://opendoors.iienetwork.org/?p=50137

Johnstone, D. B. (1993). The costs of higher education: Worldwide issues and trends for the 1990s. In P. G. Altbach & D. B. Johnstone (Eds.), *The funding of higher education: International perspectives* (pp. 3–24). New York: Garland.

Jongbloed, B., Peter Maasen, and Guy Neave (Ed.). (1999). *From the eye of the storm: Higher education's changing institution*. Dordrecht: Kluwer Academic Publishers.

Kerr, C. (1982). *The uses of the university*. Cambridge, MA: Harvard University Press.

Kerr, C. (1990). The internationalisation of learning and the nationalisation of the purposes of higher education: two 'laws of motion' in conflict? *European Journal of Education: Research, Development, and Policies, 25*(1), 5–22.

Knight, J. (1997). Internationalisation of higher education: A conceptual framework. In J. Knight & H. d. Wit (Eds.), *Internationalisation of higher education in Asia Pacific countries*. Amsterdam: European Association for International Education.

Knight, J. (1999). Internationalisation of higher education. In J. Knight & H. de Wit (Eds.), *Quality and Internationalisation in Higher Education* (pp. 13–29). Paris: OECD.

Knight, J. (2002a). The impact pf GATS and trade liberalization on higher education. In S. Uvalic´-Trumbic´ (Ed.), *Globalization and the market for higher education* (pp. 191–209). Paris: UNESCO.

Knight, J. (2002b). Trade creep: Implications of GATS for higher education policy. *International Higher Education, 28*(2).

Knight, J. (2002c). *Trade in higher education services: The implications of GATS*. London: The Observatory on Borderless Higher Education.

Knight, J. (2003). Higher education and trade agreements: What are the policy implications? In G. Breton & M. Lambert (Eds.), *Universities and globalization: Private linkages, public trust* (pp. 81–106). Paris: UNESCO Publishing.

Knight, J. (Spring 2003). Trade talk—à la four modes. Retrieved November 11, 2004, from http://www.bc.edu/bc_org/avp/soe/cihe/newsletter/news31/text002.htm

Kweik, M. (2001). Globalization and higher education. *Higher Education in Europe, XXVI*(1), 27–38.

Larsen, K., Martin, J. P., & Morris, R. (2002). *Trade in Educational Services: Trends and Emerging Issues*. Paper presented at the OECD/U.S. Forum on Trade in Educational Services, Washington, DC, Appendix B(2) 1–16.

Larsen, K., & Vincent-Lancrin, S. (2002). International trade in educational services: Good or bad? *Higher Education Management and Policy, 14*(3), 9–46.

Levine, A. (1993). *Higher learning in America, 1980–2000*. Baltimore, Md.: Johns Hopkins University Press.

Levine, A. (2001). Higher education as a mature industry. In P. G. Altbach, P. J. Gumport & D. B. Johnstone (Eds.), *In defense of American higher education* (pp. 38–58). Baltimore: Johns Hopkins University Press.

Lips, C. (2000). "Edupreneurs:" A Survey of For-Profit Education. Retrieved November 11, 2004, from http://www.cato.org/pub_display.php?pub_id=1245

Lucas, C. J. (1994). *American higher education: A history.* New York: St. Martin's Griffin.

McBurnie, G. (2001). Leveraging globalization as a policy paradigm for higher education. *Higher Education in Europe, 26*(1), 11–26.

Merriam, Sharan B. (1998). *Qualitative research and case study applications in education.* San Francisco: Jossey-Bass.

Middlehurst, R. (2002). Quality assurance and accreditation for virtual education: A discussion of models and needs. In S. Uvalic´-Trumbic´ (Ed.), *Globalization and the market in higher education* (pp. 35–44). Paris: UNESCO.

Mintzberg, H. (2000). The professional bureaucracy. In M. C. Brown II (Ed.), *Organization and governance in higher education* (5th ed., pp. 50–70). Boston: Pearson Custom Publishing.

Moll, J. (2001). International education and training services: A global market of opportunity for U.S. providers. *Export America, May,* 19–21.

Moll, J. (2002). *Trade in education and training services: Excellent opportunities for U.S. providers.* Retrieved September 23, 2004, from http://www.export.gov/exportamerica/newopportunities/

Mujica Márquez, A. (2002). The impact of globalization on higher education: The Latin American context. In S. Uvalic´-Trumbic´ (Ed.), *Globalization and the market in higher education* (pp. 83–94). Paris: UNESCO.

Mundy, K., & Iga, M. (2003). Hegemonic exceptionalism and legitimating bet-hedging: Paradoxes and lessons from the U.S. and Japanese approaches to education services under the GATS. *Globalisation, Societies and Education, 1*(3), 281–320.

National Association of State Universities and Land Grant Colleges (2003). About NASULGC. Retrieved October 15, 2003, from http://www.nasulgc.org/About_Nasulgc/about_nasulgc.htm

National Committee for Trade in Education (NCITE). (2003). Mission Statement. Retrieved October 15, 2003, from http://www.tradeineducation.org/general_info/frames.html

National Conference of State Legislatures. (March 24, 2003). Letter to Ambassador Robert Zoellick regarding negotiations proceeding under the General Agreement on Trade in Services (GATS). Washington, DC.

National Conference of State Legislatures. (January 19, 2005). Letter to Ambassador Robert Zoellick. Washington, DC.

National Conference of State Legislatures, Council of State Governments, The United Conference of Mayors, & National League of Cities. (September 23, 2003). Letter to USTR regarding state & local trade principles. Washington, DC.

National Education Association. (2004). *Higher education and international trade agreements: An examination of the threats and promises of globalization.* Washington, DC: National Education Association.

Neave, G., & van Vught, F. (1994). Government and higher education in developing countries: a conceptual framework. In G. Neave & F. van Vught (Eds.), *Government and higher education relationships across three continents: The winds of change* (pp. 1–21). Oxford: Pergamon.

Nielson, J. (November 3–4, 2003). *A quick guide to the state of play in the GATS negotiations.* Paper presented at the OECD/Norway Forum on Trade in Educational Services: Managing the Internationalisation of Post-Secondary Education, Trondheim, Norway.

OECD. *History of the OECD.* Retrieved November 12, 2004, from http://www.oecd.org/document/63/0,2340,en_2649_201185_1876671_1_1_1_1,00.html

OECD. *Marshall Plan speech.* Retrieved November 12, 2004, from http://www.oecd.org/document/10/0,2340,en_2649_201185_1876938_1_1_1_1,00.html

OECD. *Convention of the Organisation for Economic Co-operation and Development.* Retrieved November 12, 2004, from http://www.oecd.org/document/7/0,2340,en_2649_201185_1915847_1_1_1_1,00.html

OECD. (2002). *GATS: The Case for Open Services Markets.* Paris: OECD.

OECD. (2004a). *Internationalisation and trade in higher education: Opportunities and challenges.* Paris: Organization for Economic Co-operation and Development—Center for Educational Research and Innovation.

OECD. (2004b). *Policy brief: Internationalisation of higher education.* Retrieved November 22, 2004, 2004, from www.oecd.org/publications/Pol_brief

OECD/CERI. (2002). *Background document: Current commitments under the GATS in educational services.* Paper presented at the OECD/U.S. Forum on Trade in Educational Services, Washington, DC, Appendix B(3) 1–47.

Office of the United States Trade Representative. (2000, March 28). Notice and request for comments. *Federal Register, 65.*

Office of the United States Trade Representative. (2000, November 13). Notice of Meeting of the Industry Sector Advisory Committee on Services. *Federal Register, 65.*

Office of the United States Trade Representative. (2001, March 14). Notice of Meeting of the Industry Sector Advisory Committee on Services. *Federal Register, 66.*

Office of the United States Trade Representative. (2001, May 15). Notice of Meeting of the Industry Sector Advisory Committee on Services. *Federal Register, 66.*

Office of the United States Trade Representative. (2001, September 7). Notice of Meeting of the Industry Sector Advisory Committee on Services for Trade Policy Matters. *Federal Register, 66.*

Office of the United States Trade Representative. (2001, October 11). Notice of Meeting of the Industry Sector Advisory Committee on Services for Trade Policy Matters. *Federal Register, 66.*

Office of the United States Trade Representative. (2002, July 25). Notice of Meeting of the Industry Sector Advisory Committee on Services for Trade Policy Matters. *Federal Register, 67.*

Office of the United States Trade Representative. (2002, September 19). Request for comments and notice of public hearing concerning market access in the Doha Development Agenda negotiations in the World Trade Organization (WTO). *Federal Register, 67.*

Office of the United States Trade Representative. (2002, March 19). Notice and request for comments. *Federal Register, 67.*

Office of the United States Trade Representative. (2003, July 11). Notice of Meeting of the Industry Sector Advisory Committee on Services. *Federal Register, 68.*

Office of the United States Trade Representative. (2003, October 6). Notice of Meeting of the Industry Sector Advisory Committee on Services. *Federal Register, 68.*

Padilla, C. A. (2003, April 14). Letter from USTR to the Raymond Scheppach, National Governors Association regarding the GATS and higher education. Provided by the NCSL.

Papovitch, J. S. (2002). *U.S. perspectives on trade in services with a focus on education and training.* Paper presented at the OECD/U.S. Forum on Trade in Educational Services, Washington, DC.

Patrinos, H. A. (2002). *Role of the private sector in the global market for education.* Paper presented at the NUFFIC Conference Shifting Roles, Changing Rules: The Global Higher Education Market, The Hague, The Netherlands.

Pusser, B. (2001). *The knowledge economy and postsecondary education.* Paper presented in the Committee on the Impact of the Changing Economy on The Educational System: Report of a Workshop, Washington, DC, 105–126.

Rauhvargers, A. (2002). Recognition in the European region: Response to recent challenges from inside and outside. In S. Uvalic´-Trumbic´ (Ed.), *Globalization and the market in higher education* (pp. 73–82). Paris: UNESCO.

Readings, B. (1996). *The University in Ruins.* Cambridge, MA: Harvard University Press.

Robertson, S. L. (2003). WTO/GATS and the global education services industry. *Globalisation, Societies and Education, 1*(3), 259–266.

Rudolph, F. (1990). *The American college and university: A history.* Athens, GA: The University of Georgia Press.

Sadlak, J. (1998). Globalization and concurrent challenges for higher education. In P. Scott (Ed.), *The globalization of higher education.* Buckingham, UK: Open University Press.

Salmi, J. (1992). Perspectives on financing higher education. *Higher Education Policy, 5*(2), 13–19.

Salmi, J. (2003). Constructing knowledge societies: New challenges for tertiary education. In G. Breton & M. Lambert (Eds.), *Universities and Globalization: Private Linkages, Public Trust* (pp. 51–68). Paris: UNESCO Publishing.

Sauvé, P. (2002). Trade, education, and the GATS: What's in, what's out, and what's all the fuss about? *Higher Education Management and Policy, 14*(3), 47–76.

Sauvé, P. (2002). *Trade, education, and the GATS: What's in, what's out, and what's all the fuss about?* Paper presented at the OECD/ U.S. Forum on Trade in Educational Services, Washington, DC, Appendix B(1) 1–27.

Sauvé, P., & Stern, R. M. (Eds.). (2000). *GATS 2000: New directions in services trade liberalization.* Washington, DC: Brookings Institution Press.

Scott, P. (Ed.). (1998). *The Globalization of Higher Education.* Buckingham, UK: Open University Press.

Scott, P. (1998). Massification, internationalization and globalization. In P. Scott (Ed.), *The globalization of higher education*. Buckingham, UK: Open University Press.

Scott, P. (2000). Globalisation and higher education: Challenges for the 21st century. *Journal of Studies in International Education, 4*(Spring), 3–10.

Seddoh, K. F. (2002). Educating citizens in a changing global society: A new challenge for higher education. In S. Uvalic´-Trumbic´ (Ed.), *Globalization and the market in higher education* (pp. 45–60). Paris: UNESCO.

Sedgwick, R. (2002). *The trade debate in international higher education*. Retrieved March 20, 2004, from http://www.wes.org/ewenr/02sept/feature.htm

Shumar, W. (1997). *College for sale: A critique of the commodification of higher education*. Bristol, PA: The Falmer Press.

Skilbeck, M. (2001, April 27). Global trade could profit all, given the political will. *The Times Higher Education Supplement*, p. 14.

Slaughter, S. (1998). National higher education policies in a global economy. In J. Currie & J. Newson (Eds.), *Universities and globalization: Critical perspectives* (pp. 45–70). Thousand Oaks, CA: SAGE Publications, Inc.

Slaughter, S., & Leslie, L. L. (1997). *Academic capitalism: Politics, policies, and the entrepreneurial university*. Baltimore: The Johns Hopkins University Press.

Steiglitz, J. E. (2002). *Globalization and its discontents*. NY: W. W. Norton & Company.

Strauss, A. & Corbin, J. (1994). Grounded theory methodology: An overview. In N. K. Denzin & Y. S. Lincoln (Eds.), *Handbook of qualitative research* (pp. 273–285). Thousand Oaks, CA: SAGE Publications.

Stroup, S. (2002). *Closing Remarks*. Paper presented at the OECD/U.S. Forum on Trade in Educational Services, Washington, DC, 149–151.

Tooley, J. (1999). Asking different questions: Towards justifying markets in education. In N. Alexiadou & C. Brock (Eds.), *Education as a commodity* (pp. 9–20). Saxmundham, Suffolk, UK: John Catt Educational Ltd.

UNESCO.*UNESCO Education-Objectives*. Retrieved November 22, 2004, from http://portal.unesco.org/education/en

UNESCO.*UNESCO Forum on Higher Education, Research, and Knowledge*. Retrieved November 22, 2004, from http://portal.unesco.org/education.en

UNESCO. *Constitution of the United Nations Educational, Scientific and Cultural Organization*. Retrieved November 12, 2004, from http://portal.unesco.org/en/ev.php-URL_ID=3328&URL_DO=DO_TOPIC&URL_SECTION=201.html

UNESCO.*UNESCO milestones*. Retrieved November 12, 2004, from http://portal.unesco.org/en/ev.php-URL_ID=14606&URL_DO=DO_TOPIC&URL_SECTION=201.html

Urry, J. (1998). Contemporary transformations of time and space. In P. Scott (Ed.), *The Globalization of higher education* (pp. 1–17). Buckingham, UK: Open University Press.

USDOC. *Office of Service Industries*. Retrieved November 11, 2003, from http://ita.doc.gov/td/sif/Office%20of%20Service%20Industries.htm

USTR. *History of the United States Trade Representative*. Retrieved October 26, 2004, from http://www.ustr.gov/Who_We_Are/History_of_the_United_States_Trade_Representative.html

USTR. *Mission of the USTR*. Retrieved October 26, 2004, from http://www.ustr.gov/who_we_are/mission_of_the_USTR_printer.html

USTR. (March 31, 2003). *Free trade in services: Opening dynamic new markets.* Retrieved October 12, 2004, from http://www.ustr.gov/Document_Library/Fact_Sheets/2003/Free_Trade_in_Services_Opening_Dynamic_New_Markets.html

USTR. (November 5, 2002). *Zoellick notifies Congress of progress on global trade talks.* Retrieved October 13, 2003, from http://www.ustr.gov/Document_Library/Letters_to_Congress/2002/Zoellick_Notifies_Congress_of_Progress_on_Global_Trade_Talks.html

USTR. (November 5, 2002). *Zoellick notifies Congress of progress on global trade talks—House.* Retrieved October 13, 2004, from http://www.ustr.gov/Document_Library/Letters_to_Congress/2002/Zoellick_Notifies_Congress_of_Pro gress_on_Global_Trade_Talks_-_House_Letter.html

USTR. (July 1, 2002). *United States announces proposals for liberating trade in services.* Retrieved October 13, 2004, from http://www.ustr.gov/Document_Library/Press_Releases/2002/July/United_States_Announces_Proposals_for_Liberalizing_Trade_in_Services.html

USTR. *WTO services trade negotiations.* Retrieved November 4, 2004, from http://www.ustr.gov/sectors/services/gats.pdf

USTR. *America and the World Trade Organization.* Retrieved March 17, 2003, from http://www.ustr.gov/pdf/wto_usa.pdf

USTR. (2000). *Communication from the United States: Higher (tertiary) education, adult education, and training.* Retrieved February 19, 2002, from http://www.wto.org/english/tratop_e/serv_e/s_propnewnegs_e.htm#education

USTR. (2002). *Initial request for market access.* Washington, DC.

USTR. (2003). *2003–03–31 Consolidated Offer.* Washington, DC: www.ustr.gov/sectors/services/2003–03–31-consolidated_offer.pdf.

Uvalic´-Trumbic´, S. (Ed.). (2002). *Globalization and the market in higher education: Quality, accreditation, and qualifications.* Paris: UNESCO.

Uvalic´-Trumbic´, S. (2002). Globalization and quality in higher education: An introduction. In S. Uvalic´-Trumbic´ (Ed.), *Globalization and the market in higher education* (pp. 1–10). Paris: UNESCO.

Van Damme, D. (2002). Higher education in the age of globalization. In S. Uvalic´-Trumbic´ (Ed.), *Globalization and the market in higher education* (pp. 21–34). Paris: UNESCO.

van Tilburg, P. (2002). Higher education: Engine of change or adherence to trends? An inventory of views. *Higher Education Management and Policy, 14*(2), 9–26.

Ward, D. (2002). *Trade in educational services: A U.S. university response.* Paper presented at the OECD/U.S. Forum on Trade in Educational Services, Washington, DC, 41–44.

Ward, D. (2003). *Attachment to letter to U.S. Trade Representative.* Retrieved March 27, 2003, from http://www.acenet.edu/washington/letters/2003/03march/zoellick.cfm

Waters, M. (1995). *Globalization.* London and New York: Routledge.

Wendt, R. (2000). *Globalization.* Sterling, VA: Pluto Press.

Williams, H. M. (2002). The ever increasing demands made on universities in the United States by society and politicians. In W. Z. Hirsch & L. E. Weber

(Eds.), *As the walls of academia are tumbling down* (pp. 53–60). London: Economica.

Wilson, J. K. (1999). The canon and the curriculum: Multicultural revolution and traditionalist revolt. In P. G. Altbach, R. O. Berdahl & P. J. Gumport (Eds.), *American higher education in the 21st century* (pp. 427–447). Baltimore: Johns Hopkins University Press.

Wolff, R. P. (1969). *The ideal of the university.* Boston: Beacon Press.

World Bank, The. *What is the World Bank?* Retrieved October 13, 2004, from http://web.worldbank.org/WBSITE/EXTERNAL/EXTABOUTUS/0,,contentMDK:20040558~menuPK:34559~pagePK:51123644~piPK:329829~theSitePK:29708,00.html

World Bank, The. *World Bank History.* Retrieved October 13, 2004, from http://web.worldbank.org/WBSITE/EXTERNAL/EXTABOUTUS/EXTARCHIVES/0,,contentMDK:20053333~menuPK:63762~pagePK:36726~piPK:36092~theSitePK:29506,00.html

Worthington, R. (2000). *Rethinking globalization:* Production, Politics, Actions. NY: Peter Lang Publishing, Inc.

Wright, A. (2005). From ivory tower to academic sweatshop. Retrieved February 5, 2005, http://www.salon.com/tech/feature/2005/01/26/distance_learning/index_np.html?x

WTO. *Annex 1B: General Agreement on Trade in Services.* Retrieved March 17, 2003, from http://www.wto.org/english/docs_e/legal_e/26-gats.pdf

WTO. *GATS—fact and fiction.* Retrieved March 17, 2003, from http://www.wto.org/english/tratop_e/serv_e/gats_factfiction_e.htm

WTO. *The General Agreement on Trade in Services (GATS): Objectives, coverage and disciplines.* Retrieved November 11, 2003, from http://www.wto.org/english/tratop_e/serv_e/gatsqu_e.htm

WTO. *What is the WTO.* Retrieved November 11, 2003, from http://www.wto.org/english/thewto_e/whatis_e/whatis_e.htm

Yin, R.K. (2003). Case Study Research: Design and Methods. Thousand Oaks, CA: SAGE Publications.

Zusman, A. (1999). Issues facing higher education in the twenty-first century. In P. G. Altbach, R. O. Berdahl & P. J. Gumport (Eds.), *American higher education in the 21st century* (pp. 109–148). Baltimore: Johns Hopkins University Press.

Index

For Product Safety Concerns and Information please contact our EU representative GPSR@taylorandfrancis.com
Taylor & Francis Verlag GmbH, Kaufingerstraße 24, 80331 München, Germany

www.ingramcontent.com/pod-product-compliance
Lightning Source LLC
Chambersburg PA
CBHW050437280326
41932CB00013BA/2145

9780415805810